Private Library
A. C. Wenger,
No.

# Historical Geography of Bible Lands

By

JOHN B. CALKIN, M.A.

*Author of "Notes on Education," "A Geography of the World,"
"A History of the Dominion of Canada," etc.*

WITH AN INTRODUCTION

by

THE REV. ROBERT A. FALCONER, LL.D. Litt. D.

*Principal of Presbyterian College, Halifax, Nova Scotia.*

PHILADELPHIA
THE WESTMINSTER PRESS
1915

COPYRIGHT, 1904,
BY
J. H. SCRIBNER.

# ACKNOWLEDGMENTS

THE writer of this book is not an explorer nor even a traveler. It is not then at all necessary to state that the facts herein set down are not derived from personal observation. Many books have been consulted, of which those that have contributed most largely to this work are the following:—

"The Historical Geography of the Holy Land," by Prof. George Adam Smith, "History, Prophecy, and the Monuments," by Prof. J. F. McCurdy, LL. D., "Sinai and Palestine," by Dean Stanley, "The Holy Land," by John Kelman, A. M., Smith's "Bible Dictionary," Hastings' "Bible Dictionary," Davis's "A Dictionary of the Bible," "A History of the Jewish People," by James Stevenson Riggs, D. D., "A History of the Babylonians and Assyrians," by George Stephen Goodspeed, Ph. D., "A History of the Jewish People During the Babylonian, Persian, and Greek Periods," by Charles Foster Kent, Ph. D., "St. Paul the Traveler and Roman Citizen," by W. M. Ramsay, D. C. L., LL. D.

He also gladly recognizes his very great obligation for valuable suggestions from Robert Murray, LL. D., Editor of the *Presbyterian Witness*, Halifax, N. S., Robert A. Falconer, LL. D., Litt. D., Principal of the Presbyterian College, Halifax, N. S., and John Currie, D. D., Professor of Hebrew and Oriental languages, of the same college. To the valued aid thus given, Dr. Falconer has bestowed the added favor of the generous commendatory Introductory Note which stands at the beginning of the book.

# CONTENTS

|  | Introductory Note | 7 |
|---|---|---|
| I. | Introductory | 11 |
| II. | Palestine | 14 |
| III. | The Maritime Plain | 19 |
| IV. | The Shephelah | 22 |
| V. | Galilee | 25 |
| VI. | Esdraelon | 28 |
| VII. | Samaria | 31 |
| VIII. | Judæa | 37 |
| IX. | The Valley of the Jordan | 48 |
| X. | Eastern Palestine | 57 |
| XI. | The Lands of the Euphrates and the Tigris | 65 |
| XII. | Historic Sketch of Babylonia, Assyria, Persia, etc | 71 |
| XIII. | Syria | 79 |
| XIV. | Phœnicia | 84 |
| XV. | Egypt | 87 |
| XVI. | The Wilderness of the Wandering | 94 |
| XVII. | Edom | 97 |
| XVIII. | Asia Minor | 99 |
| XIX. | Greece | 108 |
| XX. | The Islands of Bible Story | 114 |
| XXI. | Rome | 116 |
| XXII. | Historic Outline.—From the Call of Abraham to the Death of Moses | 122 |
| XXIII. | Historic Sketch.—The Judges | 127 |
| XXIV. | Historical Sketch.—The Undivided Monarchy | 130 |
| XXV. | The Kingdom of Israel | 137 |
| XXVI. | The Kingdom of Judah | 140 |
| XXVII. | The Babylonian Period | 147 |
| XXVIII. | The Medo-Persian Period | 150 |
| XXIX. | The Greek Period.—333–168 b. c. | 155 |
| XXX. | The Maccabæan Period | 159 |
| XXXI. | The Roman Period | 164 |

# INTRODUCTORY NOTE

By Robert A. Falconer, LL. D., Litt. D.,
*Principal of Presbyterian College, Halifax, Nova Scotia.*

---

THERE is, it would appear, a place for such a book as is herewith presented to the public. Issued at a moderate price, containing maps without which geography becomes for the average person a tiresome and lifeless discipline, it covers all the lands of the Bible. Further, it is written by one who for many years has had wide experience both in teaching and in training teachers in a Normal School, and who therefore should know how to present what teachers most require to learn. Well-informed in matters of recent discovery and with respect to geography, the author will, we hope, find the success which his work on world-geography has met, repeated in this narrower department of the same subject.

If so much pains is bestowed, and rightly, upon the equipment of the day-school teacher, we must surely provide the best that we can offer for the furnishing forth of the Sunday-school teacher, who, at great self-sacrifice and often with little encouragement, essays a much more difficult task than the teacher in the public school. For can we do too much to relieve the difficulty of those who during the short hour on Sunday give to many children all the religious instruction that they get, and in this meager fashion try to check those influences against a religious conduct of life which crowd in upon the child by almost every avenue of his intelligence?

But this book is not meant only for teachers. It is equally well-suited for the average Bible reader. Study of the Bible is something more than meditation. It involves the effort of placing one's self in such a position as to see the life of the people who received the revelation of God which we have in the Bible. And the earthly scenes in which that life was spent contribute much toward its understanding. The Bible is not like the Koran, which claims to be "coeval with God uncreated, eternal, its first transcript having been written from the beginning in rays of light upon a gigantic tablet resting by the throne of the Almighty." It did not come from heaven at the hands of the angel Gabriel. The Bible is the story of God's revelation of himself first to the people of Israel and afterwards in his Son Jesus Christ.

God has his home on earth in the hearts of his children. Into their everyday life he came in the past and is coming to-day by his Spirit. To Israel he made himself known in an especial manner. What a marvel is that history and its changing fortunes, from the wandering tribes under the patriarchs till it closed with the fall of Jerusalem in A. D. 70! But through it all, under lawgiver and prophet, there was a constantly enlarging knowledge of the true God given here a little, there a little, line upon line, precept upon precept, whether to enslaved aliens in Egypt, to rebellious nomads in the desert, to a prosperous people almost intoxicated by the worldly ambitions of a settled country, or to those who knew the disaster of the exile and the pathos of the return, until the remnant of Israel, after an upflaring of heroism, settled into religious torpor, from which the call of John the Baptist and the gospel of Jesus could not arouse it. That nation was the house of God, and it was not finally left desolate till the temple of the Christian Church took its place.

The conditions in which the people lived had great influence on the form that the divine revelation took, and the history was largely dependent upon the physical features of the country; for Israel was placed down among the great world-powers and was a coveted prize. Babylonia, Egypt, Assyria, enter again and again into the message of the prophet. Behind the Israel of the monarchy lay Egypt, and the wonderful redemption from that land gave its meaning to all that followed. Israel was the people of Jehovah who had created them and saved them. Again the level stretches of Babylonia bred a civilization much akin to that of Israel and nursed its ancestors. Why were these Semitic peoples in their religious essentials so entirely different? It is not indeed to be explained by climate or land configuration, but the geographical position of Israel helped her to maintain her national integrity.

Geography thus becomes a primary aid when we wish to read the records of the past. It does for us what travel is able to effect far more vividly. The history of Europe is invested with greater interest for the modern mind than that of ancient empires, because the countries in which it was enacted are comparatively familiar to us. When the land has imprinted its figure upon our memory, we understand better why the currents of history ran in just such particular channels.

Again, the literature of any people is an expression of their deepest life. The Bible is a great literature, and all literature is full of allusion to its native soil. From almost every page of the Bible there starts forth some hint of land or climate. Palestine was varied in climate, resources, and beauty. There were the mountains of Lebanon topped with snow, and the steaming valley of the Jordan sunk away below the sea level. There was Galilee traversed by the highways of the world's commerce, and Judæa on its plateau with a glacis against the Orient or the Sea. So also diversified climate and habits of nature unfamiliar to our western mind present us with many a problem of interpretation. But the study of biblical geography makes that life concrete. No longer do shadowy figures move to and fro on the unreal background of a far-away world.

Geography indeed sheds more light upon the Old Testament than it does upon the New. But it is of great value for the understanding of the Gospels and Epistles also. The differences between the messages of Jesus in the Synoptics and in John are partly to be explained by the differences in the people who heard them and the countries in which they lived. Galilee was open to the world, and its people were much more receptive of new ideas. Judæa shut off from outside influence was under the control of the hierarchy in the capital. Then what did the journeys of Jesus to Tyre and Sidon and to Cæsarea Philippi mean? Geography has something to tell us. That "Woe unto thee, Chorazin!" also is significant of a busy unrecorded ministry of our Lord, for this city has dropped into oblivion. Why is Tiberias never mentioned in the Gospels? What a world lay on the borders of Galilee in the Decapolis, all but untouched by Jesus! These towns passed by in the Gospels are a witness that Jesus knew well the character of the wide world for which he brought his gospel. He did not imagine that it was to be confined to the Jewish people. He could not have got away from the Gentile even in Galilee had he so wished.

To the study of the life of Paul geography has of recent years become tributary. Scholars have made the cities to which he traveled much better known to us, and we owe a large debt to the brilliant work of Prof. W. M. Ramsay. He has taken us in his books in the footsteps of Paul, following him along the highways of commerce to the large cities of Asia Minor, Syria, and Greece, till we are lost in amazement at the work of the apostle, who had faith to undertake the evangelization of the Western World and was granted the divine power for its accomplishment.

Geography also forces other questions upon us. It enables us to realize the extent of the early conquests of the gospel. Syria, Asia Minor, Greece, Italy, Egypt, Africa, Ethiopia, Armenia were filled with Christian churches probably within two centuries after the first preaching of Christianity. We know comparatively little of its first planting in these parts. How did it come thither? Our imagination is stimulated to wonder at the incessant activity of unrecorded but faithful followers of the Lord Jesus, who carried the good news even to the ends of the then known world.

Many of these matters may not be of direct value for the ordinary teacher in the Sunday school, but they are of much indirect importance; for one must know a great deal more than is at once used in the class. If we live from hand to mouth, doling out to our scholars the pitiful scraps of knowledge we may gather from week to week from the average lesson help, those whom we are trying to teach will get no satisfactory impression of the range and movement of Bible history and the way in which God wrought out his will among the nations. The intelligent reader of the Bible also must of necessity have some comprehension of the fields on which the forces of the Kingdom of God were marshaled.

# Historical Geography of Bible Lands

## CHAPTER I

### INTRODUCTORY

The Bible is not a systematic theological treatise. In giving to the Israelites, and through them to all peoples, a revelation of his will, God did so, in large measure, by a concrete story of individual and national life, rather than in the form of didactic statement and abstract principle. In this method there is an adaptation to human need and to the great purpose to be subserved by such revelation. The religion of the Bible is a matter of conduct and character. It is a living, active force in shaping human life and in directing human action. It is emphatically something to be done. Its highest outcome is the development of character, and doing is the grand law of development. Thus the Bible is largely a story of God's providence in dealing with a people according to their varying conditions and circumstances.

In the training and developing process to which the Israelites were subjected, the lands in which they lived had an important influence. Some part of this work—doubtless a large part—was effected through direct revelation and supernatural manifestation. But in great measure it was a discipline of natural causes, of which environment was a chief factor. It is, indeed, the case with every people, that the physical features of the land in which they live have a potent influence in determining what they become, and in shaping their habits and their character. Mountain or lowland, seaside or interior, arctic snow or burning sand, well-watered, arable plains or dry pasture lands, city or country, each has its own specific influence on a people, modifies their manner of living, and leaves on them its own impress.

Without a knowledge of the country in which its events occurred, many portions of the Bible cannot be fully understood, and many portions of it lose their forcefulness and beauty. An event that seems inexplicable, in contravention of natural law, miraculous, or incredible, may, when regarded in connection with the conditions of its environment, lose its anomalous aspect and come to be seen as the very thing that should have happened. Hence it is that the study of Bible and Bible lands should go together. Especially is a full knowledge of the land needful to the teacher of Bible truth.

Bible lands are comprised chiefly in southwestern Asia, northeastern Africa, and southeastern Europe,—where the three continents of the Old World approach or join each other. They extend from Mount Ararat on the north to Mount Sinai on the south, and from the Tigris on the east to the Tiber on the west. They include Elam, Media, Persia, Assyria, Babylonia, Mesopotamia, Syria, Palestine, Arabia, Egypt, Asia Minor, Greece and Rome. As the home of the Chosen People and the scene of the greater number of the events recorded in the Bible, Palestine will be our first and chief concern in the following pages. The other countries, enumerated above, however much more grandly they may have figured in the history of the world, take a subordinate place in our scheme. Inconspicuous though it was, and intermeddling little in affairs outside its own limits, Palestine was the center of influence, from which went forth the chief determining forces that have shaped the character and history of the civilized world.

**Its Isolation.**—Isolated by its surroundings from the great centers of the world's activities, Palestine stood apart from all other lands. On the north is the great barrier wall of Lebanon, on the east is the Syrian Desert, on the south is the Desert of Arabia, and on the west is the Mediterranean Sea. The sea, in modern times a great highway of intercourse between separated lands, was, according to the ideas of the ancients, a barrier which God had interposed to keep different peoples asunder. The idea had emphasis in this case, for the Mediterranean coast of Palestine is an inhospitable shore without a harbor.

**Palestine on the World's Highway.**—Yet with all its isolation, Palestine was situated directly on the grand highway that connected the centers of ancient civilization and power. Egypt and Assyria, the two great world-powers of ancient times, lay on opposite sides, while through the low plains that skirted the highlands of Palestine and divided these highlands into sections, lay the route of travel, of trade, and of war. On the one side were India, Persia, Assyria, Babylonia, and Syria; and on the other were Egypt, Greece, and Rome. Through all the ages, along these lowlands passed between east and west the great caravans with their costly treasures.

In her highlands Palestine had a retreat from the great world-events that were being enacted at her doors. Thus she was near to and aloof from the main stream of human activity. She could, as one writer finely says, be "a spectator of the world's conflicts and not their victim." The Old Testament era was a period of types and foreshadowings of ages that were to follow. Then as now God's people were in the world but not of it. They could have such seclusion as would allow of undisturbed communion with God, and yet observe his providences in dealing with the nations. And what a constantly moving panorama were the events in which these providences were unfolded, as one after another, Assyria, Babylonia, Medo-Persia, Greece, and Rome, each in its turn, became the central figure, and then moved off the stage to make room for its successor!

**Diversity Within Small Compass.**—One other feature may be noted in this connection, showing the suitability of Palestine as the land of the Book. That feature is, great diversity within small compass. The remarkable contrast of elevation from the low-lying Valley of the Jordan, the plains of the coast, and Esdraelon, with the highlands of Judæa, Samaria, Galilee, the highlands beyond the Jordan and the Lebanons, gives corresponding diversity of temperature, plants, animals, products, industries and habits of the people. The whole earth is in a measure epitomized in this little country. Accordingly the literature of the people, its figures and illustrations, easily become intelligible to all peoples, and the Book of this land is suited to become the Book of all lands. The Hebrews were chosen and set apart as a peculiar people, not for their own sake alone or chiefly, but as the medium of a divine message to the world. Such was the word spoken to Abraham—"In thee shall all families of the earth be blessed."

## CHAPTER II

### PALESTINE

**Name.**—This country has been known by various names. Palestine, the most common name of the present day, was never given to the country in Bible times, but was thus applied early in the Christian era. The word was derived from Philistia, the name of that portion of the Maritime Plain that was occupied by the Philistines. Canaan, meaning lowland, is said first to have belonged to the coast country of Phœnicia, then to have been extended to the lowlands of Sharon and the Jordan Valley, and finally it became the name of the whole country.[1] Other names by which the country has been known are Land of the Hebrews,[2] Land of Israel[3] and Land of Promise.[4] It is often called the Holy Land.

**Size.**—One is almost amazed to find Palestine so small a country. Its size is entirely disproportionate to the place it fills in our thoughts, and to the influence it has had on the history of other lands. The length of the country on the west of the Jordan, from Dan in the extreme north to Beer-sheba in the south, is 144 miles. The breadth of this western division is about 90 miles at Beer-sheba, and, becoming narrower as one goes north, 55 miles at Jerusalem, 40 miles at the Sea of Galilee, and 25 miles in the far north. Its area is about 6,000 square miles. Eastern Palestine is about 150 miles in length, north and south, and it varies in breadth from 80 miles in the north to 30 miles in the south. The territory occupied by the tribes on this side of the Jordan was about 4,500 square miles. Thus the area of the whole land of Israel was less than 11,000 square miles. But here as elsewhere history teaches the lesson that the grandeur and influence of a country are not to be measured by the number of square miles in its area.

**The Promised Land.**—The Promised Land had a much wider area than had that of possession.[5] It included the land of the Philistines, the Maritime Plain of Phœnicia, Cœle-Syria as far north as Hamath, the territory easterly to the Euphrates, and southerly to Wady-el-Arish or "the River of Egypt." Probably during the reigns of David and Solomon the territory of Israel was larger than at any other period in the history of the nation, but even then it failed to reach the full limits of the promise. And so it has been in the Christian era as under the Mosaic dispensation;

---

[1] Num. 34:2; Acts 7:11.  [2] Gen. 40:15.  [3] 1 Sam. 13:19.
[4] Heb. 11:9.  [5] Gen. 15:18; Num. 34:1-12; Josh. 1:4; 13:1.

God's people, through lack of faith and enterprise, have never availed themselves of the fullness and richness of the promises. There has always been "much land to be possessed."

**The Lebanons.**—The Mountains of Lebanon, though not within the limits of the territory occupied by the Israelites, form such a prominent feature in the landscape, and had so marked an influence on the physical condition of Palestine and on the character of the people, as well as on their literature, that some notice of them is demanded in this sketch.

The word Lebanon means white. Lebanon is the *Mont Blanc*, the White Mountain, of Syria. The name may have originated either in the snow-clad summits of these mountains, or in the white limestone on their slopes.

The Lebanons comprise two main parallel ranges, Lebanon and Anti-Lebanon, extending northeast and southwest for about one hundred miles. These ranges are separated by a narrow highland valley, known to the Greeks as Cœle-Syria, but in modern times called Bukaa.

Lebanon, the westerly range, has an average height of about 7,000 feet and an extreme elevation, toward the northern part, of about 10,500 feet. With its lofty peaks, deep gorges, and rapid streams, it presents much fine scenery. The westerly slope, facing the Mediterranean Sea, is well watered by the vapor-laden westerly winds. To the height of 5,000 feet these slopes are very fertile, yielding wheat, olives, dates, figs, and grapes. The valleys along these slopes are dotted with villages. Of the great cedars for which Lebanon was once famous, only a few groups remain. Such variety of climate has Lebanon, that an Arabian poet said of it: "The winter is upon its head, the spring upon its shoulders, the autumn in its bosom, and at its feet slumbers the summer."

**The Maronites** are a peculiar sect of Christians who live chiefly on Mount Lebanon and in its neighborhood. They follow cattle-breeding, agriculture, and the production of silk.

**The Anti-Lebanon** range does not maintain an average height equal to that of Lebanon. Its highest point is Mount Hermon at the south of the range. The rainfall here is less copious, the rain winds from the Mediterranean having been deprived of the richness of their moisture in crossing the cold heights of Lebanon.

**Mount Hermon,** 9,200 feet above the sea level, a conspicuous object throughout a large part of Palestine, is a noted feature in Bible story. It is generally regarded as the Mount of Transfiguration. In its neighborhood was the city Cæsarea Philippi, which, so far as the gospel record states, was the most northern limit of our Lord's journeyings.[1] The summits of the mountain are covered with snow throughout a large part of the year, and they so condense the vapors with which the air is laden

---
[1] Matt. 16 : 13; 17 : 1.

The sea is the reservoir from which it draws the water vapor of its atmosphere; the mountains condense this vapor and convert it into the showers that water the land.

**Political Divisions.**—The land of Israel at the time of the settlement under Joshua was divided among the various tribes, each division taking the name of the tribe to which it was allotted. Reuben, Gad, and half of Manasseh had their portions assigned them by Moses on the east side of the Jordan. Reuben was on the south, on the Arnon, adjoining the land of Moab. Gad came next, extending to the River Yarmuk. Manasseh was on the north of this river. This eastern land, however, continued to be spoken of by its old names, Bashan and Gilead.

The other tribes were placed on the west side of the Jordan. Naphtali was in the northeast along the Sea of Galilee and the upper Jordan. Asher lay west of Naphtali, extending to the sea. Zebulun was wedged in between the southern half of Naphtali and Asher. Issachar was directly south of Naphtali and Zebulun, comprising the Plain of Esdraelon. The half tribe of Manasseh lay south of Esdraelon. Ephraim lay along the Jordan south of the western half of Manasseh. Dan was south of the western half of Ephraim, extending to the sea. Benjamin was situated south of Ephraim on the lower Jordan. Judah was between the northern half of the Dead Sea and the Mediterranean. Simeon lay south of Judah in the district known as the *Negeb* or "South Country."

On the division of the kingdom after Solomon's death, the northern portion became known as The Kingdom of Israel; sometimes also it was called Ephraim, taking the name of the leading tribe in that division. The southern division was called The Kingdom of Judah, or simply Judah.

In New Testament times, under Roman rule, the country was divided into Galilee, Samaria, Judæa, and, on the east of the Jordan, Peræa.

Galilee included the territory originally assigned to Naphtali, Zebulun, and Issachar. The territory of Asher was Phœnician and at this time formed no part of the land of Israel. Galilee was divided into Upper Galilee and Lower Galilee, Upper Galilee comprising the northern half of Naphtali, and Lower Galilee comprising that portion of Naphtali lying west of the Sea of Galilee and also Zebulun and Issachar.

Samaria, comprising the territory originally belonging to the half tribe of Manasseh and that belonging to Ephraim, was, through the scruples of Jewish rabbis, not regarded as part of the land of Israel, and the Samaritans were looked upon as heathen. This disowning of the Samaritans began at the time of the return of Judah from the captivity in Babylon. When the Assyrians carried into captivity the inhabitants of the northern kingdom, they placed other people from the East in the land. These people, although through intermarriage they became closely related to the Jews, were always regarded by them with much contempt.

# CHAPTER III

## THE MARITIME PLAIN

**Harbors.**—The coast of Palestine is remarkably regular, without indenting bay or projecting headland. Indeed there is no proper harbor on the coast from end to end. So foreign was the idea of harbor to the Hebrew mind, that there is no word for it in the language. The Hebrews cared little for foreign trade or maritime pursuits. Indeed they rarely pressed their claim to the sea limit. The coast country was for the most part left to the Phœnician, the Canaanite, and the Philistine. The Hebrew name for west was sea, and the shores of the Mediterranean were the utmost limit of the nation's aspirations in that direction. Joppa was the only port in the early days. Under Roman rule Cæsarea with its costly breakwater was built by Herod the Great.

**Divisions.**—The Maritime Plain may be divided into three sections:—The Plain of Phœnicia in the north, Sharon in the middle, and Philistia in the south.

**The Plain of Phœnicia** is separated from Sharon by Mount Carmel, which thrusts itself across the lowlands, leaving only about two hundred yards between its headland and the sea. This northerly division with its scanty limits between the foothills of Lebanon and the Mediterranean varies in width from half a mile in the north to eight miles in the south. It is divided by headlands into the Plain of Tyre in the north and the Plain of Acre in the south. In the distribution of territory among the tribes of Israel the northern part of this plain was allotted to Asher, the southern part to Zebulun. The native Phœnicians, however, were never dispossessed.[1] Tyre and Sidon, on the coast, were ancient Phœnician cities of great historic interest.

**Sharon.**—The narrow coastland between the headland of Carmel and Nahr ez Zerka or Crocodile River is called The Plain of Tanturah. The Plain of Sharon, beginning at this point with a width of about eight miles, extends southerly forty-four miles to Nahr Rubin, south of Joppa, where it is twelve miles wide. It is an undulating country with a line of low rocky hills along the coast. In the north end are marshes and miry bogs. There are also, scattered here and there, small groups of oaks, the remains of an extensive forest. This district is now inhabited by lawless Arab shepherds.

[1] Judg. 1 : 31.

The southern part of Sharon is a fruitful region, yielding wheat, oranges, lemons, pomegranates, grapes, apples, and melons.

Joppa, or as known by its modern name of Jaffa or Yaffa, though having no harbor, is the chief port of Palestine. It was at this place that the timber from Lebanon for both the first and second temples was landed.[1] From this port Jonah sailed;[2] and here also Peter had his vision.[3]

Cæsarea, thirty-two miles north of Joppa, was built by Herod the Great, when Palestine was under Roman rule. Herod lavished untold wealth on its palace, temple, theater, amphitheater and great breakwater. The apostle Paul was kept here as a prisoner for two years.[4]

Lydda (*Lod* or *Lud*) is situated in a fertile district, nine miles from Joppa, and on the northern road between Joppa and Jerusalem. Peter labored here with much success.[5]

Ramleh, fourteen miles from Joppa, on the road to Jerusalem, surrounded by olive groves, is a small but prosperous town, founded by the Mohammedans.

Philistia.—The land of the Philistines occupies the southern part of the Maritime Plain. It extends about forty miles north and south, and it varies in width from twelve to twenty-five miles. Elevated from one hundred to two hundred feet above the sea level, it is for the most part a fertile plain without trees. Along the coast is a fringe of sand hills, and on the east the undulating plains are varied by ridges of highland. The country is noted for its fruitful grain fields and rich pastures, though extensive districts have been much injured by drifting sand. At certain seasons of the year the fields are gay with poppies, pimpernels, narcissus, blue iris, and other bright colored flowers. The Philistines are supposed to have settled in Palestine shortly before the arrival of the Israelites, and like them to have come directly from Egypt.[6] The origin of the people, however, is not known. The territory occupied by them was allotted to Judah. Some portions of the country were taken by this tribe, but were held for only a short time. The Philistines were a warlike people and proved very troublesome to their neighbors. The wars between the two countries were generally along the borderland known as the Shephelah, and in the valleys leading up to the highlands of Judæa, though at times the Philistines penetrated to the very heart of the country.[7] Because of their position on the great highway traversed by the armies of Egypt and Assyria, the Philistines as a nation became extinct. The name Palestine, however, remains as a memorial of the people.

The principal cities of Philistia were Gaza, Ashkelon, Ashdod, Ekron, and Gath.

[1] 2 Chron. 2: 16; Ezra 3: 7. [2] Jonah 1: 3. [3] Acts 10: 1–16.
[4] Acts 23: 23, 24. [5] Acts 9: 32–35. [6] Gen. 10: 19.
[7] Judg. 13: 1; 16: 21, 30; 1 Sam., chs. 4, 5, 6, 13, 14, 17, 28, 29.

Gaza is situated on a hill in the southwestern corner of the country, three miles from the sea. It has existed as an important city from the earliest historic times down to the present day. Its importance has been due chiefly to its position as the halting place before entering the desert, on the road from Palestine to Egypt. The place has frequent mention in the Bible.[1]

Ashkelon was the only one of the five cities that stood on the shore. The neighboring country is very fertile, and was once famous for its excellent wine. The city is noted for important events connected with the Crusades.

Ashdod or Azotus was a strongly fortified city, three miles from the sea, on the road between Egypt and the East. It was one of the chief seats of the worship of Dagon, the fish-god. Psammetichus, king of Egypt, took the city after a siege of twenty-seven years.

Ekron, in the vale of Sorek, was the last city to which the ark was taken before its return to Beth-shemesh.[2] These two cities were connected by a direct road.

Gath has so completely disappeared that its very site is unknown. The probable situation of the city was at the foot of the highlands of Judah, ten miles east of Ashdod.[3]

Roads and Passes.—The Maritime Plain, without obstruction throughout its entire length and open at both ends, was the great route of travel between Egypt and Arabia on the one side, and Palestine, Damascus, and the far East on the other. Throughout the ages it was rather the world's highway for merchant caravans and invading armies than the country of any one people.

The route through the plain led up from the desert by way of Gaza and Ashdod through Sharon. From Ashdod northerly there were two routes. One turning coastward led to Joppa and Cæsarea; the other kept inland past Ekron, Ramleh, and Lydda.

A possible route from Sharon to Phœnicia lay along the shore round the headland of Carmel. Richard, the lion-hearted, and Napoleon led their armies by this way; but the route was difficult and dangerous. The common route was at the southeast of Carmel by Tell Keimun and the lower Kishon Valley.

The route to the Jordan Valley and Damascus lay along Wady Nar and through the Plain of Dothan, entering Esdraelon at Jenin. By this way were the Ishmaelites traveling when they fell in with Jacob's sons at Dothan.[4] There were also other passes at this end of Carmel.

[1] Gen. 10: 19; Josh. 10: 41; 11: 22; 13: 3; 15: 47; Judg. 1: 18; 16: 21; Acts 8: 26.
[2] 1 Sam. 5: 10.    [3] 1 Sam. 17: 4, 23.    [4] Gen. 37: 25.

## CHAPTER IV
### THE SHEPHELAH

BETWEEN Philistia and the highlands of Judæa there lies a middle ground, neither plain nor mountain. Consisting of groups of low rounded chalk hills, broken up by several broad valleys running crosswise from the mountains, this territory is physically distinct from the Maritime Plain. Nor are these hills the lower slopes of the mountains on the east; for they are separated from them by a deep valley running north and south. Moreover the hills of this district differ from the highlands lying east of them in being formed of a softer limestone, more easily worn down by mechanical action. This land is in Hebrew called *The Shephelah*, a word that in the common version of the Bible is translated "Low Country."[1] The Shephelah proper lies between Beer-sheba and the Vale of Aijalon. The foothills farther north, along the borders of Samaria, do not stand out by themselves, but are simply the lower slopes of the mountains.

Passing along the valley that lies between the Shephelah and the highlands of Judæa, one would have on the east precipitous heights rising from 2,000 to 3,000 feet; on the west the hills of the Shephelah are only about one fourth of that height. The broad cross valleys are well watered by small streams flowing through them to the Maritime Plain, and they are clothed with rich grainfields and fruitful olive groves. These valleys are continued by narrow, rocky defiles up into the mountains of Judæa to the central watershed.

The valleys of the Shephelah have been the scene of many encounters between opposing forces. In the early times the combatants were Israelites and Canaanites; later the wars were waged between Israelites and Philistines; then the Maccabees fought here with the Syrians; and in the time of the Crusades Richard of England and Saladin the Saracen led the opposing armies.

The **Vale of Aijalon** is the most northerly of the cross valleys. It is continued into the highlands by gorges that lead past the Beth-horons to Gibeon, and is one of the easiest routes between Joppa and Jerusalem. Along this valley Joshua pursued the Amorites on the noted occasion when he commanded the sun and moon to stand still until he had finished his day's work.[2] By this route also the Philistines invaded the land of Israel in the time of King Saul, and after a period of oppression they

[1] 2 Chron. 28: 18.     [2] Josh. 10: 1–14.

were, through the bravery of Jonathan, discomfited and driven back.[1] While they held the Israelites under their power, the Philistines, to prevent them from making instruments of war, removed all the smiths from the land.[2]

On a high point overlooking the Vale of Aijalon stood the strong city Gezer. King Horam and many of the inhabitants of the city were slain in Joshua's wars, but it does not appear that the city was taken.[3] Gezer maintained its independence down to a much later period, when it was captured and burned by Pharaoh of Egypt, who gave the site to his daughter, the wife of King Solomon.[4]

Through recent explorations at Gezer various ancient relics have been discovered. Among these are pieces of broken pottery that are considered as belonging to an age anterior to the settlement of Palestine by the Israelites.

**Wady es Surar** or **Vale of Sorek,** in the Shephelah, is continued by a defile to the highlands south of Jerusalem. At its junction with the valley running north and south at the base of the highlands is a wide, well-watered basin. The inheritance of the tribe of Dan lay between Sorek and Aijalon.[5] It was but a brief sojourn the Danites made here, so that the place became known simply as "the Camp of Dan."[6] Samson, the hero of the tribe of Dan, was born in Zorah, and in the Vale of Sorek he began his wonderful exploits. In the neighborhood was Timnath, the home of the Philistine maiden who first won the heart of Samson, and not far distant, in the valley, were the wheat fields into which Samson set loose his three hundred foxes with firebrands tied to their tails.[7] What a vein of humor the young man had, as well as a spirit of revenge!

On the south side of Sorek was Beth-shemesh to which the ark was brought from Ekron, and in full view in the vale below was the wheat field where the labors of the reapers were arrested by the lowing kine as they came up the vale.[8]

The railway between Jaffa and Jerusalem passes through Wady Surar.

**Wady es Sur** or **The Vale of Elah,** still farther south, leads up through the Shephelah to a level plain, supposed to be the battle field where David slew Goliath. From this plain two divergent wadies strike up into the mountains, one (Jindy) toward Bethlehem, and the other (Sur) toward Hebron. Off Wady Sur, on the right as you go up, is a cave region, in which, as some writers suppose, is the famous cave Adullam, for a time the headquarters of David and his forlorn four hundred.[9]

[1] 1 Sam., chs. 13, 14.  [2] 1 Sam. 13: 19–21.  [3] Josh. 10: 33; 12: 12.
[4] 1 Kings 9: 16.  [5] Josh. 19: 40–48.  [6] Judg. 13: 25; ch. 18.
[7] Judg. 15: 4, 5.  [8] 1 Sam., ch. 6.  [9] 1 Sam. 22: 1, 2.

**Wady el Afranj** and **Wady el Hesy** lie in the extreme south. Beit Jibrin or Eleutheropolis, in the former, was a place of much importance when the country was under Roman rule. On a mound in the Valley of el Hesy is Lachish, a place of historic interest.

In the Shephelah are many small villages, and ruins of villages of former ages are still more numerous. Among the rocky hills are old wine and oil presses that tell of the industries of former days. There are also remains of cloisters, churches, and other ancient structures. Then the hills, which are formed of soft limestone, are honeycombed with caves more or less excavated by human hands. All these things speak of the varied history of the land. In early Christian times apostles and evangelists preached the gospel in its cities. Peter, who visited "the saints who were at Lydda," was not the first missionary in the region.[1] Later when dire persecution arose under the Roman emperors, the Christians sought refuge in the caves with which the land abounds. The most famous cave district is toward the south near Beit Jibrin. In this neighborhood "are caves in which you may wander for hours, through cells, rooms, and pillared halls with staircases and large corridors, all cut out of the soft yellow chalk."[2]

[1] Acts 9 : 32.    [2] George Adam Smith.

## CHAPTER V
### GALILEE

THE word Galilee means a round object, a circuit, a region. The name was first given to a small district in the northeast of the Land of Israel and afterwards it was extended to a larger territory.[1]

At a certain period in its history Galilee was occupied by a people who were not of Israelite stock, and hence it was spoken of as "Galilee of the Gentiles."[2] The twenty cities given by Solomon to Hiram, King of Tyre, in compensation for materials used in building the temple were probably inhabited chiefly by Gentiles.[3]

Galilee was bounded on the north by the deep gorge of the Leontes; it extended to the eastern borders of the Jordan Valley and to the southern borders of Esdraelon. Although the Promised Land extended westerly to the Mediterranean Sea, the coast country was always occupied by Gentiles. Galilee included Mount Carmel and the eastern shores of the Sea of Galilee. It measured about fifty miles north and south and thirty miles east and west, comprising an area of about 1,600 square miles.

Upper Galilee comprised the territory between the Leontes and the parallel passing through the north end of the Sea of Galilee. It consists of a plateau about 2,000 feet high, varied with valleys and with mountains along the south side from 2,500 to 3,000 feet high. Lower Galilee is much less elevated, its plains being about 700 feet in height, and its hills less than 2,000 feet. The Galilæan highlands form a somewhat wavelike succession of hills and valleys, running east and west.

**Mount Tabor** (1,843 feet), on the northeast of Esdraelon, is of historic note. Isolated from other highlands, it appears in the distance like a truncated cone and forms a conspicuous object in the landscape.[4] It was here that Deborah and Barak assembled their forces for the contest against Sisera.[5] Some persons have thought Tabor to be the Mount of Transfiguration, but the best authorities give this distinction to Mount Hermon.

**Little Hermon** (1,800 feet), spoken of in Judges as the Hill Moreh,[6] rises abruptly from the plain on the southwest of the Sea of Galilee. Endor is situated on its northern slope. The rocky hills in its neighbor-

---
[1] Josh. 20:7.   [2] Isa. 9:1.   [3] 1 Kings 9:11.
[4] Jer. 46:18; Ps. 89:12.   [5] Judg. 4:6-14.   [6] Judg. 7:1.

hood abound in caves, one of which may have been the home of the witch visited by King Saul.[1] Endor is seven or eight miles from Gilboa where Saul's army was encamped.

**The Nazareth Range** rises by terraces from the northern borders of Esdraelon, and then slopes gently to the north and west.

Like other portions of the highlands, Galilee is of limestone formation. The region near the Sea of Galilee is volcanic, as shown by lava strewn over the surface and by hot springs near the lake. Galilee is also subject to earthquakes.

Galilee is a well-watered and fertile region. Its valleys and plains are suited for tillage and pasture, and its hills are covered with forests. The richness of the land is beautifully pictured in the blessings of Jacob and Moses on the tribes of Asher and Naphtali.[2]

After the early settlement of the tribes little reference is made in the Old Testament to Galilee. Except in the early times the tribes occupying it took no prominent part in the affairs of the nation. The references in the New Testament are chiefly to places in Lower Galilee, as Nazareth, Nain, Cana; and the cities around the lake. This was the scene of a large part of our Lord's ministry as described in the first three Gospels. The illustrations used by Jesus in his teachings here were such as appealed specially to the husbandman, the fisherman, and the merchant, while in Judæa he drew them chiefly from shepherd life and vine culture.

The tribes that settled in Galilee were an open-hearted and brave people.[3] In the time of our Lord the people here were less exclusive and bigoted, and they were thus more teachable than were those of Judæa. At the same time they were probably less cultured, and they seem to have had some peculiarity of speech or provincialism by which they could be distinguished from their Judæan brethren.[4] The disciples, with the exception of Judas and perhaps two or three others, were Galilæans.

The chief places in Galilee that need further notice were Kedesh, Safed, Shunem, Nazareth, Cana, Nain, and the cities on the shores of the Sea of Galilee.[5]

**Kedesh** or **Kedesh-naphtali** was a fortified city and a city of refuge in Upper Galilee. It was the home of Barak.[6]

**Safed**, in the mountain district of Naphtali, is not mentioned in the Bible, but it is spoken of in the Talmud as one of the holy cities of Palestine. It was the scene of noted events connected with the Crusades, and it has ruins of a strong castle built by the warriors of that period. The city was visited by an earthquake on New Year's day, 1837, causing the death of 5,000 of its inhabitants.

**Shunem**, allotted to the tribe of Issachar, was probably situated

---

[1] 1 Sam. 28 : 7–25. [2] Gen. 49 : 20; Deut. 33 : 23, 24. [3] Judg. 5 : 18.
[4] Mark 14 : 70. [5] See Chapter IX. [6] Judg. 4 : 6; Josh. 19 : 32; 20 : 7; 21 : 32.

seven or eight miles south of Mount Tabor. It is interesting from its connection with the story of Elisha.[1]

**Nazareth**, the home of Joseph and Mary and the place where Jesus was brought up, was situated in a basin-shaped valley among the hills on the borders of Esdraelon. Though shut in by these hills, it was near the great route of travel between southern Palestine and the countries on the northeast, the northern portion of the route passing through Cœle-Syria. From the heights near Nazareth can be seen many noted places in northern Palestine.

**Cana of Galilee** was near Capernaum and on higher ground.[2] The traditional site is about four miles northeast of Nazareth. It is noted as the scene of Christ's first miracle,[3] and also as the native place of the disciple Nathanael.[4]

**Nain**, situated on the northwest of Little Hermon, near its base, is memorable as the place where Jesus raised the widow's son to life.[5] The approach to the village on the northwest is by a steep, rocky pathway, along which are many caves used as sepulchers.

**Routes of Travel.**—Galilee was situated between countries that carried on large trade with each other, and the highways that lay over hills and plains brought her into contact with the people of these countries. Some of the old roads constructed by the Romans still remain. A great trade route from Damascus lay round Hermon and through Upper Galilee to Capernaum, where at one time Matthew the publican collected the Roman taxes. From this place the road passed over Esdraelon to the coast. Other roads led across Galilee between Phœnicia and Damascus.

[1] 2 Kings 4:8.   [2] John 2:11, 12; 4:46.   [3] John 2:1, 11; 4:46.
[4] John 21:2.   [5] Luke 7:11.

# CHAPTER VI

## ESDRAELON

The Plain of Esdraelon divided the western highlands into two sections. The main body of the plain, which has an average elevation of two hundred feet above the sea level, has the general form of a triangle, the angular points being at Tell el Kasis on the Kishon nine miles from its mouth, En-gannim or Jenin at the foot of the hills of Samaria, and Mount Tabor. The southwest side, along the base of Carmel, is about twenty miles long, the east and north sides are each about fifteen miles. Regularity of form, however, is much broken by the lowlands running in at various places among the hills, and by ridges thrust out from these hills into the plain.

**The Gateways.**—Esdraelon is an open plain. On the west is a gateway where the Kishon passes through the Plain of Acre to the sea. At one place this is but a narrow pass a hundred yards wide between the hills of Galilee and Carmel. Another opening lies through the Vale of Dothan at the southwest corner. On the eastern side are two openings to the Jordan Valley. By far the more important of these is the Valley of Jezreel between Mount Gilboa and Little Hermon or the Hill Moreh. The other lies between Moreh and Mount Tabor, continued by a narrow wady to the Jordan. The lowlands also form a deep recess or bay without outlet behind Gilboa.

The name Esdraelon is the Greek form of Jezreel, which means "God's Sowing," in allusion doubtless to the luxuriance of vegetation on the plain. In Bible story the main portion of the plain is sometimes called the Plain of Megiddo.

Esdraelon is divided by a slight swell into two very unequal slopes. This water-parting lies between Jezreel and Shunem. The western and longer slope is drained by the Kishon and its tributaries. The eastern slope, known as the Valley of Jezreel, is about twelve miles in length. Through it flows Nahr Jalud, a small rapid stream which falls four hundred feet in its short course.

**The Kishon** in the dry season is only a small river. Many of its tributaries are but winter torrents that during the summer are quite dry. But in the rainy season, fed by these torrents that come dashing down from the highlands on each side, the Kishon becomes a large and tumultuous river. The strong current at this season has worn a deep channel along the bed of the river, so that crossing in the rainy season is difficult and dangerous.

**The Soil** of Esdraelon is a loose loam, rich and productive for grain and for pasturage. In the rainy season portions of the plain become drenched and miry.

**Common Property.**—Esdraelon with its open gateways always invited intrusion, either of wandering shepherds seeking pasturage for their flocks, or of marauders bent on plunder. It was the battle field of Palestine and the warpath traversed in all ages by the nations of the east and of the west. Some of its battles may be briefly noticed.

**Deborah's Victory.**—Early in the period of the Judges the Canaanites held the plain, thus separating the tribes on the north from those on the south. It was at this time that Deborah of Mount Ephraim and Barak of Kedesh-naphtali gathered their forces on Mount Tabor.[1] Sisera with his army and his chariots was on the plain. During the battle that took place heavy rain set in. The horses and chariots were mired in the soft ground,[2] and Sisera fled on foot eastward and was slain by Jael, the wife of Heber the Kenite.[3] The Kishon, swollen by the floods, overwhelmed the army which fled westward down its valley.[4]

**Gideon's Victory.**—A little later in the history of Israel, Esdraelon saw another battle. This time it was the Midianites from the east that were the invaders, and their object was plunder.[5] Gideon's army was posted on the northern slopes of Gilboa at the head of the Valley of Jezreel, and the hosts of Midian were in the valley opposite by the Hill Moreh.[6] Close at Gideon's feet, in the valley, were three springs that issued from the rocks of Mount Gilboa, beside one of which, the famous Well of Harod, he chose his valiant three hundred.[7] By these three hundred the hosts of Midian and Amalek were put to flight, and chased down the Valley of Jezreel, across the Jordan, at the Fords of Beth-barah, and far away among the mountains of Gilead.[8]

**Saul's Defeat.**—Yet another conflict in this great battle field—that in which Saul and Jonathan were slain. The Philistines, who were ever as "thorns in the sides" of the Israelites,[9] had marched up the Maritime Plain and entered Esdraelon, probably by way of Megiddo, and were encamped near Shunem over against Gilboa. King Saul, with the army of Israel, took up his position on Mount Gilboa.[10] Then we have the weird story of Saul's midnight tramp some seven or eight miles over the plain, past the enemy's encampment, to the hag who told fortunes in some hiding place at Endor.[11] Little comfort got the God-forsaken monarch

---

[1] Judg. 4: 5, 6, 12, 14.　　[2] Judg. 5: 20.　　[3] Judg. 4: 11, 17–21.
[4] Judg. 5: 21.　　[5] Judg. 6: 2–6, 11.　　[6] Judg. 7: 1.
[7] Judg. 7: 1, 4–6.　　[8] Judg. 7: 24, 25.　　[9] Judg. 2: 3.
[10] 1 Sam. 28: 4.　　[11] 1 Sam. 28: 7–25.

that night. But the story need not be told here. The Philistines were victorious. Saul and his sons were slain, and their headless bodies, ghastly spectacle! were hung by the gate on the walls of Beth-shan at the foot of the Valley of Jezreel.[1]

**Josiah and Pharaoh-necho.**—Again disaster befell Israel in Esdraelon. Pharaoh-necho of Egypt, on the warpath against the king of Babylon, marching through the coast lands of Philistia and Sharon, had come through the mountain passes to Megiddo.[2] Here Josiah King of Judah sought to arrest his progress across the plain, and was fatally wounded in the attempt. Josiah had been a good king and a great reformer in his day. Such men did not always occupy the throne, and "all Judah and Jerusalem mourned for him." The prophet Jeremiah, too, "lamented for Josiah," but he sought to restrain the tears of the people for the worse ills that were to come:—

> "Weep not for the dead, nor bemoan him:
> But weeping weep for him that goeth away:
> For he shall never come back, nor see the land of his birth."[3]

**Other Battles.**—Other battles there were in Esdraelon, but their story cannot here be told. Jehu from Ramoth-gilead, driving with characteristic fury up the Valley of Jezreel, met and slew the kings of Judah and Israel at the head of the valley.[4] Battles there were here also in later days by the Maccabees, the Romans, the Arabs, the Crusaders, and by Napoleon.

**Armageddon.**—Meditating on the war that is ever being waged between the forces of right and wrong, the seer of Patmos, with the memory of Esdraelon as the battle field of his nation's history before his mind, pictures this plain, under the name of Armageddon, as the scene of a final conflict, "the battle of that great day of God Almighty" that shall forever end the struggle between good and evil.[5]

---

[1] 1 Sam., ch. 31.  [2] 2 Kings 23: 28, 29; 2 Chron. 35: 20–25.  [3] Jer. 22: 10.
[4] 2 Kings 9: 1–3, 16–27.  [5] Rev. 16: 16.

## CHAPTER VII

### SAMARIA

The Samaria of the New Testament was Mount Ephraim of the Old Testament. It was here that Ephraim, half Manasseh, and Dan had their allotment. It is the most open part of the southern section of the western highlands, and the easiest of access. Abraham came first to this region on entering the Land of Canaan. Jacob also, on returning with his family from Padan-aram, came this way, and halted here for a time. Within its borders occurred many of the great events of Old Testament times. After the captivity of the Northern Kingdom, it was, in large measure, occupied by an alien people. At the beginning of the Christian era it had long ceased to be regarded as a part of the Holy Land and was looked on with disdain as a polluted land to be religiously avoided by every true son of Israel.

Bounds.—The northern boundary of Samaria lay along the southern edge of Esdraelon; the eastern border was the Jordan; the western was the eastern edge of Sharon. The limit on the south was variable, though the usual line lay directly south of Bethel.

The earliest boundary on the south, which, with some minor changes, continued from the division of the kingdom down to the exile, lay along Wady Suweinit on the Jordan slope, the Vale of Aijalon on the seaward slope, and a connecting line between them across the plateau south of Bethel. Jericho, south of this line, belonged to the Northern Kingdom. After their return from Babylon the Jews made gradual advances northerly, till at the time of our Lord's ministry Judæa included considerable territory that had belonged to the Northern Kingdom. It was then scarcely twenty-five miles across Samaria. Yet to avoid passing through this polluted land pilgrims from Galilee generally crossed the Jordan at fords opposite Beth-shan, went down the Jordan Valley, and recrossed the Jordan near Jericho.

Physical Features.—Samaria has an average elevation of about 2,000 feet above the sea level and an extreme of over 3,000 feet. Generally it is not so much a mountain mass as a series of high ridges with intervening elevated valleys and plains. The northern half of the country is open on the east, north, and west. It descends to the Jordan Valley and to the Maritime Plain by gradually sloping ridges and broad valleys. On the north is an easy gradient through a succession of plains to

Esdraelon. The southern half of Samaria is bordered on the eastern and western sides by more precipitous banks and steep, rugged wadies.

The Water-Parting between the eastern and western slopes is far east of the middle of the highlands, giving two thirds of the whole breadth to the western side. The short descent to the depressed Jordan Valley is thus very steep, being in the southern section about 2,800 feet in the distance of nine miles. The slope on the western side is much more gradual.

The chief elevations above the general level are Mounts Carmel, Gilboa, Ebal, Gerizim, and Baal-Hazor.

**Carmel** is a singular ridge about twelve miles long, loosely connected with the highlands of Samaria by rounded hills of soft limestone, broken by more or less open valleys. It strikes one's fancy as a displacement of high land that once filled the gap of Esdraelon. The height of the ridge varies, reaching its highest point, 1,742 feet, about four miles from its northern end. The ridge terminates in a bold promontory 500 feet high, leaving a pass 600 feet wide between the mountain and the sea. At the southeast, where the ridge breaks down into low hills, lie the Valley of Dothan and various narrow passes. The seaward slopes are gradual; but on the north the descent to the Valley of the Kishon is often very steep. The mountain is of limestone formation and is honeycombed with long winding caverns. During the existence of the Northern Kingdom, Carmel was politically connected with Samaria; in later time its relations were more commonly with Galilee.

The word Carmel means park or garden. In Hebrew it is generally preceded by the word "the." It is "The Park" taking its name doubtless from the richness of its soil, its verdure, and the beauty of its groves and flowers, features of "excellency" for which it and Sharon were conspicuous.[1] Carmel was a sanctuary, a holy place, resorted to both by the worshipers of Jehovah and by the devotees of false gods.[2]

**Mount Gilboa** is a bleak barren ridge rising to about 1,700 feet at the highest, and extending about ten miles along the southern borders of Esdraelon. It is famous as the scene of the defeat and death of Saul and Jonathan, an event which gave origin to that pathetic dirge known as David's Lament, in which the bard of Israel voiced his own and the nation's grief.[3]

**Mounts Ebal** and **Gerizim,** on the line of the central watershed, are often referred to in Bible story. At their base they are less than a quarter of a mile apart. Ebal, on the north, rises to the height of 3,076 feet above the sea level; Gerizim, on the south, 2,848 feet; and the Vale of Shechem, between them, is 1,672 feet. These mountains were the scene of one of the grandest assemblages of people of which history makes record.

[1] Isa. 35:2.  [2] 1 Kings 18:19.  [3] 2 Sam. 1:17-27.

According to the command of Moses, Joshua, shortly after crossing the Jordan, led the whole body of the Israelites, men, women, and children, to this place. Here, the Levites, standing in the valley, pronounced the curses of the law on evil-doers, to which half of the tribes, standing on Ebal, responded "Amen"; then the Levites pronounced the blessings on well-doers, followed by "Amen" from the other tribes, standing on Gerizim.[1] Later, shortly before his death, Joshua again convened the tribes at the same place to receive his last words of counsel.[2]

A graphic story connected with Gerizim is that of Jotham and his parable of the trees choosing a king to rule over them. One can easily picture this wily chieftain as he stands on some projecting bluff, telling his story so full of biting sarcasm to the ungrateful men of Shechem in the valley at his feet, and then running for his life to escape their fury.[3]

In later times the Samaritans, excluded from any part in the worship at Jerusalem, erected a temple on Mount Gerizim. "Our fathers worshiped in this mountain," said the woman of Samaria to our Lord, as she pointed to Gerizim that rose near by.[4] But the temple in which her fathers worshiped had been destroyed nearly 170 years.

It is held by some writers, with much show of reason, that Gerizim was the mountain to which Abraham journeyed for the sacrifice of Isaac.[5]

**The Vale of Shechem**, between Ebal and Gerizim, slopes both easterly and westerly. The valley with its gardens and orchards, and its copious springs of water, is a place of surpassing beauty, and the surrounding country is very fertile. Within the valley is the piece of ground that Jacob purchased from the children of Hamor, and which afterwards became the burial place of Joseph.[6] Here also is Jacob's Well, at which occurred the interview between our Saviour and the woman of Samaria. "The well is deep," and the sinking of it must have cost much labor. As there is abundance of water in the place, the special purpose of the well is an interesting question. Probably to avoid quarrels with the shepherds, Jacob thought it advisable to have water supply of his own.

**Baal-Hazor**, twenty miles south of Gerizim, over 3,300 feet above the level of the sea, is one of the highest points in the land. On this mountain Absalom had an estate. where he held the great feast at the sheep-shearing, at which he caused his brother Amnon to be assassinated.[7]

**Valleys and Plains.**—A central plain along the line of the watershed, or rather a series of plains opening into each other between low hills, leads up from Esdraelon on the north, extending far through the middle of the country. Opening out from this are many cross valleys or

[1] Deut., ch. 27; Josh., ch. 8.   [2] Josh., ch. 24.   [3] Judg., ch. 9.   [4] John 4: 20.
[5] Gen., ch. 22.   [6] Gen. 33: 19; Josh. 24: 32.   [7] 2 Sam. 13: 23–29.

wadies, some on the east running down to the Jordan Valley; others on the west to the Maritime Plain.

**Wady Farah,** on the east, at first runs northerly past Gerizim and Ebal, and then curving around to the southeast, opens to the Jordan Valley near the Damieh Ford opposite the mouth of the Jabbok.

The **Plain of Dothan** strikes out westerly between the low hills that connect Carmel with the main highlands. It was in this fertile district that Joseph found his brothers guarding their flocks.[1] A few miles farther south, on the same side, is **The Barley Vale** (Wady esh-Shair) which leads down from the Valley of Shechem to the Maritime Plain. Still farther south is **The Brook Kanah,** the boundary line between Ephraim and Manasseh.[2]

**Cities.**—The principal cities and towns of Samaria were Jezreel, Beth-shan, Megiddo, En-gannim, Shechem, Tirzah, Samaria, Bethel, and Shiloh.

**Jezreel** doubtless took its name from the fertile lands spread out at its base. The city was situated on a foothill of Gilboa, which on the northeast has a steep rocky descent of a hundred feet to the plain. It commanded a wide prospect, looking westward over Esdraelon to Mount Carmel. From a tower on the eastern wall the watchman could see far down the Valley of Jezreel.[3] The city became important in the time of Ahab and Jezebel, it being their chief place of residence. The royal palace stood on the eastern wall with high windows looking down the valley.[4] Close to this wall was an open space, a depository of city offal, which was devoured by ravenous dogs, the city's scavengers. Out from one of these windows to the ground below, at the command of Jehu, was Jezebel thrown, and here at the base of the wall was her mangled body devoured by the hungry dogs.[5] Near the city are three springs, one of them the famous Well of Harod, the sources of Nahr Jalud.[6]

**Beth-shan** is situated at the foot of the Valley of Jezreel "on the brow where the valley drops down 300 feet to the Ghor" or Jordan Valley. It was allotted to Manasseh though within the limits of Issachar, but it was long occupied by the Canaanites.[7] In the time of the Maccabees the name of the city was changed to Scythopolis. It contains ruins of ancient temples and of an amphitheater.

**Megiddo** has been identified as the modern Lejjun, the Roman military station Legio. It is situated on the southern borders of Esdraelon and commands the entrance to the pass on the caravan route between Egypt and Damascus.

**En-gannim** is supposed to have occupied the site of the modern village Jenin, situated at the entrance of the highland plains on the south

---

[1] Gen. 37 : 17.  [2] Josh. 17 : 9.  [3] 2 Kings 9 : 17.  [4] 2 Kings 9 : 30.
[5] 2 Kings 9 : 30-35.  [6] 1 Sam. 29 : 1 ; Judg. 7 : 1.  [7] Judg. 1 : 27.

of Esdraelon, and on the road leading up through Central Samaria. The ancient name En-gannim means "Spring of Gardens." The gardens and orchards that surround the village and the spring that furnishes it with water still justify the name.

**Shechem** occupied a site of singular beauty on the highest part of the valley close under Mount Gerizim.[1] It was on the great thoroughfare between Jerusalem and Galilee, and was an important center with roads leading out in all directions. It is one of the earliest places mentioned in the Bible.[2] Here Rehoboam was crowned, and under Jeroboam the place became the first capital of the Northern Kingdom.[3] In later times the city got the name Neapolis (Newtown) which has become changed to the modern Nablus. It has been a common opinion that Sychar was the same place as Shechem. There are, however, good reasons for believing that Sychar was another city, situated about two miles to the northeast of Shechem.

**Tirzah**, noted for its beauty, became the second royal city of the kings of Israel.[4] Zimri, besieged in Tirzah, to save himself from capture set fire to his palace and perished in the flames.[5] The site of this city is not certainly known, but it was probably a few miles northeast of Shechem.

**Samaria** was founded by Omri, who purchased the site for two talents of silver.[6] This site, as beautiful as it is commanding, on an oblong hill, rising abruptly 400 feet above the level of the Barley Vale, in which it is situated, is about six miles northwest of Shechem. Here, on this hill, overlooked by still higher hills beyond the valley, Omri built the new city which became the permanent capital of the kingdom. The city was almost impregnable. Two sieges it sustained without yielding—one in 901 B. C.;[7] the other nine years later.[8] In 721 B. C., after a three years' siege it was captured by Shalmaneser, king of Assyria.[9] Near the beginning of the Christian era, Samaria was rebuilt by Herod the Great and named Sebaste, the Greek equivalent for the Latin Augusta, the feminine of Augustus. Some broken pillars, colonnades, and other remains of Herod's great work still exist, but the city has gone, and only a small village occupies its site.

**Bethel** ("House of God")[10] occupied an important position as a frontier town of the Kingdom of Israel. It was on the great thoroughfare between Judæa and Galilee.[11] Passes also from the Jordan Valley and from Sharon meet here. Scarcely any spot in Palestine witnessed so many remarkable events of sacred story. From a mountain on the east of Bethel,

---

[1] See Vale of Shechem, p. 33.  [2] Gen. 12:6; 33:18; 37:12.  [3] 1 Kings 12:1, 25.
[4] Song of Solomon 6:4; 1 Kings 14:17; 15:33.  [5] 1 Kings 16:18.
[6] 1 Kings 16:23, 24.  [7] 1 Kings 20:1.  [8] 2 Kings 6:24 to 7:20.
[9] 2 Kings 18:9, 10.  [10] Gen. 28:19; 35:14, 15.  [11] Judges 20:31; 21:19.

Abraham directed Lot to survey the land and choose his place of residence.[1] At Bethel Jacob saw the wonderful vision of the ladder that reached to heaven.[2] It was one of the three cities in Samuel's yearly circuit and was a holy place of resort to ask counsel of God in times of difficulty.[3] But after the division of the kingdom it was greatly debased, Jeroboam making it a center of idol worship.[4] Bethel was captured and annexed to the Southern Kingdom of Abijah, though it probably was not held very long.[5]

**Shiloh** occupied a secluded place about ten miles north of Bethel on the east of the road that leads to Shechem. The site is without any attractive natural feature. For a period of about 400 years, in the time of the Judges, Shiloh was the seat of the Tabernacle and the Ark of the Covenant, and thus became the most revered sanctuary in the land.[6] On the capture of the Ark by the Philistines, Shiloh lost its preëminence as a holy place.[7] It was at Shiloh that the Benjamites seized young women for wives after their tribe had been nearly annihilated in the great war with the other tribes.[8]

**Roads and Open Valleys.**—Roads such as are common in western lands were unknown in Palestine. The comparatively smooth plains of Samaria, however, led to the early introduction of wheeled vehicles. Its open valleys also made the country so accessible on every side, that it was more exposed to raids of the plundering tribes of the desert and to invasions of formidable enemies than its sister kingdom on the more inaccessible highlands of Judæa.

[1] Gen. 13: 1–10.
[2] Gen. 28: 10–22.
[3] Judges 20: 18, 26–28; 21: 4; I Sam. 7: 16.
[4] I Kings 12: 27–33.
[5] 2 Chron. 13: 19.
[6] Judges 21: 19; Josh. 18: 1.
[7] I Sam. 4: 3–11.
[8] Judges 21: 19–23.

## CHAPTER VIII
## JUDÆA

In the settlement of the tribes by Joshua this territory was assigned to Benjamin, Judah, Simeon, and Dan. To Benjamin was allotted the northeastern portion, bordering on Ephraim and the Jordan. South of this, along the Dead Sea, covering the whole breadth of the plateau and as much of the Maritime Plain as he could wrest from the Philistines was Judah's portion. Of Simeon we have little mention, but his allotment was the dry south land, or the Negeb, lying next the desert. Dan's portion was on the west of Benjamin, between the Valleys of Sorek and Aijalon, and extending to the sea.[1]

At the disruption on the accession of Rehoboam, this territory formed the southern kingdom which remained under the dynasty of David. The boundary line between the two kingdoms, however, is somewhat uncertain, nor did it always hold the same place.

**Name.**—In the early times each portion of the Land of Israel was called by the name of its tribe. On the division of the kingdom this southern section became known as the Kingdom of Judah and also Judah, after the prominent tribe.[2] On the return of the people from the Captivity (A. D. 536), it was called Judæa. At the same time, the word Jews came into use as the name of the inhabitants of the land, and it has been extended so as to include Hebrew people of whatever tribe.[3]

**Bounds.**—On the north this division was bounded by Samaria; on the east by the Jordan and the Dead Sea; on the south by the Desert of Arabia. On the west the border varied according as Judah or Philistia prevailed. "The Promised Land" extended to the Mediterranean.

**Historic Note.**—In the early times, succeeding the settlement of the tribes, we find little mention of this part of the country. Remote on the mountain heights and isolated by the rocky walls on their borders from the outside world, its people, little disturbed by intrusions, seem to have kept very much by themselves. They apparently took no part in the wars of Barak and Gideon, and, with the exception of the tribes of Benjamin and Dan, had no recognition in Deborah's Song of Thanksgiving.[4] Nor did they in the early days possess much martial courage. For when under the yoke of Philistia, submissive to a state of vassalage, and devoid

---

[1] Josh., chs. 15–19.  
[2] 1 Kings 15: 9.  
[3] Ezra. 4: 12; Gal. 2: 14.  
[4] Judg. 4: 10; 5: 14, 17; 6: 35.

of the spirit of free men, they were ready even to sacrifice the hero of the tribe of Dan, who was giving his life to deliver them from their oppressors.[1]

In later days the people of Judæa were bigoted and exclusive, too narrow-minded to be anything but conservative of old customs and traditions. But they did develop love of country and a spirit that would suffer self-extinction rather than loss of independence. Of this the heroism shown at the destruction of Jerusalem by Titus bears witness.

**Size of the Country.**—Indeed when one thinks of how these people held out against the great world-powers, Egypt, Babylonia, and Rome, that sought their national extinction, one is apt to forget the utter insignificance of their territory—a mere speck on the map of the world, in length, from Geba to Beer-sheba,[2] 55 miles; in breadth about 30 miles; and having an area of about 1,500 square miles, of which a large part was desert.

**Physical Features.**—Judæa is massive highland or table-land varied by shallow valleys and dome-like heights that rise above the general level of the plateau. The central and main portion is a limestone plateau two thousand feet or more above the sea. The appearance of the country is not inspiring. Stones are everywhere. The moorland plains are strewn with stones. The hills that vary the surface are devoid of trees and almost of verdure, while in many a place the underlying limestone has thrust its bare scalp through the thin soil. The valleys are often but the rocky pathway of winter torrents. Another feature does not improve the picture—the dryness of the country. In traveling through the land from one end to the other one would not find more than six or seven perennial streams.

**Mountain Heights.**—Several points of eminence rise above the general level. **Neby Samwil** (2,935 feet), five miles northwest of Jerusalem, commands a wide view. It is considered by some persons to be the Mizpah in Benjamin of the Bible, and the "great high place" and sanctuary near Gibeon, where Solomon made choice of wisdom above all other gifts.[3]

**The Mount of Olives** (2,637 feet) is a curved ridge lying on the east of Jerusalem, from which it is separated by the narrow ravine of the Kidron. Its association with Bible events gives it an interest not surpassed by any place in Palestine. It was by this way that David went when he fled from Absalom.[4] But most of all, it derives interest as the theater of many events in the life of our Lord.[5] Gethsemane was on the western slope of Olivet, near Jerusalem.

Other parts of the country, south of Jerusalem, are still more elevated.

---

[1] Judg. 15:9–13.  [2] 2 Kings 23:8.  [3] 1 Kings 3:4–9.
[4] 2 Sam. 15:23,30.  [5] Matt. 24:3; Luke 19:29–38; 24:50–53; Acts 1:12.

The highest land is between Bethlehem and Hebron. South of Hebron the country falls off through the Negeb to the lower level of the desert.

**The Heights of Benjamin.**—The northern part of Judæa, between Jerusalem and Bethel, embracing the territory allotted to Benjamin, is a land of mountain ridges and high rocky plains. The soil is shallow, stony, and ill-suited to agriculture. On either side of the central watershed, which indeed is not central, but far over on the eastern side, are deep ravines or wadies, which, on the one hand, descend by steep incline to the Jordan Valley, and on the other less abruptly to the Maritime Plain. The descent to the Jordan Valley is estimated at 3,000 feet in the course of ten miles; on the west side at 1,800 feet in twenty-five miles.

On the eastern side, beginning at the central ridge, is Wady Suweinit which halfway down unites with Wady Kelt and then descends to the Jordan Valley. Along this way lies the great route between the highlands and the valley; but the route is rather along the intervening ridges than through the gorges, which are too deep and precipitous for highways. At best it was a toilsome way, and to make the journey from the Valley of the Jordan to the heights of Benjamin was emphatically "to labor thither."[1] On the western ridge again is the more gently sloping Valley of Aijalon, which opens out from the central watershed near Neby Samwil and passes by way of Upper and Lower Beth-horon. This was in ancient times the great route of travel between the Maritime Plain and Jerusalem. These two roads, east and west, thus form a continuous route across the highlands, between the sea and the Jordan. At the central watershed this route crosses the great highway between the far north by way of Shechem and the far south by way of Jerusalem and Hebron.[2]

Benjamin was thus an open gateway. It was also the borderland between the Kingdoms of Israel and Judah. Its position in this regard led to its becoming the site of several strongholds to guard against foreign enemies and encroachments of the sister kingdom. Among the places suggestive of great national events are Michmash, which stood on the northern edge of Wady Suweinit, and Gibeah or Geba directly opposite on the south side.[3] Not far distant was Ramah, memorable as the place where in vision the prophet sees the disconsolate Rachel weeping for her fallen children.[4] Near the head of this ravine stood Ai; also on the other side of the watershed was Gibeon that guarded the gateway of the west, the scene of many noted events from the time its citizens shrewdly practiced their artifice on Joshua, to the grand ceremonial of Solomon on his accession to the throne.[5] A few miles farther west were the Beth-horons,—the Upper and the Nether.[6]

[1] Josh. 7:3.
[3] 1 Sam. 14:5; 2 Kings 23:8.
[5] Josh. 9:3–15; 2 Sam. 20:5–10; 1 Kings 2:28, 29; 3:4.
[2] See Ch. IV, p. 22.
[4] Jer. 31:15; Matt. 2:16–18.
[6] Josh. 16:3, 5.

**Battles.**—By the route from Jordan along the borders of Suweinit Joshua made his first entrance to the interior in his expedition against Ai.[1] Later, in the days of King Saul, a great battle was fought near the head of this gorge. The Philistines had come into the very heart of the country, doubtless by way of the Valley of Aijalon, and crossing over they had encamped at Michmash. The Israelites were so stricken with fear that "they hid themselves in caves . . . and in rocks, and in high places, and in pits." Some of them also fled for safety across the Jordan.[2] The little band of warriors remaining to Saul were encamped at Gibeah on the opposite side of the gorge. For them there seemed little hope; but the valor of Jonathan and his armor-bearer saved the country. These heroes crossed the gorge where two points jut out from opposite sides, clambered up the steep cliffs on their hands and knees, and, aided by the timely occurrence of an earthquake, put to flight the panic-stricken Philistines.[3]

A great battle also was fought on the western side of these highlands on that memorable day when Joshua came to the aid of his new allies, the Gibeonites.[4]

**The Jeshimon.**—This is a long, narrow district, thirty-five miles north and south and ten miles east and west, known as the Wilderness of Judah, lying along the western side of the Dead Sea. It comprises broad, barren, and rocky plains, through the middle of which torrent beds slope to the Dead Sea. These plains are divided by equally barren ridges of limestone, furrowed down their steep sides by channels of winter torrents. This is one of the dryest and dreariest regions in all the land,—no water or vegetable life save in the rainy season. Little else than marl, flint, and jagged limestone rocks greets the eye of the weary traveler. An impressive feature of this desert region is the magic change wrought in it when the rainy season sets in. For a brief period "the desert rejoices, and blossoms as the rose."[5] At this season it affords herbage for the flocks of wandering shepherds. Somewhere in this region was the cave where David cut off the skirts of Saul's robe.[6] This is supposed to be the desert to which John the Baptist retired in the early part of his ministry, and also that in which Jesus was tempted by Satan.[7]

**Mar Saba.**—The gorge of the Kidron, in its course from Jerusalem to the Dead Sea, crosses this dreary wilderness. About twelve miles from Jerusalem, on the edge of the high cliffs overhanging the narrow gorge, stands Mar Saba, a monastery of the Greek Church, founded by St. Saba in the fifth century. The place is destitute of verdure—neither

---

[1] Josh. 7 : 2–5; 8 : 1–29.   [2] 1 Sam. 13 : 1–7.   [3] 1 Sam. 14 : 1–16.   [4] Josh. 10 : 1–14.
[5] Isa. 35 : 1.   [6] 1 Sam. 24 : 1–22.   [7] Matt. 3 : 1; 4 : 1.

tree nor blade of grass, save one solitary palm in the courtyard of the monastery. At one time, long ago, the monastery was inhabited by remarkable men, some of whom were noted hymn-writers. The sixty or seventy monks who now dwell here are in no respect worthy of their predecessors. The neighboring cliffs are honeycombed with caves to which the monks retreat for meditation and prayer.

**Fertile Districts.**—Judæa has its fertile districts. Wherever water is abundant there is fruitfulness. One of these oases lies about Hebron.[1] The country round Bethlehem also is productive, yielding grain, fruit, and pasturage.[2] The vine, a staple product in Bible ages, is still extensively cultivated. So are olives and figs. But yet on the whole, as in the past, so now, it is a pastoral rather than an agricultural country. In ancient times vine-culture and the care of flocks were the characteristic industries of the land, and from these the Bible borrows many of its metaphors.[3]

Doubtless in the days of the country's prosperity the land was far more productive than it is at present. The hills were terraced and carefully cultivated. The stones, gathered out of the soil, were built into walls and towers to guard the vineyards and the fields.

**Ruins.**—The ruins of ancient villages that crown many a hilltop are evidences of the country's former resources. "Above all other countries in the world," says Dean Stanley, "Palestine is a land of ruins." Of Judæa he says, "There is hardly a hilltop of the many that are within sight which is not covered by the vestiges of some fortress or city of former ages." But while on the east of the Jordan these remains of a former civilization have in many cases come down to the present day with comparatively little dilapidation, in Judæa they are more frequently masses of stones with little left to show their ancient architectural form.

**En-gedi.**—Midway along the heights that overlook the Dead Sea on the west is one of the most marvelous transitions, from a dreary, barren desert to a fertile oasis, that one can imagine. At the edge of the desert the land suddenly drops 400 feet and then slopes down to a broad fruitful garden land half a mile square, hanging like a picture facing the sea. Small grainfields, vineyards, orchards, and melon patches take the place of rocks. This is En-gedi.[4] The magic power of water has wrought the change. At the base of the cliffs on the upper side of the oasis the fountain bursts forth from its rocky prison and carries life and beauty along its pathway to the Dead Sea. Once the place was famous for its balsam trees and its palms. Hence came one of the names of the fortified town that stood here—Hazazon-tamar or "Hazazon of the Palm."[5]

[1] Num. 13 : 23–27.
[3] John 10 : 11 ; 15 : 1 ; Ps. 23 : 1 ; 80 : 8.
[5] Gen. 14 : 7 ; 2 Chron. 20 : 2.
[2] Ruth 2 : 1–8 ; Luke 2 : 8.
[4] Song of Solomon 1 : 14.

En-gedi is accessible by a sloping pathway from the beach on the margin of the Dead Sea, and by a steeper stairway from the desert. A route into Judæa from the Land of Moab lies round the south end of the Dead Sea and along the shore to En-gedi. From the summit of the banks the route varies, either southwest by Hebron, northwest direct to Jerusalem, or between these to Tekoa. This latter route was the one taken by the Moabites and Ammonites in the time of Jehoshaphat.[1]

**Masada.**—A few miles south of En-gedi, back of the desert, on the rocky heights that rise precipitously 1,700 feet above the shores of the Dead Sea, stands Masada, one of the strongest natural fortresses in the world. It is 1,300 feet higher than the adjoining land, except at one place where it is but 400 feet above a neck of rock running out from a wady that makes down from the desert. Thus isolated, it can be reached only by men in single file along rude steps cut in the rock. From its summit, a plateau 700 yards long and about 200 yards wide, the view is magnificent, including the whole of the Dead Sea and the long mountain wall of Moab beyond.

The Maccabees first made a fortress of this rock. Herod the Great in a time of danger fled hither. He strengthened the fortifications, built a gorgeous palace, cut reservoirs in the rock for holding rain water, and made caverns for storing wine and other supplies.

In A. D. 70, when Jerusalem was destroyed by the Romans, a band of Jews, the remnant of the garrison of Jerusalem, fled to this place with their wives and children. But when they saw that the Romans were about to gain possession of their stronghold, rather than fall into the hands of the enemy, these determined men first killed their wives and children; then ten of their number, chosen by lot, killed the others; one of those remaining killed the nine; and finally the last man took his own life.

**The Negeb.**—A tract of country in the southern part of Judæa, along the borders of the Arabian Desert, is in the authorized version of the Bible called the "South," and also the "South Country."[2] The primary meaning of the word thus translated is dryness. As this territory is emphatically "a dry, parched land," it became known as the "Dry Country." Then as the Dry Country lay on the south, it came to be synonymous with that point of the compass, in the same way as the Sea was also the west. This Dry Country meant to the Israelite the same as South Country. In the revised version of the Bible the word is left untranslated, and given as a proper name, The Negeb.

The Negeb broadens out from the narrow highlands on the north through undulating plains to "the Desert of the Wanderings." It is especially a pasture land and is chiefly dependent for its water supply on

---

[1] 2 Chron., ch. 20.   [2] Gen. 13: 1; 24: 62; 1 Sam. 30: 1; Ps. 126: 4.

artificial wells and cisterns. It was allotted to the tribe of Simeon.[1] The character of the country demanded nomadic life. Hence the people of this tribe were wandering shepherds, and they finally became identified with the roving shepherds of the desert.[2]

A great wady traverses the Negeb from Hebron to Beer-sheba, and thence by way of Gaza it passes to the sea. This was the route of travel from Beer-sheba to Egypt and to Sinai. By this way went Abraham and the sons of Jacob in their journeys between these places.

**Cities.**—While almost every hilltop in Judæa was the site of a small village there were no large cities in the land. In addition to those towns already spoken of a few others claim notice.

**Jerusalem** has for its modern name el Kuds esh-Sherif, shortened to el Kuds. Its earliest recorded name was Salem or Shalem.[3] It was afterwards known as Jebus.[4] It stands on the crest of the highlands about 2,600 feet above the sea level, about thirty miles from the Mediterranean Sea and eighteen miles from the Jordan. Its site is a promontory or tongue of land extending southeasterly from the main watershed and separated from the highland mass, except on the north and northwest, by deep ravines that sink 500 feet below the general level. The Valley of the Kidron comes down on the east between Jerusalem and the Mount of Olives, and then descends southeasterly through the Wilderness of Judah. The Vale of Hinnom opens out on the west of the city, and curving round extends along the southern border, joining the Kidron at Siloam near the southeast corner. The lower part of this ravine was called Tophet or "Place of Fire," and also Gehenna. It was used as a place for burning the refuse of the city. Aceldama, or the "Field of Blood," and the "Hill of Evil Counsel" lie across the gorge of Hinnom on the south.

The promontory is cleft by a third ravine, known as the Tyropœon, which runs southeasterly from its central part to its southeast corner where it unites with the other two gorges. The Tyropœon again divides into two branches. The main branch curves around westerly, extending across the western side of the promontory nearly to the Vale of Hinnom. A shallower branch takes a more northerly course. The Tyropœon is nearly filled up by the *débris* that has accumulated in it through the ages. The eastern side of the promontory is also crossed by a slight depression.

The site of the ancient city thus comprised four hills. In the southwest, lying between the Tyropœon and the Vale of Hinnom was Mount Zion, measuring about 3,000 feet by 1,800 feet, and rising to the height of 2,540 feet. This was the "Upper City." The City of David and Zion were different names applied to the same locality.[5] It seems probable

---

[1] Josh. 19: 9.     [2] 1 Chron. 4: 24–43.     [3] Gen. 14: 18; Ps. 76: 2.
[4] Judg. 19: 10–12.     [5] 2 Sam. 5: 7–9; 1 Chron. 11: 4–7.

that these were other names for Jerusalem as it was in the time of David. There has, however, been much controversy on these points.

On the northwest, between the two arms of the Tyropœon, is Acra, 2,490 feet high. In the southeast, lying between the Tyropœon and the Kidron Valley, is Mount Moriah, on the northern portion of which stood Solomon's Temple. The southern portion of this section, extending to the junction of the three valleys, was called Ophel. On the north of Mount Moriah is the section known as Bezetha.

The deep ravines on all sides but the north were during the ages a natural defense for the city, and invading enemies have always made their attacks on the unprotected side. The natural strength of the city probably explains the fact of the Jebusites' keeping possession of it so long. Trusting, no doubt, to these defenses, the citizens sent a mocking message to David during his successful siege.[1]

The original condition of the site of Jerusalem has been greatly changed by artificial leveling down and filling up, and also by the accumulation of the *débris* of many centuries in the ravines. In recent years, through the pick and spade of the explorer, many features of the ancient city have been discovered.

**The Pool of Siloam.**—The water supply of Jerusalem was partly from natural springs and partly from rain water collected in reservoirs. The Pool of Siloam on the southeast of Jerusalem, near the mouth of the Tyropœon Valley, is a reservoir which received its water in intermittent supplies through an underground aqueduct from a natural spring on the northeast of the city. Through this aqueduct, about a third of a mile in length and varying in height from sixteen inches to five or six feet, a party of explorers, led by Sir Charles Warren, crept through mud and water on their hands and knees, occupying about four hours in the task. They carried lights with them that they might be able to take measurements. A lad, who afterwards made the same journey, reported that he had seen writing on the wall of the aqueduct. This report led Professor Sayce and others, equipped with material for taking impressions, to crawl through again. The Hebrew inscription which they thus found simply indicated the meeting place of the two parties of miners who started their work from opposite ends of the aqueduct.

Mount Moriah originally consisted of a sharp-pointed rock, rising many feet above the surrounding neighborhood. To make a level surface for the temple site, walls were built perpendicularly seventy feet high from the foot of the hill on the east and west sides nearly to the summit of the rocky point. The intervening space was filled with stones and earth. The temple area was inclosed by a wall. Near its center is a raised platform ten feet above the general level, covering about five acres, paved

[1] 2 Sam. 5 : 6–8.

with white marble. The native rock rises through this platform to the height of fifteen feet. This sacred rock, according to tradition, is the place where Abraham was about to sacrifice Isaac,—later the threshing-floor of Araunah, and still later the site of the Holy of Holies.

The Mohammedan structure, usually called the Mosque of Omar, though not really a mosque, the most beautiful building in Jerusalem, now occupies the spot where it is supposed Solomon's Temple once stood. The building is an octagon in form, each side being about sixty feet long. The lower part of the walls is of white marble, and the upper portion is covered with beautifully-colored porcelain tiles. The windows are of richly-colored glass of the sixteenth century, and the mosaic adornment of the interior is of surpassing beauty.

Jerusalem has witnessed many sieges.[1] It was taken by Nebuchadnezzar in 597 B. C., and again in 586 B. C. It fell under the power of Alexander the Great in 332 B. C. Subsequently it was ruled alternately by the Ptolemies of Egypt and the Seleucidæ of Antioch. About 63 B. C. it came under the Romans. Rebellion against Roman rule led to the destruction of the city by Titus, A. D. 70, after a siege of 143 days.

Within the past quarter of a century Jerusalem has doubled its population, having at the present time between 40,000 and 50,000 inhabitants, of whom 30,000 are Jews. The city is connected with Jaffa, on the coast, by railway.

**Bethany,** now known by the name el-Azirîyeh, is situated about two miles from Jerusalem, on the eastern slope of the Mount of Olives, and on the road to Jericho. It is but a small village, deriving its interest from the events connected with the latter part of our Lord's life. It was here that he raised Lazarus[2] from the dead, and it was at Bethany that he found a resting place the last few nights before the crucifixion.[3]

**Bethlehem** is six miles from Jerusalem, a little to the east of the road between that city and Hebron. It is one of the oldest towns in Palestine and comes into notice first under the name of Ephrath or Ephratah.[4] Apart from personal associations of the deepest interest, it never attained very great distinction. It was "little among the thousands of Judah."[5] But it had a distinction all its own as the city of Boaz, of Naomi, of Ruth by adoption, and of David.[6] Above all is it memorable as the birthplace of Jesus.[7] Among its features pointed out to the traveler are the Cave of the Nativity, which is the traditional birthplace of Jesus, the Well of David, reputed to be the well from which the three brave warriors brought water for David to drink.[8] The rugged hills on the east of the town are

---

[1] 2 Kings 24 : 11–15 ; 25 : 4.
[2] John 11 : 1–44.
[3] Matt. 21 : 17 ; Mark 11 : 12, 19.
[4] Gen. 35 : 16 ; 48 :7.
[5] Micah 5 : 2.
[6] Ruth 1 : 1–19 ; 1 Sam. 16 : 1–13.
[7] Luke 2 : 1–7.
[8] 2 Sam. 23 : 15–17.

probably the pasture lands where David guarded his father's flocks,[1] and where a thousand years later other "shepherds were abiding, keeping watch over their flocks by night."[2] A short distance from Bethlehem, near the highway, is shown the tomb of Rachel.[3]

Hebron, twenty miles south of Jerusalem, 3,040 feet above the Mediterranean, is situated in one of the most fruitful districts of Judæa. It is a very old city—one of the oldest in the world.[4] It was a favorite residence of Abraham, being known at that time as Kirjath-arba, and it was also called Mamre. Here Sarah died and was buried in the Cave of Machpelah. This same cave became the last resting place of Abraham, of Isaac, of Jacob, and of Leah.[5] Over this cave at the present day stands a Mohammedan mosque, from which Christians are strictly excluded. As a special act of courtesy the Prince of Wales, now Edward VII, accompanied by Dean Stanley and others, was permitted by the governor of Jerusalem, in 1862, to enter the mosque.

In the valley near the town are several reservoirs for water, which are of great antiquity. The largest is 130 feet square and fifty feet deep.

Hebron was one of the six cities of refuge. Here David was anointed king over Judah, and for seven years and a half this city was his capital.[6]

Beer-sheba, twenty-seven miles from Hebron, noted among other things as marking the southern limit of the Land of Israel, was on the great road between Palestine and Egypt. It was at different times the home of Abraham, Isaac, and Jacob. Its position on the borders of the desert made its great wells, of which there are seven, a frequent resort. The largest of these wells is ten feet in diameter. Near the wells are stone troughs round which shepherds still gather with their flocks at evening time as of yore.

**Routes of Travel.**—Reference has already been made to the principal roads through Judæa. The great highway north and south lies through the middle of the country between Bethel and Beer-sheba, passing by way of Jerusalem and Hebron. By it Abraham and Jacob journeyed; and also Joseph when sent by his father to visit his brothers at Dothan.

Different routes led from the coast, of which perhaps the most important is that by the Valley of Aijalon and the Beth-horons. Another lies by Wady Surar, through which runs the railway between Jaffa and Jerusalem.

From the Jordan Valley is the route lying near Wady Suweinit by way of Michmash. A common but arduous road between Jericho and Jerusalem passes by way of the Mount of Olives. By this way pilgrims from Peræa and Galilee were accustomed to travel when visiting the temple. By it

---

[1] 1 Sam. 16:11.     [2] Luke 2:8-15.     [3] Gen. 35:19, 20
[4] Num. 13:22.     [5] Gen. 49:29-32.     [6] 2 Sam. 2:1-11.

also our Lord traveled on his last journey to Jerusalem. Of this route has been said,—"When taken upwards, a more hot and weary way it is impossible to conceive between blistered limestone rocks, and in front the bare hills piled high without shadow or verdure."[1] Another route leaves the valley five miles south of Jericho and forking on its way sends one branch to Jerusalem and the other to Bethlehem. Then there is the route between the coast of the Dead Sea and the Jeshimon by way of En-gedi.

[1] George Adam Smith.

## CHAPTER IX

## THE VALLEY OF THE JORDAN

THE great depression or rift, of which the Jordan Valley forms the central portion, is a remarkable feature of Palestine. In different parts of the world there are districts below the sea level. Such a tract of country is found in Asia near the Caspian Sea; there is one in the northwest of the Sahara in Africa; and there is one in the southeast of California. None of these depressions, however, exceeds 300 feet below the sea level, whereas the Valley of the Jordan through its last sixty-five miles is from 682 feet to 1,292 feet below the sea.

This wonderful valley extends from the foot of the Taurus Mountains through the valley of the Orontes, Cœle-syria, the Jordan Valley, the Dead Sea, and Wady Arabah to the Gulf of Akabah, a distance of about 550 miles.

**How the Valley was Formed.**—In the remote ages, geologists tell us, the whole of Palestine was covered by the ocean. Then by means of forces generated within the crust of the earth there came an uplifting process, accompanied by lateral pressure on each side, east and west. The limestone that had been formed on the bed of the sea was thus thrown up above the water in great folds, forming an eastern and a western highland ridge, with this valley between them. While this lifting-up process was going on there occurred a fracture or "a fault," as geologists call it, along the edge of the valley, causing a falling in of its floor, and a deepening of the valley. The land round the mouth of the Jordan and the surface of the Dead Sea are 1,290 feet below the sea level, while the bordering highlands rise to nearly 3,000 feet above that level.

The whole valley, from the Taurus Mountains to the Gulf of Akabah, is divided by two watersheds into four slopes. One of these watersheds is in Cœle-syria and forms the northerly slope of the Orontes and the southerly of the Leontes and the Jordan. The other watershed is in Wady Arabah sixty-five miles from the Dead Sea, sloping northerly to this sea and southerly to the Gulf of Akabah. This watershed is 640 feet above the sea level. But for this elevation the gulf would extend through the valley to Lake Huleh, forming a long narrow arm of the Red Sea.

**Sources of the Jordan.**—The Jordan is formed by the union of four small streams which take their rise in the Lebanons. The longest of these streams by forty miles, having its origin farthest up the valley at an elevation of 1,700 feet above the sea, is the Hasbâny. The most beautiful is Nahr Banias. The largest branch is the Leddan. The Jordan thus in its short course descends nearly 3,000 feet. This great fall gives it a very rapid current, and probably has also given the river its name, the word Jordan meaning "Descender."

**Paneas.**—Nahr Banias flows in almost river-like proportions from a mass of bowlders, 1,100 feet above the sea level, at the base of Mount Hermon. These waters have their source in a cave or grotto a hundred yards farther back in the mountain side. In ancient times this grotto and its fountain were sacred to the worship of Baal, the god of the Phœnicians. A town grew up near by which was called Baal-gad.[1] The Greeks, at a later period, dedicated the place to the worship of Pan, the god of the shepherds, giving the grotto the name Paneion and changing the name of the town to Paneas. After the place had fallen under the power of Rome, Herod the Great, who ruled Palestine, built here a temple in honor of his patron the Emperor Augustus Cæsar. Philip the tetrarch, Herod's son, greatly enriched the city, and renamed it Cæsarea. To distinguish it from a place of the same name on the coast it was called Cæsarea Philippi. In the course of time the city took again its old name Paneas, which in modern times, through the pronunciation of the Arabs, has become Banias. The town was once strongly fortified and commanded the great highway through Cœle-syria.

This historic city, that has changed its name so many times, famous as a seat of worship of false gods, is memorable as the northern limit of our Lord's journeyings with his disciples. Near by also is Mount Hermon, which probably is the Mount of Transfiguration.[2]

**Dan.**—The Leddan rises in a mound called Tell el-Kâdi, about five miles south of Banias. Kadi has the same meaning as the word Dan. For this reason and on account of the general fitness of the place, the opinion has arisen that Tell el-Kâdi is the site of ancient Laish which was taken by the Danites and was afterwards known as Dan.[3] According to another view Banias occupies the site of Laish.

**Lake Huleh**, or the "Waters of Merom,"[4] an expansion of the Jordan a few miles below the union of its various sources, is about four miles long, and its surface is seven feet above the level of the Mediterranean. Extensive marshes on the north of this lake are covered with a rank growth of papyrus.

On leaving Lake Huleh the Jordan is sixty feet broad and fifteen feet deep. It flows rapidly through a narrow gorge for ten miles to Lake Tiberias, having in this distance descended 675 feet. Two miles below

---

[1] Josh. 11:17; 12:7.  
[2] Matt. 16:13-20; 17:1-8.  
[3] Judg., ch. 18.  
[4] Josh. 11:5, 6.

Huleh is the Bridge of Jacob's Daughters on the great caravan route between Acca (Acre) and Damascus.

The Sea of Galilee is known by various names,—Sea of Tiberias, Lake of Gennesaret, and Sea of Chinnereth.[1] It is thirteen miles long, seven miles in extreme breadth, and about 200 feet deep. Its surface is 682 feet below the level of the Mediterranean. On the east side the banks rise from the shore to the height of 1,000 feet and more. On the west side the hills of Galilee descend to the lake by terraces ending in cliffs of moderate height. In some places there is but a narrow fringe of lowland between the water and the banks, but in general there is a broader belt of low coast land from several hundred feet to half a mile in width. At the north end the highlands come down by a gradual slope, forming on the northwest the beautiful and fertile Plain of Gennesaret.

The country round is volcanic and subject to earthquakes. The land is strewn with lava and pumice stone, and warm sulphur springs are found on some parts of the coast. The neighborhood is destitute of trees, and in general it wears a desolate and deserted aspect. The lake, as of yore, is full of fish, but scarce a fisherman's boat disturbs the water.

The Sea of Galilee, little noticed in the Old Testament, was the scene of many interesting events recorded in the Gospels. It was in the olden time, and it must ever be, a delightful feature in that land of heat and drought. How often Jesus and his disciples resorted to this water! and most refreshing it must have been to them after their long and wearisome walks over the hot dusty hills of Galilee.

In our Saviour's time the lake and its surroundings were full of life and action. There are said to have been on the lake coast nine cities having from ten to fifteen thousand inhabitants, including Capernaum, Chorazin, Bethsaida, Tiberias, Magdala, and Tarichex. Their industries were varied, comprising cultivation of the soil, fishing, curing fish, tanning, and dyeing. The fields, then fruitful, yielded grain, figs, olives, and other fruit. The lake abounded in fish of such excellent quality as gained them a name even in the world's capital, the imperial city of Rome. Nearly all these cities have now disappeared and the very site of some of them cannot be determined.

Tiberias, as the capital of Galilee, was the most prominent of the lake cities in the time of our Lord, though we have no record of his having visited the place. Its inhabitants were chiefly Gentiles, the Jews having a prejudice against the city because it occupied the site of an ancient burial ground, and because of the foreign customs that prevailed there. The city was built by Herod Antipas, who adorned it with a splendid palace and fortified it by a strong castle. Tiberias was famous for the

[1] Josh. 12:3.

warm springs in its neighborhood. It is the only place of any importance now on the lake. (Population, 5,000.)

**Taricheæ** was famous for its fish-curing establishments. Its name is a Greek word, meaning a pickling-place.

**Capernaum,** the city which Jesus adopted as his home, was on the northwest shore of the Sea of Galilee. The exact site is matter of dispute. Some scholars have selected Khan Minyeh, about five miles from the mouth of the Jordan, as the probable place where the city stood. Others prefer Tell Hum, two or three miles nearer the river. Here are found extensive ruins, including those of an ancient synagogue, seventy-five feet in length and sixty-five in breadth, which, it is supposed, may be the place where Jesus taught the people and healed the man "with an unclean spirit." Capernaum stood on a great thoroughfare. Roads led out from it in all directions—northeasterly to Damascus and the cities on the Euphrates and Tigris; easterly to Gilead; southerly to Shechem and Jerusalem; southwesterly to Egypt; and westerly past Nazareth to the Mediterranean coast.

**Bethsaida** was on the east side of the Jordan near its entrance into the lake. The site of **Chorazin** is only matter of conjecture.[1] The ruins of **Umm Keis,** near the mouth of the Yarmuk, are supposed to mark the site of **Gadara.**

Violent winds are of common occurrence on the Sea of Galilee, and they are several times spoken of in the Gospels.[2] These winds are caused by the air over the lake becoming more highly heated than that over the neighboring highlands. Then the cooler heavier air rushes down the gorges along the shores of the lake, causing the great storms that were so much dreaded by the Galilæan fishermen.

**The Ghor.**—The valley between the Sea of Galilee and the Dead Sea, by the Arabs called the Ghor, that is "the Rift," is sixty-five miles in length. The river within this portion of the valley, by reason of its numerous short windings, is about two hundred miles long. The fall through this course is six hundred and ten feet. It is greatest near the Sea of Galilee, where, for a few miles, it is forty feet in the mile. On either side the highlands rise abruptly from two thousand to three thousand feet above the valley. Throughout a large part of the valley the breadth does not exceed four miles, but opposite Beth-shean, where the Jalud from the Valley of Jezreel joins the Jordan, the breadth is eight miles, and at Jericho it is fourteen miles.

The Jordan has many affluents, the largest of which are on the eastern side. The Yarmuk, which flows in four miles below the Sea of Galilee, nearly doubles the volume of the Jordan. The Jabbok, flowing from Gilead, enters the Jordan about halfway between the Sea of Galilee

---
[1] Matt. 11:21.    [2] Matt. 8:24; Mark 4:37; Luke 8:23.

and the Dead Sea. On the western side are the Jalud from the Valley of Jezreel and the Farah from the Vale of Shechem.

Many springs and small streams flowing in from the banks and spreading their waters over the valley so thoroughly irrigate the soil, that, with the intense heat prevailing here, the vegetation in many parts is luxuriant. In some places are malarial swamps, and elsewhere are stretches of desert, barren from lack of moisture or from the presence of salt in the soil.

**The Zor.**—Within the Ghor is a narrower and deeper valley, twenty feet below the outer valley at the north end and two hundred feet deeper at the south end, and from one fourth of a mile to two miles in breadth. This inner valley, called the Zor, is a jungle of herbaceous plants, shrubs, and trees, suited to the hot climate. It is also a covert for wild animals—boars, leopards, bears, and wolves. Lions, once found in the Zor, are now extinct, but their bones are sometimes found here.

On account of its luxuriant vegetation the Zor is spoken of in the Bible as "the pride of the Jordan," or as in the authorized version, "the swelling of Jordan."[1]

Within the Zor and at a still lower level flows the rapid, tortuous, and muddy Jordan from one hundred to two hundred feet wide,—that is at ordinary seasons. But in the rainy season the river, greatly swollen, overflows its banks and takes the whole breadth of this inner valley for its bed or flood plain.[2] The wild animals are then driven to the adjoining higher lands. These annual floods have strewn the valley with driftwood and covered it with deposits of mud. By erosion they also have worn away the banks on each side, leaving them irregular and ragged. Like a fortress wall and a moat round a castle, the deep valley of the Jordan, its precipitous banks, and its rapid current served as a defense to the country.

**Fords.**—The Jordan is from three to ten feet deep. In ancient times there was not a bridge from one end of the river to the other. In fact there were no bridges in the whole of Palestine nor is there a word for bridge in the Hebrew language. There are many fording places, especially along the upper course, where the river can be crossed. The Ford of Abarah (Bethabara) is opposite Beth-shean on the road between Esdraelon and Gilead. Damieh Ford below the junction of the Jabbok with the Jordan is on the road between Nablus (Shechem) and Gilead.

The Jordan has no commercial value as a highway, nor did it enkindle an ardent patriotism in the mind of the Israelite. When an exile in a foreign land, it was not the memory of this river that awakened in him earnest longings for the home far away. It was rather the thought of

---

[1] Jer. 12:5; 49:19; 50:44; Zech. 11:3.   [2] Josh. 3:15; 1 Chron. 12:15; Jer. 12:5

Mount Zion and Jerusalem and the associations that clustered round them that stirred his memory and opened the fountain of his tears.[1] But he did remember Jordan as a barrier to be got over, and as an opposing force to be overcome. He remembered its swellings, the overflowing of its banks, its turbulence, and the struggles which it imposed. The Jordan was to Jeremiah the very climax of difficulty.[2] And so through all the ages has this river been thought of as a barrier and an object of dread. And thus it has become the type and symbol of that last struggle through which the spirit breaks loose from its clay tabernacle and passes to the heavenly Canaan.

For different reasons there have been few towns in the Jordan Valley. The summer heat is intolerable, sometimes rising to 118°. Many parts of the valley are malarial. Like the Plain of Esdraelon the valley is exposed to invasions of the robber tribes of the desert. The wild beasts of the jungle were also a source of danger.[3]

Jericho, the first city captured by the Israelites after crossing the Jordan, is supposed to have stood on a mound a mile and a half above the modern Jericho. Excavations at this place have unearthed portions of an ancient sun-dried brick wall and fragments of ancient pottery. The city taken by Joshua was surrounded by high walls and its gate was closed every night at dark.[4] The surrounding district was once exceedingly fertile, yielding the choicest tropical products. Its groves of palms gave Jericho the name "City of Palm Trees."[5] The great wealth of the city may be inferred from the rich spoil found here at the time of the conquest.[6]

The siege of Jericho is the most remarkable thing of its kind on record. While the falling of the walls was brought about through the special interposition of God, it may have been effected instrumentally by the simple human agency described in the story, rather than by what is properly called miraculous power. City walls in that age were not built to resist battering rams. The regular step of the vast host that marched round the city may have set up a vibratory motion that so affected the stability of the walls that the great shout which closed the last day's march was sufficient to cause their fall.

The rebuilding of the city was denounced by Joshua with solemn curse, and we are told in later history how it befell him who ventured to brave the curse.[7]

In the time of our Lord, Jericho was an important and wealthy city. Herod the Great fortified it, built in it splendid palaces, and derived large revenue from its taxes. It was here that this infamous tyrant died.

**The Dead Sea.**—The remarkable water known in modern times as the Dead Sea is spoken of in the Bible as the Salt Sea, Sea of Arabah or

---
[1] Jer. 12:5; 49:19; 50:44; Ps. 137.   [2] Jer. 12:1.   [3] Deut. 7:22.
[4] Josh. 2:5, 15.   [5] Deut. 34:3.   [6] Josh. 6:19; 7:2.   [7] Josh. 6:26; 1 Kings 16:34.

Sea of the Plain, and the East Sea.[1] It occupies the lowest part of the rift, 1,292 feet below the level of the Mediterranean. Its length is fifty-three miles and its average breadth is ten miles. At the north end it is 1,300 feet deep, but at the south end its depth is only about twelve feet. Its size and depth are somewhat increased when the Jordan is in flood. Besides the Jordan it receives several smaller streams, chiefly from the eastern side, of which the Arnon is the largest.

At varying distances from the margin of the water steep banks rise to the height of 4,000 feet above the beach. The eastern shore is broken but once, where it is cleft by the deep gorge of the Arnon. A tongue of land indents this shore, forming the promontory of El Lisan, fifty feet high. The rocky wall on the western side is furrowed at short intervals by narrow gorges that make down from the Wilderness of Judæa.

The Dead Sea gives off its water only by evaporation, which owing to the great heat of the valley is very copious. Like all lakes that have no outlet its waters are very salt. Ordinary sea water contains from four to six per cent of saline matter. The Dead Sea has from twenty-four to twenty-six per cent, or over six times as much as the water of the ocean. A gallon of water from the Dead Sea weighs one fifth more than distilled water.

All river water contains some salt. The streams flowing into the Dead Sea probably have more than the usual quantity, and as no salt passes out, it has been accumulating through the ages. A portion of the salt in these waters is also derived from Jebel Usdum, a mountain of rock salt at the southern end of the sea. Water trickling from this mountain or hill is ever carrying some of its salt to the sea.

The Dead Sea, like the Sea of Galilee, is subject to violent winds. Owing to the great density of its waters, however, it is not so easily disturbed by the wind, and hence the waves here are not so high as they are on the Sea of Galilee. For the same reason the waves, when once aroused, are very strong and beat with great violence against opposing objects. This great density also makes the waters of the Dead Sea very buoyant so that one can easily float upon them, but cannot easily swim in them.

No fish or other animal is found in these waters, and the shores are generally barren and desolate. The name Dead Sea, therefore, though not a Bible name, is a very fitting one. The stories told by some travelers that birds, attempting to fly across this sea, fall dead before they reach the opposite shore, are without foundation. During the rainy season grass and flowers are seen growing very near the margin of the sea.

**The Cities of the Plain.**—Somewhere on the borders of the Dead Sea, the exact place is uncertain, stood the Cities of the Plain that were

[1] Josh. 3: 16; Deut. 4: 49; 2 Kings 14: 25; Ezek. 47: 18; Joel 2: 20; Zech. 14: 8.

destroyed in the time of Abraham. Some persons have even maintained that this sea had its origin at the time of their destruction, it having been caused by the sinking of the ground on which the cities stood. Geologists, however, clearly show that the sea existed ages before the time of this tragic event. Indeed there is good evidence that the waters of the sea once covered a larger area than they do at the present time. Yet it may be that the site occupied by these cities is now submerged beneath a portion of the Dead Sea. Sir William Dawson takes this view and thinks that the cities were situated at the north end of the sea. His theory as to the way the destruction was brought about is given in the following paragraphs: —

"We learn from the narrative that the destruction was sudden and unexpected. That it was caused by brimstone and fire, that these were rained down from the sky, that a dense column of smoke ascended to a great height, like the smoke of a furnace or limekiln, and that along with or immediately after the fire, there was an emission of brine or saline mud capable of encrusting bodies (as Lot's wife) so that they appeared as mounds (not pillars) of salt. The only point in the statement in regard to which there can be doubt, is the substance intended by the Hebrew word translated brimstone. It may mean sulphur, but there is some reason to suspect that, as used here, it may rather denote pitch.

"The description is that of a bitumen or petroleum eruption similar to those which, on a small scale, have been so destructive in the oil regions of the United States of America. They arise from the existence of reservoirs of compressed inflammable gas along with petroleum and water, existing at considerable depth below the surface. When these are penetrated, as by a well or bore-hole, the gas escapes with explosive force, carrying petroleum with it, and when both have been ignited, the petroleum rains down in burning showers, and floats in flames over the ejected water, while a dense smoke towers high in the air, and the inrushing draught may produce a vortex, carrying upward to a still greater height, and distributing still more widely, the burning material."

References in the Bible to this awful visitation of the divine displeasure are numerous.[1]

**Crossing the Jordan.**—Without the intervention of miracle or contravening of natural law, the dry pathway for the Israelites across the river-bed may be accounted for in either of two ways. It might have been brought about by the undermining of some mound or bank up the river, causing a landslide across the river-bed and forming a temporary dam. Such occurrences in regard to other rivers have taken place, and it is recorded that a landslip of this kind took place above the Ford

[1] Gen., ch. 19; Deut. 29: 23; Isa. 1: 9, 10; 3: 9; 13: 19; Jer. 23: 14; 49: 18; 50: 40; Lam. 4: 6; Ezek. 16: 46, 53; Amos 4: 11.

Damieh on the Jordan in the year 1257, arresting the stream for several hours.

Again the phenomenon might have been caused by some seismic disturbance, such as an earthquake, by which the land above the crossing place was elevated, forming a ridge or mound across the valley, that for the time arrested the flow of water. Thus through the arrangement of divine providence the coincidence of movement of the Israelites and the staying of the water might have been effected in either of these ways.

**Ezekiel's Vision.**—Ezekiel's vision of the Dead Sea and certain neighboring territory is given in a remarkable word picture.[1] The torrent Kidron or Wady en Nar flows along the eastern side of Jerusalem between the city and the Mount of Olives. It pursues its course southeasterly, passing Bethlehem on its right and continuing through the crags and scorched barrens of the Wilderness of Judæa. Finally its scanty waters,—when there are any, for it is but a winter torrent,—end their course by dashing over the precipitous rocks that guard the western shores of the Dead Sea. They end their course and are forever lost in the bitter waters of this sea, having no more influence in sweetening them than has a shower of rain on the waters of the ocean. These are the facts.

Ezekiel's vision tells a different story. Through the creative power of an inspired imagination he pictures a new scene to illustrate the power of divine grace in changing the human heart and in vivifying and beautifying a dead world. At first the prophet sees the waters of Kidron flowing as a little stream from under the threshold of the temple. As they move on, they swell in volume, at first rising to the ankles of him who would wade through them. They flow on for a thousand cubits, and now they have risen to the knees; another thousand and they reach to the loins; yet another thousand and they have become a mighty river that cannot be forded. Having seen the progress and increasing volume of the waters, the prophet is called on to mark their effect on the objects with which they have come in contact. And what a change! Along the banks of the river on the one side and on the other side, where there had been only barren rocks, there are now "very many trees. . . . By the river upon the bank thereof, on this side and on that side, shall grow all trees for meat, whose leaf shall not fade, neither shall the fruit thereof be consumed: it shall bring forth new fruit according to his months, because their waters they issued out of the sanctuary: and the fruit thereof shall be for meat, and the leaf thereof for medicine." The waters fall into the sea—that sea so fatal to life—and its waters are healed. "And there shall be a very great multitude of fish, because these waters shall come thither: for they shall be healed; and every thing shall live whither the river cometh."

[1] Ezek. 47 : 1–12.

## CHAPTER X

### EASTERN PALESTINE

EASTERN PALESTINE lies between Mount Hermon and the River Arnon, and between the Jordan and the Desert. Its length, north and south, is 130 miles, and its breadth, east and west, varies from 30 to 80 miles.

**Physical Features.**—This is wholly a highland country—an extension of Anti-Lebanon—having an average elevation of about 2,000 feet above the sea level. These highlands are most impressive when viewed from the western side where they rise from the low level of the Jordan Valley, stretching their long level line against the eastern horizon. On the eastern side, the country, without deep rift or barrier wall, lies open and slopes away to the desert. The northern and southern portions are tablelands; the central portion is more varied by mountain ridges and valleys. The whole country is furrowed by deep ravines.

**Rivers.**—As compared with Western Palestine, this eastern division is a well-watered country. Rains are more frequent and the streams are larger and more numerous. Three important rivers, the Yarmuk, the Jabbok, and the Arnon, flow across the country from east to west. They flow through deep gorges, the first two discharging their waters into the Jordan, the last-named into the Dead Sea.

**The Yarmuk** has a volume equal to that of the Jordan before the union of the two. The **Jabbok**, now called the Zerka, is a brawling, crooked stream, flowing through a valley of great fertility. It was on the banks of this river that Jacob wrestled with the angel.[1] **The Arnon**, known at the present day as Wady Môjib, flows through a gorge in some parts 1,700 feet deep, at the bottom 120 feet wide, but two miles wide at the top of the sloping banks. This river formed the southern limit of Eastern Palestine. **The Zerka Maain**, identified with Nahaliel[2] ("Valley of God") flows through a deep ravine a few miles north of the Arnon. It is remarkable for the hot sulphur springs of Callirrhoe in its wild rocky chasm. In the neighborhood was the strong fortress Machærus where it is thought John the Baptist was beheaded. **Wady Heshbon** is a deep cleft leading down to the Plain of Moab, near the fords at Jericho.

**Divisions.**—At the time of the invasion of this land by the Israelites the country was known as comprising three divisions, Bashan, Gilead, and Moab. Bashan occupied the northern part between Mount Hermon and the Yarmuk; Gilead was situated between the Yarmuk and Wady Hesh-

---

[1] Gen. 32: 22–31.   [2] Num. 21: 19.

bon twenty-five miles south of the Jabbok; Moab properly lay south of the Arnon, yet the boundary was variable, sometimes lying as far north as the Heshbon.

Bashan.—This division is mostly an open, treeless plateau, healthy, well-watered, and productive. It is a volcanic region, and the stones on the surface are basalt and lava. The western side is a hilly district, once famous for its oak forests, some remains of which still exist. Along the edge of the Jordan Valley are several extinct volcanoes. This portion of the country, now called Jaulan, included ancient Geshur and Maachah. Geshur formed a small independent kingdom. One of King David's wives was the daughter of the king of Geshur, and her son Absalom was for some time an exile in this land.[1]

On the eastern side of Bashan is a district known as Lejjan which has been described as "a petrified ocean." It has numerous extinct craters, and is thickly strewn with lava, which seems to have been changed suddenly from the liquid to the solid state. In some places the lava still presents the wave-like forms of its molten condition. Elsewhere the rocks are broken, leaving wide fissures and crevasses. The district is wild and forbidding.

The Lejjan is regarded as the Trachonitis [2] of the Roman period and also as the more ancient Argob. The three names are of similar signification, meaning stony or a heap of stones.

The whole region of Bashan has in a general way been called Hauran. Hauran proper, however, is a more limited district in the middle of Bashan between Jaulan and Lejjan. The southern part of the district is by the Arabs called en Nukra, "the Hollow Hearth," from its relatively low situation.

In early times and down to the Christian era Bashan was a populous country. It contained many strong cities, remarkable remains of which still exist. Sixty cities are said to have been taken by the Israelites from Og, King of Bashan.[3] Many of these ancient cities were wholly or in part under ground. The houses were built of stone, not the walls alone, but the roof, the ceiling, and the doors. **Edrei**, on the borders of Lejjan, is one of the most remarkable of these cities. It was originally built in caves and crevasses formed by volcanic action, with its streets, houses, shops, and market place under ground. The battle of the Israelites with Og, King of Bashan, was near Edrei. **Kanatha** or **Kanawat** has also notable remains of its ancient buildings, including temples, amphitheaters, and baths.

Gilead.—The name Gilead is sometimes used in a general way to include the whole land of Israel beyond the Jordan.[4] It is more commonly

---

[1] Deut. 3:14; Josh. 13:13; 2 Sam. 15:8; 1 Chron. 2:23.
[2] Luke 3:1.   [3] Deut. 3:4.   [4] Josh. 22:9.

limited to the territory between the Yarmuk and Wady Heshbon. It is quite different from Bashan in its physical features. It is more elevated, and it is crossed by well-wooded mountain ridges with broad fertile valleys intervening. The surface rock is no longer basalt and lava, but limestone. The mountains are much broken by deep ravines. The valley of the Jabbok divides Gilead into two sections. Through this valley runs the ancient highway that comes down from Shechem and crosses the Jordan at Damieh Ford. The rugged country continues to Wady Heshbon, but on the south side of the Jabbok the forests become more scattered and finally disappear.

Gilead is a very fertile country, suited to the production of grain, grapes, olives, and other fruit. Its pasture lands are rich and extensive. This land was famous also in ancient times for its spices, aromatic gums, and medicinal plants.[1]

**The Mishor.**—Between Wady Heshbon and the Arnon lies a territory distinguished from Gilead by the name of "the plain country," the Mishor, or the Mishor of Medeba.[2] This land is quite different in its physical features from that on the north side of Wady Heshbon. The Mishor, as the name implies, is a plain—a table-land. The whole country between the Jabbok and the Arnon, including South Gilead and Mishor, is in modern times called the Belka.

**Memorable Events.**—In Gilead there are many places of great historic interest, though few of them have been fully identified. Mount Nebo, a peak of Mount Pisgah, from whose summit Moses got his view of the Promised Land, has its position so definitely indicated that one cannot go far wrong in fixing it in a commanding promontory that thrusts itself out from the general mountain into the Jordan Valley "over against Jericho."[3] The highlands here are cleft by wild gorges in which the foot of man never treads, and are a suitable place for that sepulcher which has forever been kept hidden from human vision.[4]

These same heights were the stations from which Balaam looked out upon the camp of Israel. On several high places in succession he offered sacrifices on his seven altars, seeking inspiration for words of cursing against God's chosen people. But all in vain! As the seer beheld the tribes of Israel abiding in their tents in the plains lying at his feet, his only message was one of benediction. "How goodly are thy tents, O Jacob, and thy tabernacles, O Israel! Blessed is he that blesseth thee, and cursed is he that curseth thee."[5]

These stations to which the king of Moab brought Balaam were probably holy places, sacred to the worship of Baal and other gods of the Moabites. Explorers in these lands find to-day on certain heights in this

---
[1] Gen. 37 : 25 ; Jer. 8 : 22.   [2] Deut. 4 : 43 ; Josh. 13 : 9, 16 ; 2 Sam. 24 : 5, 6.
[3] Deut. 34 : 1.   [4] Deut. 34 : 6.   [5] Num. 24 : 5, 9.

neighborhood ancient altars and monumental stones, memorials of the ancient worship. It is common to find seven stones standing in a circle. Seven was a sacred number and carried with it some special significance or power.[1] There appear to have been three forms in the religious use of stones, the menhir, the dolmen, and the circle. The menhir is a single, tall stone, rough or partly dressed, erected as a memorial or an emblem. A dolmen consists of tall unhewn stones set on end with a large flat stone placed on top so as to form a table. The circle comprised a number of stones set upright in the form of a circle. The Israelites used stones in connection with the worship of Jehovah. Their altars were made of unhewn stones.[2] Jacob set up a stone pillar at Bethel and called it "God's House."[3] The Israelites in crossing the Jordan took twelve stones from the bed of the river and set them up as a memorial at Gilgal on the western shore.[4]

**Conquest of the Land.**—The Israelites on leaving the desert entered the Promised Land on this eastern side. The territory between the Arnon and the Jabbok, that is Mishor and South Gilead, had been occupied by the Moabites and Ammonites, but shortly before the arrival of the Israelites, Sihon, King of the Amorites, coming from Western Palestine, had dispossessed them, and was then occupying the country. Sihon refused to allow the Israelites to pass through his territory, though Moses promised to do no damage and to pay for everything they used, even the water they drank.[5] This refusal led to war, in which Sihon was defeated. Thereupon Og, King of Bashan, alarmed by this invasion of the land, attacked the Israelites. He, too, was utterly routed near the strong city of Edrei.[6] The whole land from the Arnon to Mount Hermon thus fell to the invaders.

**Allotment to the Tribes.**—The tribes of Reuben and Gad were specially fond of pastoral life and they "had a very great multitude of cattle." They were greatly pleased with the well-watered and fertile land of Gilead, which they "saw was a land for cattle," and they asked Moses to give it to them as their portion of the Promised Land.[7] This request was granted on condition that their fighting men cross the Jordan and assist the other tribes in gaining possession of Western Palestine. Subsequently half of the tribe of Manasseh obtained their portion on similar terms.

The territory allotted to Reuben lay between Wady Heshbon and the Arnon, that is the Mishor, comprising about 400 square miles. The tribe of Gad was placed on the north of Reuben between Wady Heshbon and the Yarmuk, the territory including about 1,300 square miles. To Manasseh was given the land of Bashan, comprising about 2,600 square

---

[1] Num. 23 : 1, 14, 29.   [2] Ex. 20 : 25.   [3] Gen. 28 : 22.   [4] Josh. 4 : 5-9.
[5] Num. 21 : 21-26 ; Deut. 2 : 26-30.   [6] Num. 21 : 33-35 ; Deut. 3 : 1-8.   [7] Num. 32 : 1-33.

miles. The bounds of these tribes, however, were subject to much change from inroads made by the neighboring heathen peoples. Sometimes, too, the Israelites were the invaders and enlarged their territory. Thus they crossed the Arnon and obtained lands and cities from the Moabites and Ammonites.[1]

**Social Condition.**—The isolation of the tribes on the eastern side of the Jordan from their brethren on the western side, and their strictly pastoral life were unfavorable to their advancement. Hence they failed to reach the same standard of civilization as did the tribes of Western Palestine. Their most prominent characters, well exemplified in Jephthah and Jehu, were of a rugged type, bold and unconventional. Their character and habits were influenced largely by their environment. Exposed to frequent raids from their lawless neighbors of the desert, they not only learned the art of self-defense, but developed the disposition to become aggressors.[2]

**Eastern Palestine in the Time of Our Lord.**—At the time of our Saviour this whole land was known under the general name of Cœlesyria. The name Peræa was applied to that portion of this territory that lay between the rivers Jabbok and Arnon, and corresponded to the Belka of modern times. But this term was somewhat vague, and it was sometimes given to territory as far north as the Yarmuk. In its political relations Peræa was connected with Galilee. Its people, like those of Galilee, were principally Jews; whereas those on the north of the Yarmuk were mainly of Greek origin. Philip's tetrarchy lay on the north of the Yarmuk, and included Gaulanitis, Batanea, Trachonitis, and Auranitis. The region on the east and south of Eastern Palestine was known as Arabia.

**Cities.**—Jabesh-gilead was an important city during the early history of the Israelites. It comes prominently into notice at the time of the strife which led to the almost utter extinction of the tribe of Benjamin.[3] The citizens of Jabesh failed to respond to the call to join in the war against Benjamin. Their punishment was severe, resulting in the general massacre of all the inhabitants except 400 unmarried women. At a later period, when Jabesh was threatened by the Ammonites, it was succored by the prompt action of King Saul.[4] This favor was requited by the men of Jabesh at the time of Saul's death, by the rescue of the bodies of Saul and his sons from the Philistines.[5] The site of Jabesh-gilead is occupied by the modern ed-Deir in Wady el-Yabis.

**Rabbah**, Rabbath, or Rabbath-Ammon, situated on the south side of the Arnon, was the chief city of the Ammonites. Against Moab and Ammon, as descendants of Lot, the Israelites had not intended to make war.

---

[1] 2 Sam. 12: 26–31.   [2] Gen. 49: 19.   [3] Judg., chs. 19, 20.
[4] 1 Sam. 11: 1–5.   [5] 1 Sam. 31: 8.

They were commanded by God not to disturb them.[1] But these people were the aggressors. They hired Balaam to curse Israel, and showed a hostility that forfeited all regard and broke up peaceful relations.[2] After a long siege, conducted by Joab in the reign of David, Rabbah was taken. Near the close of the siege, Joab having gained possession of that part of the city that contained the reservoirs or water supply, and thus practically ended the struggle, sent for David to come and take command and so secure to himself the glory of capturing the city.[3] In the time of our Saviour this place was known as Philadelphia. Interesting remains of the city as it was at that time still exist.

**Ramoth-gilead** was an important city and stronghold, commanding the region Argob. It was also a city of refuge. The exact site of the city is not known.[4] It was the home of that remarkable man Jehu who wrought such ill to the house of Ahab and to the worshipers of Baal.[5] The city was the center of long war between the kings of Israel and Syria.

Famous in the history of this land were **Succoth, Peniel,** and **Mahanaim,** situated near each other in the neighborhood of the lower course of the Jabbok. **Aroer,** on the banks of the Arnon, was the Beer-sheba of Eastern Palestine.

**The Decapolis.**—At the beginning of the Christian era certain cities of Palestine whose inhabitants were chiefly of Greek origin were united in a confederacy for mutual defense, trade, and other purposes. Originally there were ten of these; hence the confederacy was called Decapolis (ten cities). Authorities differ as to some of these cities, but the following ten are those usually regarded as forming the original union: Scythopolis (Beth-shean), Pella, Dion, Gerasa, Philadelphia, Gadara, Raphana, Kanatha, Hippos, and Damascus. Others were subsequently added.

The cities of Decapolis were situated on the great roads that ran across Eastern Palestine, or on that great highway between Damascus and Akabah that lay along the borders of the desert. Only Scythopolis, the ancient Beth-shean, was on the west of the Jordan. Each city included within its jurisdiction a large outlying territory. Thus around Gadara was the country of the Gadarenes. The Decapolis, however, did not comprise a continuous territory between its various cities; nor were the cities wholly independent of the Roman tetrarch or governor of the province.

The Greek inhabitants of these cities were a cultured people, and there were among them many men of distinction, well advanced in Greek learning and art. They rebuilt old cities and built new ones after the model of the cities of Greece. These cities had paved and colonnaded

---
[1] Deut. 2:9, 19.  [2] Num., ch. 22.  [3] 2 Sam. 11:1; 12:26-31.
[4] Deut. 4:43; 1 Kings 4:13.  [5] 2 Kings, chs. 9, 10.

streets, large amphitheaters, theaters, splendid temples, forums, baths, and mausoleums. In some cases water was brought long distances through stone pipes. The aqueduct which supplied Gadara with water has been traced far east to the neighborhood of Edrei. Some of these cities had large artificial ponds, in which sham sea fights were exhibited for the amusement of the people.

Much intercourse was kept up between the Decapolis and Galilee. Our Lord and his disciples visited this region. They would often come in contact with its citizens, and among other things they would thus learn to speak the Greek language.

This remarkable region, once so populous and full of life, has now but few inhabitants. Most of the cities have perished, and their sites, if they can be determined at all, are marked simply by an arch, the line of a colonnade, a few columns of a temple, the remains of a *naumachia*, or perhaps only a heap of ruins.

**Moab.**—The Land of Moab lies properly between the River Arnon and Wady Kerak, fifteen miles south of that river. It is to be noted, however, that the Moabites at times occupied territory north of the Arnon and claimed it as their own.[1] This territory is table-land similar to the Mishor on the north of the Arnon. It was a small but fertile country, famous in ancient times for the countless number of sheep that fed upon its rich pastures.

The relations of Moab to Israel were generally hostile, and many conflicts between the two peoples are recorded in the Bible. Incidents of a different kind, however, are related. In a time of severe famine in the Land of Israel, Elimelech, his wife Naomi, and their sons found refuge among the Moabites.[2] This sojourn led to Ruth's adoption of Bethlehem as her home and to her coming into the line of ancestry of King David and of David's Lord.[3] A feeling of blood tie may have influenced David during King Saul's persecution to intrust his aged parents to the protection of the king of Moab.[4] Later, when David occupied the throne, we find him waging a bitter war against Moab.[5] It has been conjectured as the cause of this change of attitude, that the king of Moab may have been false to his trust.

Early in the time of the Judges the Moabites marched northwards and seized Jericho which they held for eighteen years. Again, during the reign of Ahab, Moab was tributary to Israel. On the death of Ahab, however, the king of Moab asserted his freedom.

About this time, in the reign of Jehoshaphat, the Moabites, Ammonites,

---

[1] Judg. 11 : 12–18.  [2] Ruth 1 : 1.  [3] Ruth 1 : 16–19; 4 : 9–13; Matt. 1 : 5–16.
[4] 1 Sam. 22 : 3, 4.  [5] 2 Sam. 8 : 2.

and other allies invaded the Kingdom of Judah.[1] They marched round the south end of the Dead Sea ; thence northerly along the beach and up the pass of En-gedi to Tekoa. But the allies quarreled with one another, and Jehoshaphat had only to gather up the spoil that his enemies left on the field.

During the same reign, probably a little later, the combined forces of Israel and Judah invaded the Land of Moab.[2] They marched southerly through Judæa into Edom, where they were joined by an Edomite force. The allies then invaded Moab from the south. Disaster befell the Moabites. Looking out early in the morning toward the camp of the allied army they saw what appeared like brooks of blood. In reality it was water reflecting the rays of the morning sun. Mistakenly supposing that the enemy had destroyed each other, as their own men had done on a former occasion, the Moabites rushed forward, eager for plunder. It was only to fall into the hands of a foe prepared to receive them. Terrible slaughter ensued. The whole land of Moab was laid waste. Crops were destroyed, stones were scattered over the fields, forests were cut down, wells of water were filled up, and towns were demolished. Finally the king of Moab took shelter in his capital Kir-hareseth.

**Kir-hareseth** or **Kir-haresh** (Nest in the Rock), the capital of Moab, supposed to be the modern Kerak, was a natural fortress of great strength. It was built on a promontory about 2,700 feet high that extends out into the deep Wady Kerak, connected with the plateau by a narrow ridge. The entrance to the city originally was by tunnel. To this fortress King Mesha betook himself. During the siege he tried a bold move. With a strong band of warriors he made a sally against his assailants. In this he failed. In his extremity he invoked the aid of his gods by sacrificing his son upon an altar erected on the walls of the city in sight of the allied army. Shocked by such a spectacle, the kings of Israel and Judah raised the siege and departed to their own land. Thus Mesha was left to believe in the efficacy of his sacrifice.[3]

In the early part of the twelfth century the Crusaders built a strong fortress at Kerak, with high massive walls and towers. Curious and interesting remains of their work here are still in existence.

---

[1] 2 Chron. 20: 1-26.     [2] 2 Kings 3: 4-27.     [3] 2 Kings 3: 26, 27.

## CHAPTER XI

### THE LANDS OF THE EUPHRATES AND THE TIGRIS

ON the east of Palestine beyond the great Arabian Desert and south of the highlands of Armenia is the Land of the Twin Rivers. The upper or northern half of this territory was, by the Hebrews, called Aram Naharayim or "Aram of the Two Rivers." Later, by the Greeks, it was called Mesopotamia, that is "Mid-river-land."[1]

**Physical Features.**—From the highlands of Armenia, some 7,000 feet above the sea level, there stretches southerly a vast plain 700 miles to the Persian Gulf. The upper or northern half of this country is a region of limestone and gypsum, with a gentle slope toward the south. At the north this section, diversified by mountain spurs and valleys, is well watered and fertile, but toward the south it is dry steppe land, better suited to grazing than to tillage. The rivers have cut deep channels or canyons through the section, two or three miles wide and 300 feet deep.

The southern half of this great plain is a low alluvial region which has, through the ages, been reclaimed from the sea by the action of the rivers. This process is still going on. The rivers are ever bearing away the highlands piece-meal and depositing their burden along the margin of the ocean. The land is thus moving forward and extending its domain at the rate of about seventy-five feet each year. The country here is very level and is but slightly elevated above the river-bed. Indeed near the sea it is so low that water and land commingle in swamp and marsh. This alluvial plain is without mineral or stone of any kind. Excellent clay for brickmaking is abundant; also bitumen which, from earliest times, has been used as a cement or mortar to bind the bricks together.

In ancient years the alluvial plain was a wonderfully fertile region. It yielded dates in great abundance; also figs, grapes, and other fruit. But its chief product was wheat, of which it is said to have yielded two hundredfold. Its productiveness in grain, however, was dependent on artificial watering. The summer season is here dry and hot, and the whole country was in the olden time intersected with canals connected with the rivers thus supplying water for irrigation.

**The Two Great Rivers** of the country, the Euphrates and the Tigris, rise 150 miles apart in the highlands of Armenia,—the former on the north of Lake Van, the other on the south of this lake. At first the course of

---

[1] Some writers question the correctness of the dual form Naharayim, preferring instead the plural Naharin. This would give "Land of the Rivers."

the Euphrates is southwesterly, as if it were making for the Mediterranean Sea; then bending round it flows southeasterly, and the two rivers converge until they enter a common channel and as one river pass on to the Persian Gulf.

When yet the world was young this plain became the chosen home of different branches of the human family. Various portions of the country are connected with Bible story.[1] In one place men thought to build a city and a tower that would forever bind them together.[2] Here, in "Ur of the Chaldees," was the birthplace of Abraham.[3] Elsewhere was Nineveh, to which Jonah was sent to preach repentance to the people.[4] This was the land of exile where the Jews hung their silent harps upon the willows,[5] where Ezekiel "by the river Chebar," saw his wonderful vision,[6] and Daniel and his three friends had such varied experiences of trial and triumph.[7]

This wonderful land, once populous, the seat of great cities, of powerful empires and of the world's earliest civilization,—this land that once held supremacy over the world is to-day a land of barrenness and of ruins. Where once were waving grainfields wandering Bedouins seek pasturage for their flocks and herds. The great cities, long sought for in vain, are now being exhumed from mounds of earth that through the centuries and the millenniums accumulated over them. "The innumerable canals which in bygone ages, like so many nourishing veins, crossed the rich alluvial plain, bringing life and joy and wealth to every village and field, are choked up with rubbish and earth."[8]

**Searching for the Lost Cities.**—For ages men inquired,—Where are the great cities of this land with their palaces and temples and lofty walls that history tells us of? Then they began to ask,—What are these great mounds of earth that we see scattered up and down throughout the land? Coming nearer and observing broken pottery lying round and masses of brickwork cropping out from the mounds, they set to work with pick and shovel. It was scarcely a century ago that the work of excavation began in Babylon and Nineveh (1820). Comparatively little was done, however, in this great field of exploration until near the middle of the past century. Since that time among the distinguished men who have been prominent either in the work of excavation or in translating the inscriptions that have been discovered are Paul E. Botta, Sir Henry Austen Layard, W. K. Loftus, Sir Henry Rawlinson, George Smith, H. Rassam, A. H. Sayce, H. V. Hilprecht, Dr. Peters, and J. H. Haynes.

**Excavated Cities.**—The ancient cities at which the work of excavation has been carried on comprise Nineveh, Calah, and Dur-sharrukin in

---

[1] Gen. 10: 9–12, 22; 11: 27.　　[2] Gen. 11: 1–4.　　[3] Gen. 11: 27–31.
[4] Jonah 1: 1, 2.　　[5] Ps. 137: 1, 2.　　[6] Ezek. 1: 1–28.
[7] Dan. 1: 3–6.　　[8] Hilprecht, "Explorations in Bible Lands."

Assyria; Babylon, Borsippa, Eridu, Ur, Nippur, Ellasar, and Erek in Babylonia; and Susa or Shushan in ancient Elam. Among the varied objects discovered in these cities are ancient palaces and temples, bas-reliefs and sculptures representing war scenes, hunting scenes, sacrifices to the gods, soldiers leading away captives, impaling them, or flaying them alive, and various exploits of the kings; winged bulls, winged lions; ornaments of gold, silver, precious stones, and ivory; copper, bronze, and glass vessels; shields, swords, saws, hammers, and many other things too numerous to mention. But of special importance are the ancient temple libraries that have been unearthed.

The "Black Obelisk," of Shalmaneser II, found at Calah, is one of the most interesting "finds." This is a block of black marble about seven feet high, with bas-reliefs representing historic events and war scenes. An inscription states, "I (Shalmaneser) received tribute of Jehu."

A slab of stone, found in the hall of Sennacherib's palace at Nineveh, depicts the siege of Lachish by this king at the time of his invasion of Judah (701 B. C.). Assyrian warriors are shown impaling prisoners and flaying them alive. A long procession of captives appears advancing toward Sennacherib. The haughty monarch sits on a throne, and above his head is inscribed, "Sennacherib, King of the Universe."

Limestone and alabaster, being plentiful in Assyria, largely took the place of brick as building material. Temples and palaces were the principal buildings and were erected on platforms of earth or brick faced with stone. The palaces were of one story with thick walls, and their apartments consisted of halls, galleries, and chambers, built around an open court. The temple was usually a *ziggurat* or stage-tower, consisting of a series of solid masses of brick, built up in stories or stages one upon another. The whole structure presented the form of a pyramid. The base was rectangular, with the angular points directed toward the cardinal points of the compass. Each story was built on the one next below, but receding from the edge, so as to rest on a smaller base and leave a platform or shelf on all sides. At the top was the shrine of the chief god of the city, and on the lower shelves were shrines of inferior gods. A winding staircase led from the base to the summit.

**Libraries.**—The libraries found in these ruined cities are vast collections of inscribed clay tablets. Carefully-prepared clay was fashioned into tablets of various sizes—the common size being about six inches long, two inches wide, and one inch thick. Sometimes, instead of tablets, the clay was made into little cones or prisms. The writing was done with a stylus while the clay was soft. The tablet or block was then dried in the sun or baked in a kiln. The characters are short, straight lines with a triangle or wedge-shaped form at one end, or sometimes at both ends.

From the frequent recurrence of this wedge form the term cuneiform or wedge-shaped is applied to the language and literature as well as to the characters.

For many years the strange cuneiform writings were a sealed language. Behistun, a great rock 1,700 feet high on the road between Hamadan and Bagdad furnished a "Rosetta Stone." In deciphering a trilingual inscription (in the languages of Assyria, Persia, and Elam) on this rock Sir Henry Rawlinson discovered the key to the cuneiform language.

The subjects treated of in the tablets include history, the wars, building operations, and other exploits of the kings, religion, mythology, astronomy, astrology, medicine, and law. They comprise a mythical story of the creation and of the deluge; also the laws of Khammurabi of the time of Abraham. Some of these laws closely resemble those of Moses.

**Babylonia** comprised the alluvial territory on the south, between the rivers, and extended to the desert on the west of the Euphrates. In the extreme south, near where the rivers come together, was Kaldi or the Land of the Chaldees, which in its history was often closely identified with Babylonia.

**Cities.**—**Bagdad,** on the Tigris, the capital of the Turkish province of Mesopotamia, is a comparatively modern city, founded in A. D. 762. It is said to have had at one time a population of 1,500,000. Though now having only about 180,000 inhabitants, it is still an important city. The proposed German railway through this valley will connect Bagdad with the Persian Gulf.

**Babylon,** situated on both sides of the Euphrates, now represented by mounds near the modern city Hillah, was surrounded by a double wall, the outer one 350 feet high and 85 feet thick, and making a circuit of 55 miles. It is said to have been the capital of the Babylonian Empire under Khammurabi (2297-2254 B. C.), and to have attained its greatest glory under Nebuchadnezzar (604-561 B. C.), who built temples and palaces, and in many ways adorned the city. Among his works were the great temple of Bel or Bel-Merodach and the "Hanging Gardens," the site of which is supposed to be included in the northern mound now called Babil.

**Eridu** (Abu Sharein), situated in the desert on the west of the Euphrates, was a very old city and the seat of a famous oracle.[1] Its ruins comprise the remains of a pyramidal tower crowned with a sacred chamber for religious rites.

**Borsippa,** represented by the ruins of Birs or Birs Nimrud, is in the

---

[1] Eridu is generally, though incorrectly according to Hilprecht, placed on the east of the Euphrates.

neighborhood of Babylon.  The remains of its stage-tower or temple, 153 feet high, supposed by some to be the "Tower of Babel," are among the finest specimens of the kind in all the land.

**Ur** or "Ur of the Chaldees" (Mugheir or Mugeyer of the present day), is situated on the right or west bank of the Euphrates.  The surrounding country is lowland, so that during the annual flood of the Euphrates from March to June the ruins are on an island.  This city was the center of worship of the moon-god Sin.  The stage-tower or temple of Sin in this city, about 70 feet high, has a base of 198 feet in length and 133 feet in breadth.  Ur was the native place of Abraham.[1]

**Nippur** (now called Niffer), on the great canal or "River Chebar," in the middle of the plain south of Babylon, was a noted religious center for the worship of the god Bel.  Among the recent discoveries made here is a great temple, the work of many kings, with its wonderful library of clay tablets.  These tablets are of different ages, some being as early as 2000 B. C.

**Ellassar** or **Larsam** (Senkereh), thirty miles north of Ur, contained a temple of the sun-god Shamash.

**Erek** or **Urek** (Warka) was devoted to the worship of the goddess Ishtar.

**Assyria** proper was situated along the middle course of the Tigris, extending to the highland region on the east of the river.  Southerly it extended through the higher undulating tracts to the flat alluvial plains of Babylonia.  The eastern section, through which flow the main tributaries of the Tigris, is very fertile.  Western Assyria is drier and less fruitful, especially the southwestern portion.  The term Assyria was often applied to a much larger territory.

**Nineveh** (made the capital of Assyria by Sennacherib about 700 B. C.) was situated on the east bank of the Tigris opposite the modern Mosul.  The site is now occupied by two mounds, Kuyunjunek and Nebi Yunus, which were explored by Layard, Rassam, and George Smith.  Unearthed by their excavations were several royal palaces, the walls of which were adorned with sculptures representing the exploits of ancient kings.  Sennacherib's palace in Nineveh is said to be the greatest ever built by an Assyrian monarch.  Although the whole building has not been excavated, seventy-one rooms have been explored.

**Calah**, represented by the ruins of Nimrud on the Tigris eighteen miles south of Nineveh, was one of the early capitals of Assyria.[2]  The ruins show remains of splendid temples and palaces, rich in bas-reliefs representing the exploits of the ancient kings.  In one of the palaces was

[1] Gen. 11 : 31.         [2] Gen. 10 : 11.

found a storeroom filled with implements of war and bronze vessels of beautiful design. Many of the relics of Calah, including the famous "Black Obelisk," are now in the British Museum.

**Dur-sharrukin**, built by Sargon, eighteen miles northeast of Nineveh, was surrounded by a wall fifty feet high. Sargon erected here a vast palace, covering an area of twenty-five acres, the walls of which were adorned with bas-relief representations of his wars.

**Media** occupied the highland district on the south and southwest of the Caspian Sea. The territory is now included in Persia.

**Achmetha** or **Ecbatana**, supposed to be the modern Hamadan, was the capital of Media. It was the summer residence of the Medo-Persian kings, and public documents seem to have been kept here.[1]

**Elam** comprised the territory on the east of the lower course of the Tigris. It is a fertile region of varied scenery,—mountains, valleys, and ravines. In ancient times it formed the center of a great empire.

**Susa** or **Shushan** was the capital of Elam and afterwards of the Medo-Persian Empire. The site of the city is occupied by several large mounds. This city was the scene of the story of Esther and Mordecai as told in the Book of Esther. Explorations were made here over half a century ago by Loftus and Sir Fenwick Williams of Kars. The most remarkable feature of the ruins is the great palace, the central hall of which was 200 feet square and the roof was supported by thirty-six columns sixty feet high.[2] In this famous capital was held what was perhaps the world's first great exhibition.[3]

Probably the most important discovery made among the ruins of Shushan is the *stele* or sculptured slab on which is inscribed the law code of Khammurabi, the Amraphel, King of Shinar, of the time of Abraham. This famous code comprises 280 edicts which the great conqueror asserted he received from the sun-god Shamash. Many of these laws closely resemble some of those in the Mosaic code.

**Persia** proper in ancient times was a small country south of Media and east of Elam. For the most part it was an arid, barren region. On the borders of the mountains were fertile valleys, which produced famous wines. The Persians immigrated to this country from a region near Lake Urumiah on the east of the Caspian Sea.

**Persepolis**, one of the capitals of Medo-Persia, has among its ruins the remains of magnificent palaces and pavilions. Thirteen columns sixty-four feet high that belonged to one of these palaces are still standing.

---

[1] Ezra 6:2.    [2] Esther 1:2.    [3] Esther 1:3, 4.

## CHAPTER XII

## HISTORIC SKETCH OF BABYLONIA, ASSYRIA, PERSIA, ETC.

THE story of the lands of the Euphrates and the Tigris, in disconnected fragments of fact and legend, goes back five thousand years before the Christian era. Some of the earliest postdiluvian records of the Bible relate to these lands. It is, however, to the clay tablets discovered in the buried cities, a hundred and sixty thousand of which are now in the various museums of the world, that we owe the chief part of our knowledge of their history. From these sources authentic history may be traced to Sargon who ruled in Agade in Northern Babylonia about 3800 B. C.

In the early times the country was the seat of many petty states, each comprising a small territory round a central city. As in other lands there grew up a rivalry among the rulers of these principalities that led to the supremacy of the stronger over the weaker and eventually to consolidation into more powerful kingdoms. Then there followed wider conquests until the leading kingdom became an empire. In this process of empire-building the city was the state—not merely the center of power, but the power itself.

A conquered state, unless it proved very troublesome, was allowed the management of its own internal affairs. So long as it paid the tribute imposed and furnished its quota of men for the wars of the suzerain, all was well. But if a people strenuously resisted, or having once submitted afterwards rebelled, no form of punishment was too severe. Reconquest was followed by demolition of fortifications, if not utter destruction of the city. The principal inhabitants were often deported to some distant part of the empire, and other people were brought in to occupy their place. Captive kings were sometimes shut up in cages and exposed like wild beasts to public view, or they were, like horses, harnessed to the victor's chariot and driven through the streets. In extreme cases noted captives who had given trouble were flayed alive, and their skins were nailed to the city walls.

The Babylonian and Assyrian empires grew to vast proportions, but they never were very thoroughly consolidated. The various states were held together by military force. Insurrections and reconquests were of frequent occurrence.

The Babylonians and Assyrians, belonging to what is known as Semitic stock, were kindred in origin and language to the Hebrews.

Their history is closely interwoven with each other. They were a deeply religious people, but they differed from the Israelites in being polytheists. Their pantheon was a hierarchy, but the power of the greatest gods was limited to certain places or spheres of action. Anu was the god of heaven, Bel was the god of earth, and Ea the god of the abyss. Each city had its own god who was the chief deity for that place. Ea was supreme in Eridu, Sin in Ur, Marduk in Babylon. This belief in the limitation of the power of a god is well illustrated in the case of the people deported from the east to the cities of Samaria.[1] The kings of Babylon and Nineveh believed that they were the vicegerents of the gods, and they showed their loyalty to them by the grandeur of the temples which they built, and their confidence in them by their many and importunate prayers for divine aid. The most sacred shrine with the image of the supreme god was placed in the topmost story of the lofty temple-towers, evidently for the purpose of getting as near to heaven as possible. In prayer the suppliant stood, with both hands outspread before him, his prayer comprising ascription of glory to the god, confession of sin, and petition for aid. The Babylonians were solicitous of the future, which they sought to discover through augury, omens, and dreams.

**Old Babylonia.**—The earliest City-States that appear in the dawn of historic record were in the lower Tigro-Euphrates Valley. Among these states Babylon was not prominent. This city, however, takes its place as the chief seat of power early in the twenty-third century B. C. (about 2285), when Khammurabi, identified as "Amraphel" of Abraham's time,[2] gathered the scattered principalities under his rule and made it the capital of a great empire. This empire, known as the Old Babylonian Empire with its capital at Babylon, continued, though with many changes of dynasty and sometimes under foreign rule, for over fifteen hundred years (2385–733 B. C.). Sargon I, whose reign dates back to about 3800 B. C., having his capital at Agade (Akkad), ruled over a people considerably advanced in civilization.

**The Assyrian Empire.**—Meanwhile an offshoot had sprung from the Babylonian stock, which, dependent for centuries, then a rival, came at length to overshadow the parent stem. At an early date, before the time of Khammurabi, a colony from Babylon migrated north and founded a city called Asshur on the west bank of the Tigris. This city named after the chief god of the people, gave name to the country and became its first capital.

[1] 2 Kings 17 : 24–29.                                          [2] Gen. 14 : 1.

In religion, language, and general customs the Assyrians resembled the Babylonians. They were, however, more warlike than the parent people, and they were more barbarous in their treatment of those whom they had vanquished. While they revered the gods of Babylonia, they regarded Ashur as their national god and gave him the highest place in their pantheon.

For several centuries the Assyrians yielded allegiance to the mother country, but they became independent some time during the seventeenth century B. C. Shalmaneser I, who reigned toward the close of the fourteenth century, added largely to his territory by conquests in the north and west along the upper course of the Tigris and the Euphrates. He also founded a new capital, Calah, forty miles north of Asshur, on the east of the Tigris. Tiglath-pileser I, who lived two hundred years later, was also a great warrior. Four clay cylinders, found at the corner of a ruined temple at Asshur, all bearing the same inscription, give an account of his exploits. Ashurnasirpal, who came to the throne about 884 B. C., the annals of whose reign are inscribed on a stone slab found in a temple at Calah, was a monarch of great renown.

Among other details of Ashurnasirpal's doings he tells in these records how he flayed alive a governor of a captured city and hung his skin on the city walls. This king built for himself in Calah a great palace 350 feet square.

Shalmaneser II, succeeded Ashurnasirpal (860 B. C.). His exploits are recorded on the Black Obelisk found at Nimrud and now in the British Museum in London. He defeated the allied forces of Benhadad of Damascus, Ahab of Israel, and other confederate kings. At a later period he conquered Hazael of Damascus, received tribute of Jehu, King of Israel, and reduced Babylonia to the position of a vassal state.

Tiglath-pileser III, Shalmaneser IV, Sargon, Sennacherib, Esar-haddon, and Ashurbanipal were among the greatest of the Assyrian kings. The Hebrew nations as well as other peoples of Western Asia were made to feel the weight of their power. Tiglath-pileser carried into captivity many of the Israelites on the east of the Jordan.[1] Shalmaneser invaded the Kingdom of Israel again, and Sargon completed its conquest by the capture and destruction of Samaria and the deportation of its principal inhabitants[2] (721 B. C.).

Sargon had trouble in Babylon. A Chaldæan prince, named Merodach-baladan, seized the throne in this southern metropolis and having made an alliance with the Elamites set the king of Nineveh at defiance. It would appear also that this usurper used his influence with Hezekiah, King of Judah, to cause disaffection toward his suzerain, the king of Assyria.[3]

[1] 1 Kings 15: 29.   [2] 2 Kings 17: 5; 18: 9-12.   [3] 2 Kings 20: 12, 13.

One of the grandest schemes of Sargon was the building of the city Dur-sharrukin for a royal residence.

Sennacherib's exploits in Western Asia during the reign of Hezekiah are of great interest to Bible students. The early part of his reign was disturbed by rebellion in Babylon, led by Merodach-baladan. Having quieted matters here, Sennacherib marched into Western Asia where the suzerainty of Assyria had been thrown off by various princes. His first move in this quarter was against Phœnicia, which, with the exception of Tyre, he readily brought to submission. With part of his army he then marched through Philistia, capturing the cities Gaza, Ashkelon, Ekron, Lachish, and Libnah, and also defeated an Egyptian army sent to the aid of these cities. Another division of his army marched through the land of Judah, capturing "forty-six walled cities and the smaller cities round about them without number."[1] The conqueror further states,—"Two hundred thousand one hundred and fifty people, small and great, male and female, horses, mules, asses, camels, cattle, sheep without number, I brought forth from their midst and reckoned as spoil." Having thus overrun the country, the invading army blockaded Jerusalem.

Thoroughly alarmed Hezekiah sent to Sennacherib, who was then at Lachish, asking for terms of reconciliation. The amount demanded was large, but by stripping the temple of the precious metals, Hezekiah was able to make prompt payment, and the Assyrian army was withdrawn. Shortly after, thinking, perhaps, the conditions he had imposed were too easy, Sennacherib sent a messenger to Hezekiah, demanding surrender of the city. Filled with consternation, Hezekiah turned to Isaiah for counsel. The prophet told him to give no heed to the demand, for he should have help from Jehovah. And so we read,—"The angel of Jehovah went forth, and smote in the camp of the Assyrians a hundred and four score and five thousand; and when men arose early in the morning, behold, these were all dead bodies."[2] It is commonly supposed that the Assyrians were smitten by pestilence.

Panic-stricken, Sennacherib with the remnant of his army hastened to the east where he found his authority seriously imperiled. Merodach-baladan was again in Babylon, and this city together with the surrounding country, aided by the Elamites, was in a state of rebellion. The great king's resources were severely taxed, but in the end he gained complete triumph over his foes. He captured Babylon, razed it to the ground, burned what was combustible, and then turned the waters of the Euphrates in upon the ruins. In the destruction of this city much that was of great interest and value in Babylonian literature, science, and art, perished.

Sennacherib was a great builder as well as warrior. Among his other

[1] 2 Kings 18 : 13.    [2] Isa. 37 : 36; 2 Kings 19 : 35; 2 Chron. 32 : 21.

works he rebuilt Nineveh, which had fallen into decay, and made it the capital of Assyria. But in the midst of his triumphs, the victim of conspiracy, his life was suddenly ended. As he stood praying in the temple of his god, he was assassinated by two of his sons.[1]

Esar-haddon, who succeeded Sennacherib, brought the empire to the summit of her power and glory. His first and most beneficent work was the restoration of Babylon which his father had destroyed. He built a great palace in Nineveh, for which it is said twenty-two vassal kings contributed materials. He was also famous as a builder of temples. His wars in the west were in the main crowned with success, even the kingdom of the Nile being added to his empire. Manasseh, King of Judah, son of Hezekiah, was among his vassals. Only the sea-girt city of Tyre baffled his power and skill; it he failed to capture. The territory of Northern Israel was repopulated during the reign of Esar-haddon by the deportation of people from the east.[2]

Next on the throne was Ashurbanipal, whose reign was much disturbed by insurrection both in Babylon and in the west. But he put down the insurgents with a strong hand. He was also a famous builder of temples and palaces. His great palace in Nineveh was richly decorated with sculpture of a high order. A bas-relief represents him in his garden, feasting with his queen, while near by suspended on a tree is the head of a captive king. The record tells us that on one occasion he was drawn to the temple of his favorite goddess Ishtar by four kings harnessed to his chariot. The clay-tablet library of this king, a large part of which is now in the British Museum, is said to surpass all other similar Assyrian collections.

There were yet two more kings on the Assyrian throne, and then, amid all its splendor and triumph, this great empire suddenly came to an end. Pharaoh-Necho of Egypt threw off the yoke and became aggressive. Marching through Palestine he was opposed by Josiah, King of Judah, whom he slew at Megiddo.[3] Continuing northerly, he met and defeated the Assyrian forces at Carchemish.

Meanwhile the Medes, now a formidable power in the east, had been regarding the Assyrian land with covetous eye. Cyaxares, King of Media, and Nabopolassar, of Chaldæan stock, the Assyrian viceroy of Babylon, whose son Nebuchadnezzar had married the daughter of Cyaxares, formed an alliance against the king of Assyria. The allied forces besieged and took Nineveh, which they utterly destroyed. According to tradition the king, determined not to fall into the hands of his enemies, heaped up his treasures in a great funeral pyre, four hundred feet high, and seating himself upon it with his wives, set it on fire and perished in the flames. The

---

[1] 2 Kings 19 : 37.   [2] Ezra 4 : 2.   [3] 2 Kings 23 : 29; 2 Chron. 35 : 20–23.

Assyrian Empire was divided between the conquerors, the northern half falling to Cyaxares, the southern to Nabopolassar.

**The New Babylonian or Chaldæan Empire** (606–538 B. C.).—The New Babylonian Empire, called also the Chaldæan Empire, extended westerly to the Mediterranean Sea. Nabopolassar sent his son Nebuchadnezzar into Syria to secure the loyalty of the vassal states in that quarter, over which Pharaoh-Necho of Egypt was trying to establish his power. Having defeated this sovereign at Carchemish and pursued him to the borders of Egypt, Nebuchadnezzar received the homage of various tributary kings, including Jehoiakim, King of Judah,[1] and returned hastily to Babylon to take possession of the throne made vacant by the death of his father.

Nebuchadnezzar's brilliant reign lasted for forty-three years. Among his exploits were the destruction of Jerusalem,[2] a thirteen years' siege of Tyre, and his building operations in Babylon, including city walls, ramparts, temples, and that "wonder of the world," "The Hanging Gardens of Babylon"—terraced grounds built up, it is said, to solace his Median wife for the loss of the rugged scenery of her native land. He also restored the dilapidated temples in the various cities of Babylonia, and added greatly to the canal system for the improvement of agriculture.

On the death of Nebuchadnezzar the glory of the empire soon departed. There followed during the reigns of his son and grandson, a few years of internal strife. Then a usurper, named Nabunaid or Nabonidus, obtained the throne. The facts relating to the closing years of the empire are not well known. Nabonidus was not a warrior. The building of temples, the care of the gods, and gathering up archaic records were more in accord with his taste. In restoring old temples he cleared away the ruins to the very foundations that he might find the long-hidden inscriptions of the original builders. Thus, at Sippar, in rebuilding the temple of Shamash the sun-god, he came upon records placed there by the builder Naram Sin about 3750 B. C. But while he was thus engaged his foes were planning the destruction of his empire.[3]

The Medes, who held the empire on the north, true to the old alliance with Nabopolassar, had continued friendly during the rule of his dynasty in Babylonia. But now that the power had passed into other hands their King Astyages began to look across the border with hostile intent. While he was preparing for movement in this direction, one of his own vassals, Cyrus the Persian, rebelled against him, overturned his throne, and established the Medo-Persian Empire.

Through the conquest of Media by Cyrus (549 B. C.) Persia became the dominant power on the north of Babylonia. The exploits of Cyrus

---

[1] 2 Kings 24 : 1.   [2] 2 Kings, ch. 25.   [3] See page 77.

filled the nations with alarm. Not the neighboring empire of Babylonia alone, but distant Egypt, Lydia, and Greece were disturbed by his warlike movements. These powers formed an alliance for the guarding of mutual interests. Before they could concentrate their forces, however, Cyrus marched into Asia Minor, defeated Crœsus the king of Lydia, annexed his kingdom to his own great empire, and carried off the captive king.

The next great movement of Cyrus was the invasion of Babylonia. Nabonidus and his son Belshazzar appear at this time to have ruled conjointly, and the cares of government were entrusted to the latter. Cyrus laid siege to Babylon, then in charge of Belshazzar, and captured it without striking a blow.[1]

The story of Cyrus's diverting the Euphrates to a new channel and taking his army into the city by the river-bed is without foundation. There was treachery within the city. The priests of Marduk, the chief god of Babylon, being indignant, it is said, because Nabonidus was giving Shamash, the sun-god, equal honor with Marduk, opened the city gates and gave free admission to the Persian army (539 B. C.). Thus ended the third and began the fourth of the great world powers of Asia.

**The Medo-Persian Empire.**—The Persians, differing from the dominant peoples who preceded them, were of Aryan stock. They were a people of softer manners than the Assyrians and Babylonians and ruled those whom they conquered with less severity. The king was indeed supreme lord, and, as shown in the Book of Esther, had absolute power over the lives and property of his subjects. Yet Persian rule was comparatively mild and tolerant.

Cyrus treated his new subjects in Babylonia with great clemency and took pains to conciliate them by showing due respect to their gods and their religion. Exiles who had been deported to Babylonia he permitted to return to their own land. The Jews, though not wholly exceptional in this regard, were shown special consideration. Cyrus issued a remarkable edict,[2] allowing them to return to Jerusalem, and rebuild the city and temple. He also restored to them the sacred vessels of the temple which Nebuchadnezzar had taken away.

The religion of the Persians was a dualism. They believed in two great spiritual powers—Ahuramazda or Ormazd, the good spirit, and Ahriman, the evil spirit. Ormazd was the giver of life and the source of all good things. Ahriman was the death-dealer, the source of all evil things,—poverty, war, disease, sin, and death. He kept under him many evil spirits to carry out his wicked purposes.

The Persians had no images, but they regarded the sun, moon, stars,

---

[1] Dan. 5 : 30, 31.   [2] Isa. 44 : 28; 45 : 1-4; Jer. 25 : 10; 33 : 7-10; Ezra 1 : 1-11.

fire, and all light-giving bodies as emblems of deity. Their worship was simple without sacrifice, and consisted chiefly in praise and prayer. Their sacred book, made up largely of religious rules, hymns, and prayers, is called the Avesta.

The Medo-Persian Empire was short-lived, existing only about two hundred years. Cyrus was succeeded by his son Cambyses, an erratic prince, whose wild schemes secured for him the title of madman. He conquered Egypt, however, and added it to his vast empire—the greatest the world had yet seen, extending from the Ægean Sea and the Nile on the west, to the river Indus. Darius I consolidated the empire, divided it into provinces, and organized a system of government. He attempted the conquest of Greece, an enterprise in which he utterly failed. Xerxes, who is supposed to be the Ahasuerus of the Book of Esther, at the head of the largest army the world had ever seen, made a similar expedition into Greece with like disastrous results (480 B. C.). After him came Artaxerxes Longimanus (the "long-handed"), who ruled the empire in the time of Ezra and Nehemiah (466–425 B. C.). It was in his reign, about seventy-five years after the edict of Cyrus, that Ezra went to Jerusalem.

Artaxerxes II, on account of his wonderful memory, was called Artaxerxes Mnemon. His brother Cyrus, whom he had made governor of Asia Minor, revolted and made that famous expedition against him described in Xenophon's Anabasis. In the great battle of Cunæ Cyrus was defeated and slain (401 B. C.). The last of the Persian monarchs was Darius III, who was defeated by Alexander the Great, 331 B. C.

## CHAPTER XIII
### SYRIA

The name Syria is given in the English Bible for the Hebrew Aram.. It is a vague term, applied sometimes as the name of a large territory including Palestine, Phœnicia, and the region lying north of these countries. In a very restricted sense it is used as the name of Damascus and a small tract round that city. More properly it was the name of the country north of Palestine, and extended from the Euphrates on the east to Phœnicia, the Mediterranean Sea, and Asia Minor on the west.

The northern portion of Syria is elevated, the eastern is level, extending to the Arabian Desert. The Amanus and Taurus Mountains are on the northwestern border. The Mountains of Lebanon and Anti-Lebanon are parallel ranges on the north of Palestine. Between these ranges is the long narrow valley called Cœle-syria (Hollow Syria). The chief rivers in this section are the Litany, the Orontes, and the Barada or Abana.

Cœle-syria varies in breadth from three or four miles to fifteen miles, and is in some places broken by projecting spurs of the Lebanon ranges. At its northern end it curves round to the west and opens out to the Mediterranean. It has two slopes, a northerly and a southerly, is watered by the rivers which flow through it in opposite directions, and is one of the most fertile and beautiful regions in all Syria. This valley was always an important route of travel between the countries on the Euphrates and Tigris and those on the seaboard. In ancient times it was the seat of noted cities, among which were Baalbec and Hamath.[1]

The **Litany** or **Leontes** rises in a small lake six miles south of the ruins of Baalbec, flows at first southerly, and then turning westerly breaks through Lebanon by a narrow defile and finally discharges its waters into the Mediterranean five miles north of Tyre. It forms the northern boundary of Western Palestine.

The **Orontes** rises near Baalbec, flows northerly through the rich valley of Cœle-syria until arrested in this direction by Mount Amanus it turns westerly, and after a course of 200 miles flows into the Mediterranean.

The **Abana** or **Barada** rises in Anti-Lebanon and flows easterly, at first through a narrow valley between parallel ranges and then, passing

[1] Amos 6:2.

out into the open plain, it divides into many small streams. On its way it gives of its waters to Damascus and to the fruitful cornfields and orchards of this delightful plain, making "the desert rejoice, and blossom as the rose." No wonder that Naaman was so jealous for the honor of this river and that he exclaimed with intensest scorn, "Are not Abana and Pharpar, rivers of Damascus, better than all the waters of Israel?" After this river has irrigated the plain and converted it into one of the most beautiful and fertile regions in the world, its surplus waters are carried forward and lost in a marsh or lake on the borders of the desert.

**Political Divisions.**—In the early ages Syria comprised many small city-states, that is, districts of country round a central ruling city. Generally some one or more of these states or kingdoms stood out more prominently as a seat of power, but no one ever rose to such ascendancy as to consolidate the whole under a single ruler. They were generally at war, either with each other, or they formed an alliance against a foreign foe who sought to obtain supremacy over them.

An example of such a confederacy against an invader is shown by the Assyrian records, when twelve kings united to fight Shalmaneser II of Assyria. The Assyrian king, having established his power over Carchemish and other states of Northern Syria, moved against the little kingdoms of the south. Ahab, King of Israel, Benhadad of Damascus, the king of Hamath, and nine other kings of lesser note met "the great king" of Assyria at Karkar on the Orontes (854 B. C.). Shalmaneser said he gained the battle, but he told of no city captured or tribute received.

The most important cities and centers of power were Damascus, Carchemish, and Hamath.

**Damascus**, about 130 miles northeast of Jerusalem, is situated in a fertile plain at the foot of Mount Hermon. It was at the head of the most important small state of ancient Syria, and probably no other city of the present day can trace its history so far back in the annals of the world. In Bible story it is often spoken of under the name Syria. The city was frequently captured and plundered by its enemies, but it speedily reasserted itself, recovered from spoliation, and became prosperous. Its vitality was due in part to the fertility of the surrounding country and in part to its being on the highway of trade. Caravans between Egypt and Phœnicia on the west and Palmyra and the Euphrates on the east passed through the city.

Of the routes of travel which passed through Damascus one lay along the present road to Beirut; another lay through Cœle-syria; another passed south of Hermon and thence across Galilee, or over Esdraelon, or down the Jordan Valley; and yet another traversed the margin of the desert on the east of Bashan and Gilead to the Gulf of Akabah. Only during the period of the Seleucidæ and the Roman period which followed it, when the new city of Antioch rose to supremacy, did Damascus fall into decay. But Damascus revived and flourished again after Antioch had become a heap of ruins. In the Apostolic age Damascus was the home of many Jews and was the seat of a synagogue. It was here that Paul was baptized. The modern name of the city is el Shams. It is still a large city, but the diversion of trade through the Suez Canal has greatly impaired its prosperity.

**Carchemish** stood on the upper Euphrates, and it is now represented by the ruins known as Jerablus. It was for centuries the capital of the Hittite kingdom in Northern Syria. Holding a commanding position on a common route of travel, it was a city of much importance. For a time it was an object of contention between Egypt and Assyria. It was captured by Pharaoh-Necho after the battle of Megiddo (608 B. C.),[1] but it was retaken by Nebuchadnezzar three years later.[2]

**Hamath,** on the Orontes, near its middle course, and near the northern limits of the Land of Promise, has frequent notice in the Old Testament.[3] Its king sent a present with congratulations to David on his defeat of the king of Zobah.[4] It was subject to Israel in the time of Solomon, but having afterwards become independent, it was recaptured by Jeroboam II.[5] Still later it was among the places taken by Sennacherib.[6]

**Baalbec** ("City of Baal" or "City of the Sun," the word having the same meaning as the Greek *Heliopolis*), situated in Cœle-syria about thirty-five miles northwest of Damascus, was a center of Baal worship. It is famous for its ancient ruins, including two temples.

**Palmyra** or **Tadmor** ("City of Palms"), situated in an oasis in the desert about 150 miles northeast of Damascus, was an important halting place on a caravan route between the east and the west. It is now famous for its ruins, including a temple of the Sun and long lines of colonnaded streets.[7]

**Riblah** was situated in a fertile plain on the east bank of the Orontes about thirty-five miles northeast of Baalbec. It was a camping ground or center of operations both of the Egyptians and Babylonians while carrying on their wars in the neighborhood. It was here that Pharaoh-Necho took up his position after his victory at Carchemish. Nebuchadnezzar also had his headquarters at Riblah at the time of the siege of Jerusalem and of Tyre.

**Antioch,** situated 300 miles northwest of Jerusalem, on the Orontes sixteen miles from its mouth, was founded by Seleucus Nicator about 300 B. C. It was the capital of Syria under the Seleucidæ and also of the Roman province of Syria. In population and importance it was the third

---

[1] 2 Chron. 35 : 20–24.　　[2] Jer. 46 : 2.　　[3] Num. 13 : 21 ; 34 : 8.
[4] 2 Sam. 8 : 9, 10.　　　　　　　　　　　　[5] 2 Chron. 8 : 4 ; 2 Kings 14 : 28.
[6] 2 Kings 18 : 14 ; 19 : 13.　　　　　　　　[7] 2 Chron. 8 : 4 ; 1 Kings 9 : 18.

city in the Roman Empire, ranking next to Rome and Alexandria. Its principal street was lined from end to end with colonnades. The city was called "Antioch the Beautiful" and "The Crown of the East." Its great trade drew to it many Jewish colonists, who enjoyed all the privileges of citizens. The city was notoriously immoral, and yet it is famous as the birthplace of Gentile Christianity. In Apostolic times it became a leading center of Christian influence, and the city has been called "The Cradle of the Church." It was here that "the disciples were first called Christians"—a name generally supposed to have been given as a nickname. The people of Antioch are said to have been noted for their low wit. Antioch (Atakia) is now a town of about 6,000 inhabitants.

**Daphne**, a suburb of Antioch, five miles distant, was famous for its groves, fountains, baths, and temples. Apollo and Artemis were the gods specially honored. Daphne was an asylum for persons seeking refuge from the arm of the law, and hence it was thronged with runaway slaves, debtors, and criminals of all classes.

**Seleucia**, at the mouth of the Orontes, was the port of Antioch.

**Historic Sketch.**—The relations of the kingdoms of Syria to the Israelites were varied though generally hostile. Damascus, Rehab, and some other states were conquered by David, and they probably remained vassal states throughout his reign.[1] Damascus regained its independence in the time of Solomon.[2] The northern kingdom of Israel and Damascus, bordering on each other, were often in conflict, though on occasions they were allies against a common foe. During a war between Israel and Judah, Benhadad, King of Damascus, who had been in alliance with Israel, was persuaded by presents from Asa, King of Judah, to change sides.[3] Shortly after, Benhadad took several cities from Omri, King of Israel, and he seems also to have exercised a sort of sovereignty in Omri's new capital Samaria.[4] Again in the reign of Ahab a formidable invasion of the Land of Israel was made by Benhadad II, with thirty-two vassal kings under his leadership. Samaria was closely besieged, and matters were looking serious, when a band of spirited young men led a sally against the foe and put them to rout.[5] Within a few months the Syrians returned with a large army, greatly outnumbering that of Israel. Again they were defeated with great slaughter, and Benhadad himself was taken prisoner. But the wily Syrian by skillful diplomacy extricated himself and made a treaty which he probably failed to carry out.[6] For three years there was peace, and then the war was renewed. Ahab seems to have been the aggressor. His object was the recovery of Ramoth-gilead on the east of the Jordan.[7] On this occasion the kings of Israel and

---

[1] 2 Sam. 8 : 3–6, 13 ; 10 : 6.  [2] 1 Kings 4 : 21 ; 11 : 23–25.
[3] 1 Kings 15 : 19 ; 2 Chron. 16 : 3.  [4] 1 Kings 20 : 34.
[5] 1 Kings 20 : 1–21.  [6] 1 Kings 20 : 22–34.  [7] 1 Kings 22 : 1–38.

Judah were allies. They were defeated and Ahab was slain. Once more, in the reign of Jehoram, Benhadad invaded the Land of Israel. While investing the city of Samaria, which was reduced by famine to dire extremity, the Syrians hearing some unusual noise, possibly caused by an earthquake, panic-stricken, fled in the utmost confusion, leaving behind them all their treasures and supplies.[1]

Subsequently Hazael, who had assassinated Benhadad and succeeded him as king of Damascus, defeated the allied forces of Israel and Judah at Ramoth-gilead and reduced Israel to a state of vassalage.[2] The king of Judah saved his capital from siege by sending rich presents to Hazael.[3]

During the reign of Benhadad III, of Damascus, Joash, King of Israel, gained a succession of victories and recovered lost territory from the Syrians.[4] Still further conquests were made by Jeroboam II, who gained for Israel both Damascus and Hamath.[5] About 100 years later the kings of Israel and Damascus appear as allies against Judah.[6] Ahaz, King of Judah, invited the aid of the king of Assyria.[7] Tiglath-pileser, who had already been waging war in Syria, glad of this opportunity of renewing his schemes of conquest, promptly acceded to the request. The result was the final overthrow of Damascus and the deportation of its inhabitants into Assyria.[8]

[1] 2 Kings 6 : 24–33 ; 7 : 1–20.   [2] 2 Kings 8 : 28 ; 10 : 32, 33 ; 13 : 3–7.
[3] 2 Kings 12 : 17, 18.   [4] 2 Kings 13 : 25.   [5] 2 Kings 14 : 28.
[6] 2 Kings 15 : 37.   [7] 2 Kings 16 : 5–9.   [8] Amos 1 : 5.

## CHAPTER XIV

### PHŒNICIA

ANCIENT Phœnicia comprised a portion of the low coast country between the Mediterranean Sea and the Mountains of Lebanon. Phœnicia proper was about twenty-eight miles in length, and it varied in breadth from one mile to five miles. The importance of the country and its influence on the affairs of the world were greatly out of proportion to its area.

Phœnicia varied in extent at different periods. At one time it included the country along the Mediterranean coast for a hundred miles or more. The territory was within the limits of "the Promised Land," but it was never conquered by the Israelites. The name Phœnicia does not occur in the Old Testament, and it is found but three times in the New Testament.[1] By the ancient inhabitants the country was called Kenaan or Canaan, which means lowland.

The **Climate** is subtropical, and the soil is fertile, yielding abundantly such fruits as oranges, lemons, figs, peaches, and pomegranates.

The **Inhabitants**, who are usually in the Bible called Zidonians, were intelligent and skilled in the mechanic arts. They excelled as shipbuilders and silversmiths. They discovered the art of making glass from sand found on the coast, and they extracted a rich purple dye, known as "Tyrian purple," from a peculiar kind of snail, that was in great demand. The Phœnician women also were skilled in embroidery.[2]

The Phœnicians were a seafaring and commercial people. They visited countries that in ancient times were considered remote, as Spain, England, Arabia, and India, bringing back the products of these lands. Restricted within narrow limits at home, some of their people went abroad and formed new settlements. Carthage in Northern Africa, the great rival of Rome, was a Phœnician colony.

The Phœnicians were near neighbors of the Israelites. The two peoples were generally on friendly terms and they carried on considerable trade with each other. King Solomon when building the temple obtained timber and skilled workmen from Phœnicia, giving wheat and oil in exchange.[3] He is said also to have ceded twenty cities of Galilee to Hiram, King of Tyre.[4] Ahab, King of Israel, married a Phœnician princess.

The language of the Phœnicians was a dialect of Hebrew. The

---

[1] Acts 11 : 19 ; 15 : 3 ; 21 : 2.
[2] Homer, "Iliad," XXIII, 743, 744 ; "Odyssey," IV, 614–618 ; "Iliad," VI, 289–295.
[3] 2 Chron. 2 : 16 ; 1 Kings 5 : 9.   [4] 1 Kings 9 : 11–13.

alphabetic system of written language is said to have been invented by them, and to have been adopted afterwards by other peoples.

The Phœnicians worshiped Baal and Ashtoreth as their principal deities. The name Baal, which signifies owner or proprietor, seems to have been a common name of deity, applied to various gods in different lands, sometimes even to the true God, Jehovah.[1] A distinguishing epithet was often appended to the word to indicate more exactly the personality or the function of the god, as Baalzebub, the fly-god of the Philistines; Baal-peor, "the god of the opening," worshiped by the Moabites. The plural of the word is Baalim. Ashtoreth or Astarte, the goddess of love, often represented by a sacred tree, was worshiped in sacred groves. Sexual impurity of the grossest kind formed part of the worship. Ashtoreth was one of the false gods adopted by Solomon,[2] and the worship of Baal was introduced into the kingdom of Israel by Jezebel, the wife of Ahab.

Phœnicia was not a single state under one government, but a confederacy of cities, of which Tyre and Sidon were the most important. The other principal cities were Arvad, Gebal, Tripolis, Berytus, Zarephath, and Accho. In the early times Zidon was the leading city, but later it was surpassed by Tyre. When in the time of the Judges the Phœnician colony at Laish was destroyed by the Danites, it is stated that being far from Zidon it had no deliverer. Zidon is here spoken of as the proper source of help, though Tyre was considerably nearer.[3]

**Tyre**, about eighty-five miles north of Joppa and about thirty miles from Nazareth, stood originally on the mainland. It was strongly fortified and resisted the siege of Nebuchadnezzar for thirteen years. At a later period the city was built on a small island about half a mile from the shore. On the land side it was protected by a wall 150 feet high. This new city was taken by Alexander the Great, after a siege of seven months.

Hiram, King of Tyre, was closely connected in business affairs, both with David and Solomon. He and Solomon were allied in some maritime adventures on the Red Sea.[4] At a later time the Tyrians brought on themselves severe denunciations for selling Hebrew captives into slavery.[5]

**Zidon** or **Sidon**, about twenty miles north of Tyre, is spoken of in the time of Joshua as "great Zidon."[6] While under Persian rule the Zidonians rebelled, but suffering disastrous defeat, they sent a delegation of five hundred of their leading men to ask clemency of the Persian king. All were put to death. Rather than fall into the hands of the cruel monarch, the citizens set fire to their houses, and with their families perished in the flames.

---

[1] Hosea 2 : 16.    [2] 1 Kings 11 : 5.    [3] Judg. 18 : 28.
[4] 1 Kings 9 : 11–13.    [5] Joel 3 : 4–8; Amos 1 : 9.    [6] Josh. 11 : 8; 19: 28.

**Arvad** (Aradus), on a small island two miles from the mainland, was farthest north of the Phœnician cities.[1]

**Tripolis** was the Greek name of a Phœnician city of which the native name is not certainly known, though some writers suppose it to have been Kadytis. It was the meeting place of the representatives of the different states of the confederacy. Each of the three cities, Tyre, Zidon, and Arvad, had within the city its special quarter inclosed by a fortified wall. The modern city is called Tarablous.

**Gebal** (Byblus) was devoted to the worship of Adonis. The Gebalites were skilled shipbuilders.[2]

**Zarephath**, the Sarepta of the New Testament, was the home of the widow that entertained Elijah.[3]

**Beirut**, the modern Berytus, is a city of later origin.

**Accho** (also **Acco** and **Acca**), the Ptolemais of the New Testament, and Acre of the present day, was assigned to the tribe of Asher,[4] but its native inhabitants were never dispossessed. It was visited by Paul when on his way to Jerusalem.[5]

[1] Gen. 10: 18; Ezek. 27: 8.  [2] Ezek. 27: 9.  [3] 1 Kings 17: 9.
[4] Judg. 1: 31.  [5] Acts 21: 7.

## CHAPTER XV

### EGYPT

THE common Bible name of Egypt is Mizraim, a dual form of Mazor. This form of the name, which means "The Two Egypts," is supposed to designate the two natural divisions of the country, Upper and Lower Egypt. Other names used in the Bible are the Land of Ham,[1] Rahab,[2] and Pathros.[3] The ancient Egyptian name was Kam-t (black), taken probably from the color of the alluvial soil.

Situated in the northeast of Africa, Egypt consists of two natural divisions, Upper Egypt comprising the narrow winding valley of the Nile above the delta from two to twelve miles in breadth, and Lower Egypt, comprising the broad level plain along the Mediterranean, known as the Delta.

These two divisions include about 11,342 square miles; the arable lands occupy only about two thirds of that area. On each side of the country is barren desert covered with drifting sand. The narrow fertile valley of the Nile in Upper Egypt is bordered by rocky cliffs.

**The Nile**, flowing through the whole length of the country without a single tributary, is the only river. On entering Lower Egypt the river divides into two principal streams, which in their onward course subdivide and finally flow into the Mediterranean Sea.

The Nile has its origin in the great lakes of Central Africa. Owing to heavy tropical rains near its sources, in the rainy season it is greatly swollen, and for several months of the year inundates the low-lying delta. In Lower Egypt the overflow begins toward the end of June, and for three months the waters continue to rise, attaining in some parts of the country a height of twenty-five feet or more above the ordinary level of the river. At this season the country resembles an inland sea. Near the mouth of the river the rise is very much less. Toward the end of November the land has become sufficiently dry for sowing the grain. The harvest time is in March.

Egypt is a very fertile country, and from the earliest times it has been famous for the production of grain. The ancients spoke of it as "the granary of the world." Large quantities of wheat were taken from Egypt to Rome. The vessel in which Paul sailed for Rome was laden with Egyptian wheat.[4]

[1] Ps. 78:51; 105:23, 27.
[3] Isa. 11:11; Jer. 44:1, 15.
[2] Ps. 87:4; Isa. 51:9.
[4] Acts 27:6, 38.

Rain sometimes falls in Lower Egypt near the Mediterranean, but agriculture is wholly dependent on irrigation. The great productiveness of the country is due entirely to this artificial watering from the river and canals which lead out from it, and to the rich black deposit that remains after the annual inundation has subsided.

Besides grain of different kinds, Egypt yields flax, cotton, melons, onions, and various tropical fruits, including dates, oranges, and lemons. The papyrus, a sort of reed, once abundant and used as a writing material, is now scarce.

The Nile, besides watering the country and giving a highway for travel, abounds in fish.

**Goshen,** the land assigned by Pharaoh to the Israelites, was a fertile district on the east of the delta between it and the Red Sea. Through neglect it is now a barren plain covered with sand that has drifted in from the desert. In ancient times a canal ran across the district from the Nile to the Red Sea. A strip of coast country here is gradually subsiding, allowing the Mediterranean to encroach upon the land. On the other hand, at the head of the Gulf of Suez a district has risen, so that a territory once covered by the sea is now dry land.

**Cities.**—The two most important cities of ancient Egypt were Memphis and Heliopolis or On, situated near each other, near the head or apex of the delta. Among the other cities were Ipsambul, Thebes, Zoan, Pithom, Rameses, Tahpanhes, Migdol, and Pelusium. Alexandria, though of much later origin, may yet be called an old city.

**Cairo,** the present capital of Egypt and the largest city in Africa, is situated near the head of the delta about a mile east of the Nile. The city was founded in A. D. 970. It is noted for several splendid mosques and a Mohammedan university. In the neighborhood are the famous pyramids of Egypt and the sites of the ancient cities Memphis and Heliopolis.

**Memphis,** the ancient capital, was situated on the western bank of the Nile ten miles south of Cairo. It is said to have been built by Menes, the founder of the first dynasty of Egyptian kings. The city was abandoned and fell into ruins during the early occupation of the country by the Mohammedans. Near Memphis was the Serapeum where the sacred bulls were buried.

**Heliopolis** or **On** was situated about four miles east of the apex of the delta. It was noted as a seat of Egyptian learning and of the worship of the sun-god Ra. Among the remains of the ancient city are massive walls and a granite obelisk.

**Thebes,** situated on the Nile on the site now occupied by the village of Luxor, succeeded Memphis as the capital of Egypt. Among its noted remains are the magnificent ruins of the Temple of Luxor. This temple was 1,200 feet in length and was many centuries in building. Another great structure was the Palace of Karnak with its famous Hall of Columns. Some of the pillars of this hall, still standing, are over seventy feet high and have capitals sixty-five feet in circumference. Here also are the gigantic "Statues of Memnon," so called. They are two colossal sitting figures of Amenhotep III, who lived about 1,500 B. C. The figures were hewn from a single block of granite; they are forty-seven feet high and rest on a pedestal ten feet in height. The tombs of the kings in the cliffs west of Thebes are of great interest. They consist of vast chambers cut out of the solid rock and contain elaborately-sculptured pillars, and rock-cut tombs of the ancient kings.

**Der-el-Bahari,** on the west bank of the Nile near Thebes, is noted for the remains of a great temple built about 1,000 B. C. The sculptures on its walls represent military triumphs. In an inner chamber the French explorer Maspero, in 1881, discovered several mummies of the Pharaohs, including Set I and Rameses II, which for some reason had long before been removed from the tombs of the kings. These mummies are now in the museum in Cairo.

**Ipsambul** or **Abu-Simbel,** the ancient Abuncis, situated in Nubia above the first cataract, is famous for its two rock-hewn temples, built on the face of a cliff by Rameses II. The temple extends into the rock about 200 feet and the walls of its chambers are decorated with sculptures representing the military exploits of the king. In the front of the larger temple are four colossal figures, about sixty-six feet high, representing Rameses II.

**Zoan** or **Tanis,** in the northeast of the delta, was a very ancient city and the capital of the Hyksos kings.[1] It is supposed that Joseph resided in this city. In the ruins of Zoan there have been discovered fragments of the largest colossus ever known, representing Rameses II. From the parts found the height of the colossus is estimated to have been ninety-two feet, or including the pedestal, 125 feet. The statue was broken up by one of the later kings, and parts of it were used in the construction of a gateway.

**Pithom,** one of the store-cities built by the Israelites, is supposed to have been near Zoan.

**Pelusium** was the frontier fortress near the isthmus. It was here that Cambyses defeated the Egyptian king and brought Egypt under Persian rule.

**Tahpanhes,** situated near the northeastern border of Egypt, was a city of some importance at the time of the overthrow of the Kingdom of Judah by Nebuchadnezzar. The prophet Jeremiah came hither with a company of his fellow-countrymen under the lead of Johanan.[2]

[1] Num. 13: 22.   [2] Jer. 43: 7–13; 44: 1.

**Migdol** was on the route of the Israelites at the time of the exodus.

**Alexandria**, founded by Alexander the Great, 332 B. C., on the Mediterranean at the northwest of the delta, was the capital of Egypt during the rule of the Ptolemies. It became famous during this period as a seat of Greek learning and also for its great library. Many Jews settled here during this period and the Greek version of the Old Testament known as the Septuagint was made in this city. Alexandria grew rapidly and became next to Rome the largest city in the Roman Empire.

**The Pyramids.**—The most remarkable pyramids are those of Ghizeh near Cairo. They are vast stone structures erected as tombs of kings during the period of the fourth dynasty, the date being variously estimated from 2450 to 4235 B. C. One of these pyramids, known as the Great Pyramid, is the largest work ever made by man, and of the so-called "Seven Wonders of the World" it alone remains. Its base is nearly square, each side measuring 756 feet, and the original height was 481 feet. It covers an area of thirteen acres, and it is said to have employed 100,000 men twenty years in its construction. The stones, some of which are thirty feet long and five feet thick, are joined by cement harder than the stones themselves. The sepulchral chamber is made of polished granite which was brought down the Nile from quarries 500 miles distant. The entrance to the chamber was most carefully concealed.

The great **Sphinx** stands near the Great Pyramid. It is ninety feet long and seventy feet high, having the body of a lion and a human head, cut out of solid rock, except the forelegs, which are of masonry.

**People.**—The ancient Egyptians belonged to the Hamitic race. They were intelligent and progressive, far in advance of most people of their time. While kind and hospitable to strangers, they thought themselves superior to other people. They treated their women with great respect. Agriculture was regarded by them as an honorable pursuit, but shepherd life was held in contempt.

The Egyptians were skilled in geometry, arithmetic, astronomy, chemistry, sculpture, architecture, and in the making of glass, pottery, fine linen, and embroidery, and in the art of embalming. The vast stones which they handled indicate wonderful command of mechanical power.

Embalming as practiced by them was an expensive process, beyond the means of any but the wealthy class. Funeral ceremonies were conducted with much pomp and accompanied by great lamentation. The period of mourning lasted seventy-two days.[1]

The ceremonies connected with the burial of Jacob were according to Egyptian custom.[2] It is remarkable that the *cortège* which accompanied the remains of Jacob to Hebron, instead of taking the direct road to Hebron, made a circuitous route round the south end of the Dead Sea

[1] Gen. 50: 3.  [2] Gen. 50: 2.

and thence northerly through the land of Moab, crossing the Jordan where the Israelties under Joshua entered the Promised Land.[1]

The early written language of the Egyptians was a sort of picture-writing combined with certain characters or symbols, something like a rebus. The Greeks, who could not read this language, called it hieroglyphics or "sacred sculpture." The walls of the temples, the stone monuments, and the tombs were covered with hieroglyphic inscriptions. In course of time the language fell into disuse, and the art of reading it was lost.

This picture-writing perplexed the linguists of modern times, until they found a key to its meaning in the famous Rosetta Stone, discovered by French soldiers while making excavations near the Rosetta mouth of the Nile. This stone, now in the British Museum, is of black basalt and contains three inscriptions having the same meaning—one in hieroglyphics, one in demotic characters, and a third in Greek. By the comparison of the different writings a clew to the hieroglyphic language was obtained.

The **Telel-Amarna Tablets** were also an interesting "find" among ancient records. These tablets of clay, like those found in Babylonia, and inscribed in the same characters, were discovered in 1887, 8 in the ruins of an ancient royal palace at Telel-Amarna in Middle Egypt. On being translated they proved to be letters on public affairs, which were sent to the king of Egypt by the kings of Babylonia and other states of Western Asia.

The ancient Egyptians were a very religious people. They had splendid temples, the walls of which were covered with sculptures, paintings, and hieroglyphics. The priests were skilled in the learning of their day, and they practiced many mysterious rites. Of their hundreds of gods, Ra, the sun-god, stood highest. He was often represented as a hawk-headed man. Osiris with his wife Isis and his son Horus formed a triad of high rank. Set, the author of all evil, was the Egyptian Satan between whom and Osiris was waged eternal warfare. The Egyptians did not worship images. Various animals, however, as bulls, dogs, cats, crocodiles, snakes, and insects, especially the *scarabæus*, were regarded with great reverence as representatives of the gods, and to kill one of them was a fearful sin. The soul of Osiris was believed to dwell in some bull to be recognized by certain colored spots on the animal. When the sacred bull died, his body was with much ceremony embalmed and placed in his tomb, and search was made for his successor in which the god had taken up his abode.

The Egyptians believed in the immortality of the soul and in its reunion with the body. This may explain their practice of embalming the dead. They also believed in a day of judgment when every one should be rewarded according to his deeds. Osiris was the guardian of the dead, and

[1] Gen. 50: 10, 11.

he, with forty-two other gods associated with him as judges, would at the day of judgment determine the final award.

**The Book of the Dead** was a most remarkable feature of the Egyptian religion. This curious document, a copy of which was deposited with the mummy in the tomb, contains a funeral ritual, comprising a series of prayers to be offered during the embalming process. It gives an account of the experiences of the disembodied soul from the time it enters the spirit-world—all its travels and perils until it falls in with and is reunited to the body; how it is then ferried across the river, enters the Elysian Fields, and stands before Osiris and the solemn conclave of Judges. Here the candidate gives an account of his life, his good and bad deeds. If he can declare that he has not stolen, has been cruel to no one, has not been idle, unjust, or envious, has not spoken ill of the king or of his father; if he can say that he has given the gods their due, has fed the hungry, given drink to the thirsty, and clothes to the naked, he is admitted to the realms of eternal bliss.

**Historic Sketch.**—The sources of ancient Egyptian history are mainly the writings of Herodotus and of Manetho, an Egyptian priest who lived about 250 B. C., the Bible, and the records of the monuments. The early chronology of events is very uncertain and varies greatly with different authorities. According to some writers authentic history goes back to about 5000 B. C.; others, more moderate, prefer to deduct about 2000 years from this estimate. The difference is due to the way in which Manetho's statements respecting the dynasties are understood. This writer classifies the kings under thirty-one dynasties, and gives the length of the period of each, but there is uncertainty as to whether these dynasties were in all cases successive over one united kingdom, or in some instances are to be understood as contemporary over different states in Upper and Lower Egypt. The records of the monuments favor the former view.

Menes, the first historic king, founded Memphis as his capital, and protected it by great dikes from inundations of the Nile. The kings of the fourth dynasty were famous builders. Cheops of this dynasty built the Great Pyramid of Ghizeh.

After a long period, of which the records give but scanty information, Egypt emerges from its obscurity with the twelfth dynasty upon the throne (2300 B. C.). Memphis has now given place to Thebes as the capital. The era of the "Theban kings," as this period was called, was most illustrious, and Egyptian civilization then reached its highest point. Following this brilliant period is that known as the rule of the Hyksos or Shepherd Kings. Nomadic tribes from Arabia or Syria invaded the country and established their rule over the native Egyptians. They were a barbarous people and did much damage to the monuments of the country's early civilization. Gradually, however, influenced by the people whom they had conquered, they adopted their manners and became more civilized. It was probably during the period of the Shepherd Kings that Joseph was elevated to power at the Egyptian Court, and his father removed to Egypt.

The expulsion of the Hyksos, which took place about 1525 B. C., was followed by what is known as the New Empire under the eighteenth dynasty. Architecture and learning again flourished, and there was introduced a policy of warfare with Syria and Assyria. Thothmes III, one of the greatest kings of this dynasty, extended his conquests to the Euphrates. By him was built a large part of the great Temple of Karnak at Thebes, and those obelisks were erected which in modern times have been transported to distant cities—Constantinople, Rome, London, and New York.

The rule of the nineteenth dynasty extends over a very brilliant period, in which Set I and Rameses II stood preëminent. They carried on war against the Hittites on the north of Palestine and captured their capital Carchemish. Records of the exploits of these kings are found on the rocky cliffs in Asia Minor. The Hall of Columns in the Temple of Karnak was built by Set I. This king also made for himself the finest of the rock sepulchers. Rameses II, in carrying on his building operations, demolished the works of his predecessors and used the materials for his own structures. His reign, extending over a period of sixty-eight years, was one of the longest in the history of the world. It is supposed that Set I was the king "who knew not Joseph,"[1] the Pharaoh of the Oppression, and that Rameses II was the king in whose court Moses was brought up, and that his son Manephta was the Pharoah of the Exodus. The mummies of Set I and Rameses II were discovered in 1886 and are now in the museum of Bulak in Cairo.

For several hundred years after the Exodus the Israelites had little intercourse with Egypt. King Solomon carried on trade with Egypt and married an Egyptian princess, receiving as dowry the city of Gezer.[2] Peaceful relations between the two countries were of short duration. During the reign of Rehoboam, Shishak of Egypt invaded Judah and plundered the new temple that Solomon built in Jerusalem.

During the closing centuries of Egypt's national life her kings were often involved in unequal contest with Assyria and Babylonia, and the country was thus at different times reduced to the position of a tributary state. The later kings of Judah, when assailed by these eastern powers, sought aid from Egypt, an alliance which was severely denounced by the prophets Isaiah, Ezekiel, Hosea, and Jeremiah. Finally, in 525 B. C., Egypt was conquered by Cambyses, the king of Persia, and ceased to be ruled by native kings.

[1] Acts 7: 18.      [2] 1 Kings 9: 16.

## CHAPTER XVI

### THE WILDERNESS OF THE WANDERING

The triangular region south of the Negeb, having Egypt and the Gulf of Suez on the west and the Arabah and the Gulf of Akabah on the east, comprises the land in which the Israelites journeyed for forty years after they left Egypt. At the north an east-and-west line from the borders of Egypt to the Dead Sea measures about 200 miles, and a north-and-south line between the Mediterranean and Ras Mohammed, the southern headland of the Sinaitic peninsula, 225 miles. The territory thus limited has an area of about 23,000 square miles.

This whole region is a desert table-land of varying elevation, rising toward the south into mountain masses over 8,000 feet above the sea level. The northwestern portion of this territory, adjoining the Mediterranean Sea, is the Wilderness of Shur, south of this is the Wilderness of Paran, of which the modern name is et Tih ("the wandering"), and the southern portion is the wilderness of Sinai.

The Gulf of Suez is shallow toward its northern end, and it once extended farther up toward the Mediterranean than it does at the present day. It is supposed that the Israelites crossed this water near Suez where it is less than a mile in breadth. The Gulf of Suez, little traversed in ancient times, now connected by the Suez Canal with the Mediterranean Sea, is the great thoroughfare between Western Europe and India, China, Japan, and Australia.

A low coast land fringes this gulf—very narrow on the south, but broadening out somewhat toward the north. Its northern portion is the Wilderness of Etham, the southern portion is the Wilderness of Sin. It was along this coast land that the Israelites journeyed, when, after leaving Egypt, they entered the wilderness. Here was Marah with its bitter waters, and five or six miles farther south was Elim with its twelve springs of sweet water and its threescore and ten palm trees.

The Gulf of Akabah, now of little account in the world's commerce, was in the times of Solomon and Jehoshaphat the gateway of Israel's foreign trade. The highlands on this coast approach very near and descend precipitously to the water.

**Elath** or **Eloth** ("The Palms"), a city of the Edomites, stood at the head of the Gulf of Akabah on the site now occupied by the village of **Akabah.**

**Ezion-geber,** where the Israelites encamped before they came to

Kadesh, and where Solomon afterwards had his naval station, was near the head of the gulf.

The mountains of the Wilderness of Sinai, impressive in their grandeur and in their silence, are wild, bare, and desolate. "They are the Alps of Arabia—but the Alps planted in the desert, and therefore stripped of all the clothing which goes to make up our variegated drapery of oak, and birch, and pine, and fir; of moss, and grass, and fern which to landscapes of European hills are almost as essential as the rocks and peaks themselves."

This mountain region contains valuable minerals. Hundreds of years before the time of Moses the Egyptians came here for copper.

The chief of these mountain peaks are in three clusters, represented by Mount Serbâl in the northwest of the Wilderness of Sinai, near the coast plains; Mount St. Catherine twenty miles or more from Serbal on the southeast; and Um Shomer, the highest of all, still farther south.

**Mount Serbal** (6,712 feet), rising abruptly from the maritime plain on the west and from the oasis of Feiran on the north, culminating in its five peaks, is accounted the grandest, though not the highest, mountain of the peninsula. Some learned men have held that this is the mountain from which the law was given to Moses.

The **Sinai Group**, comprising Jebel Mûsa (Mount of Moses), and Jebel Katherîn (Mount St. Catherine), are beautifully-colored masses of granite, gneiss, and porphyry, rugged and bare and awful in their silent grandeur. The names Sinai and Horeb in Bible usage seem to be interchangeable terms, or the one is a general name for the whole group and the other specific for a single peak.

**Jebel Musa** (7,363 feet) is the traditional "Mount of the Law," and the one accepted by the best authorities as the Sinai or Horeb of the Bible. The northern peak of this mountain, called Râs es-Sufsâfeh, "head of the Willow," taking its name from a tree growing in one of the ravines, is supposed to be the place where the law of Moses was given. On the north side of this mountain and approaching close under its precipitous cliffs 1,500 feet high, is the great plain er-Râhah, over a mile long and nearly half a mile wide, where "Israel camped before the mount."

**Mount St. Catherine** (8,540 feet) stands near Jebel Mûsa, on the southwest. Some writers indeed speak of the two as one mountain with two main peaks. At the foot of the mountain, in a ravine, is the monastery of St. Catherine founded in 527 by the Emperor Justinian. It was in this monastery that Tischendorf, in 1844, discovered the Sinaitic Codex, a Greek manuscript of the Old and New Testaments, made in the fourth century. The number of monks here at one time was between three and four hundred, but at the present day it does not exceed thirty.

Mount St. Catherine is said to have taken its name from Catherine, the

Christian martyr of Alexandria, who was first tortured on the "Catherine Wheel" and then put to death. According to legend her body was transported to this mountain and buried here by angels.

This whole wilderness is a dry and desert land. The highlands are broken by wadies, through which for a few weeks in the year during the rainy season, flow rushing streams, but they are, for the most part, at other times dry, barren, and desolate. Yet there are "occasional spots of verdure" where may be found herbage, acacias, palms, and even cultivated gardens with rich tropical fruits. These spots of "living green" have their origin in some scanty spring which has its hidden seat under a mountain cliff, from which a little rill descends with life-giving influence to the lower valleys.

Here and there is an oasis in a basin-shaped hollow into which converging waters from the surrounding heights find their way. Such a spot is Wady Feiran at the northern base of Mount Serbâl. This spot, supposed to be the Rephidim of Exodus, the scene of the famous battle between Israel and Amalek, is the most fertile place in all the wilderness. Its fruitfulness may account for the keenness of the struggle of the opposing armies for its possession.

There is evidence that this land had a richer vegetation and a larger population in ancient times than it now has. The Amalekites, who inhabited the wilderness when the Israelites passed through it, seem to have been a numerous and powerful people. At the present time the population consists of about six thousand Bedouins.

**Kadesh-barnea.**—The Israelites remained about a year in the neighborhood of Mount Sinai. They then marched northeasterly to Kadesh-barnea. Their course lay along the western side of the highlands that skirt the shores of the Gulf of Akabah and the Arabah, through a limestone desert. The incidents of the journey are recorded in the book of Numbers.

The location of Kadesh-barnea has been difficult to determine. The most probable place is that identified by Dr. H. Clay Trumbull—an oasis about ninety miles south of Hebron. This is described as a place of great beauty and richness, with abundance of water, and shrubs, flowers, and fruit in profusion. It was here that the Israelites remained while the twelve spies explored the Promised Land.

## CHAPTER XVII
### EDOM

EDOM or Mount Seir, in the New Testament called Idumæa, is a mountainous country on the east of the Arabah. It is separated from the Land of Moab on the north by the brook Zered. Ancient Edom was about one hundred miles long and twenty miles in breadth. The mountains, composed of limestone, igneous rocks and red sandstone, are deeply cleft by narrow winding valleys and glens, from which in places the steep cliffs of gorgeously-colored rocks almost exclude the light of day.

**Mount Hor** ("the mountain") is situated on the northwestern border of Edom on the east of the Arabah.[1] It rises in two peaks of bare rock 4,800 feet above the level of the Mediterranean, and 4,000 feet above the Arabah. On the summit of one of these peaks is a Mohammedan chapel built over the traditional site of Aaron's tomb. The mountain derives its chief interest from its being the place where Israel's first high priest died and was buried, and from the wide prospect on all sides which its summit commands. Close beneath it on the west but hidden from view by the rocks is Petra. A rival peak, also called Mount Hor, is situated about thirty miles northeast of this mountain.

**The Arabah** has its greatest elevation, about 500 feet above the sea level, at a point nearly opposite Mount Hor. From this point it slopes southerly to the Gulf of Akabah and northerly to the Dead Sea.

The valleys and terraced hillsides of Edom were very fertile, yielding grain, fruits, and rich pasturage. Thus was fulfilled Jacob's blessing to Esau,—"Behold, thy dwelling shall be the fatness of the earth, and of the dew of heaven from above."[2]

The Edomites were accustomed to hew out dwellings for themselves in the soft sandstone of the cliffs.

**Bozrah**, represented by the modern village Buseireh, about ten miles south of the Dead Sea, was the ancient capital of Edom.

**Ezion-geber** and **Elath** were ports at the head of the Gulf of Akabah, used by Solomon as the headquarters of his fleet.[3]

**Petra** or **Selah**,[4] situated in a mountain glen and accessible only through a narrow defile, is about twenty miles south of the Dead Sea. It is famous for its architectural remains cut out of the solid rock and for the beautiful colored cliffs overhanging the glen. Among these remains are its

[1] Num. 20:23; 33:37.　　[2] Gen. 27:39.
[3] 1 Kings 9:26.　　[4] 2 Kings 14:7.

rock-hewn Roman temple, its theater, capable of seating 3,000 spectators, and its tombs. The history of the place goes back to the time of Abraham. Chedorlaomer with his allies swept over the region of Mount Seir, then inhabited by a people named Horites ("mountaineers").[1]

**Historic Sketch.**—The Edomites throughout their history kept up the traditional hostility of their ancestor against the descendants of Jacob. They refused to allow the Israelites, when journeying through the wilderness, to pass through their territory.[2] They were conquered by David, held in subjection by Solomon, and for the most part were subject to Judah while that kingdom existed.[3] At the time of Judah's captivity, they joined the Chaldees and thus brought on themselves severe denunciations of the prophets.[4] During the period of Judah's captivity they dispossessed the Amalekites, who inhabited the territory south of the Negeb, and seized several places in the south of Judæa. A people known as Nabathæans, descended from Ishmael,[5] then took possession of Edom, forming here a strong kingdom afterwards known as Arabia Petræa. Aretas, king of this country, was father-in-law of Herod Antipas.[6]

[1] Gen. 14:6.
[2] Num. 20:14–21; Judg. 11:17, 18.
[3] 2 Sam. 8:14; 2 Kings 8:20; 14:7; 2 Chron. 25:11, 12; 28:17.
[4] Ps. 137:7; Ezek. 25:12–14.
[5] Gen. 25:13; 1 Chron. 1:29; Gen. 36:3.
[6] Matt. 14:3, 4; Acts 4:27.

## CHAPTER XVIII

### ASIA MINOR

The great peninsula on the west of Asia known as Asia Minor nearly corresponds with the portion of the Turkish Empire called Anatolia. On the east it lies open to the continent of Asia; on all other sides it is bounded by the sea: on the north, the Black Sea or the Euxine, known to the Romans as Pontus Euxinus; on the west the Straits of Constantinople or the Bosphorus, the Sea of Marmora, anciently called the Propontis, the Dardanelles or the Hellespont, and the Ægean Sea; on the south the Mediterranean Sea, called by the Romans Mare Internum and by the Hebrews the Great Sea. The territory thus bounded has an area of about 150,000 square miles.

**Physical Features.**—For the most part Asia Minor is an elevated plateau between two and three thousand feet high on the western side, and on the eastern side rising to nearly twice that height. The highlands in many cases rise abruptly from the sea. On the north the principal coast plains are the river deltas. On the west are many projecting headlands and inlets of the sea; and near the coast are many small islands. Here the plateau is broken by several river valleys, of which the valley of the Hermus and that of the Meander extend farthest inland. The southern coast is fringed throughout its greater length by a narrow strip of lowland.

**The Taurus Mountains** border the plateau on the south. At their western end these mountains lie very near the sea; farther east they recede, leaving a wider coast plain. This range, which has an extreme elevation of about two miles above the sea level, is rough and rugged, and is furrowed by deep gorges, the pathway of rapid winter torrents.

**The Anti-Taurus Mountains,** in the east of the peninsula, are parallel with the Taurus and farther inland.

**The Amanus Mountains,** lying along the borders of Cilicia and Syria, are outliers of the Taurus range.

A pass through the Taurus Mountains, known as the "Cilician Gates," has from remote ages been a common route of travel between Cilicia and the interior. A pass through the Amanus, called the "Syrian Gates," connects Cilicia and Syria.

The principal **rivers** are the Kizil Irmak (the ancient Halys) and the Sakaria (Sangarius), flowing into the Black Sea; the Sarabat (Hermus), the Cayster, and the Meander, flowing into the Ægean Sea.

Numerous **lakes,** some of which are salt and have no outlet, are scattered over the interior.

**Climate.**—On the highlands the summers are hot and dry, the winters are cold with heavy fall of snow and rain. The low coast lands along the Mediterranean are hot, damp, and at certain seasons malarious.

**Products.**—A large part of the plateau is better suited to grazing than to tillage, and in some districts the Angora goat is one of the most profitable domestic animals. Among the cultivated products are wheat, maize, the vine, olives, figs, opium and licorice. The figs of commerce come chiefly from Asia Minor.

**Historic Sketch.**—Asia Minor is famous both in history and in legend, and so commingled and overlapping are the realms of fact and fiction that it is often difficult to determine where the one ends and the other begins.

One of the myths of this many-storied land tells how once upon a time Jupiter and Mercury were entertained by the pious Philemon and his wife, Baucis, in the very region where afterwards Paul and Barnabas were mistaken for the same divinities. Another tells how Marsyas was flayed alive by the angry god Apollo because the daring youth had beaten him in a musical contest, flute against lyre.

Ancient Troy, city of the faithless Laomedon, scene of the exploits of Hercules, and fated kingdom of Priam, had its seat in the northwest, on the Ægean Sea. In this region also was Lydia, the realm of Crœsus, whose fabulous riches continue even to this age of multi-millionaires to be the ideal standard of wealth.

Asia Minor has been called the bridge between Asia and Europe. Over its highlands were great roads between the east and the west, by which traveled merchant caravans and vast armies. By this way came Darius and Xerxes for the conquest of Greece. By the same route Alexander the Great marched when he set out on his more successful expedition for the conquest of the eastern world. But the greatest of all the victors that crossed this bridge was Paul the missionary, who came from the east and planted the standard of the cross on the shores of Europe.

At the dawn of history Asia Minor was the seat of many petty kingdoms, the bounds of which were frequently changing, according to the fortunes of war.

The territory of the ancient Hittites extended from the Euphrates on the east into Asia Minor. The modern village of Boghaz-keui, identified as ancient Pteria, has interesting remains of an old Hittite city. On the walls of the rock-hewn chambers of a ruined palace found here are curious Hittite sculptures.

At an early date many Greek colonies were established along the coast of the Ægean Sea, forming an Asiatic Greece. Among these were twelve cities founded by Ionian Greeks, from whom the district took the name Ionia. Prominent among these cities were Smyrna, Ephesus, and Miletus. The coast north of Ionia, including also the island of Lesbos, was settled by Æolians. Again, on the south of Ionia, were Dorian colonies. One of their cities was Halicarnassus.

Perhaps the people of greatest prominence in the early history of Asia Minor were the Phrygians and the Lydians. Phrygia occupied the central portion of the plateau north of the Taurus Mountains. Its capital was Gordium, near the river Sangarius, noted as the place where Alexander the Great "cut the Gordian Knot." The Phrygians worshiped the goddess Cybele, called by the ancients "The great mother of the gods." Her priests were the Corybantes, and the festivals in her honor were celebrated with wild dances, accompanied by highly-exciting music peculiar to the Phrygians. One of the early kings of these people was Gordius who tied the legendary Gordian Knot. His son Midas, according to another myth, was endowed by one of the gods with the gift of turning to gold anything he touched.

Lydia was originally a small state bordering on the Ægean Sea. It afterwards extended its bounds, absorbing the neighboring territory including the Greek cities of the coast and Phrygia on the east. Sardis, near the river Hermus, was its capital. In culture the Lydians surpassed all the other states of Asia Minor. Like the Phrygians they had a peculiar music, and they were noted for their skill on the flute and the harp. The last king of Lydia was Crœsus, remarkable for his great wealth and also as a patron of learning. Among the distinguished men who visited his court were Solon, the Athenian lawgiver, and Æsop, the writer of fables. Legend informs us that Crœsus was told by the oracle of Delphi that if he made war against the Persians he would destroy a great empire. Deceived by this ambiguous response, he engaged in a war against Cyrus of Persia, resulting in his own utter defeat and the overthrow of the Lydian Empire.

With the conquest of Lydia by Cyrus the whole of Asia Minor fell to Persia (546 B. C.). It continued to form a part of the Persian Empire until that great empire was destroyed by Alexander the Great (331 B. C.). On the death of Alexander (323 B. C.) the southern portion of the peninsula became a part of the Syrian Empire under the Seleucidæ. There remained four independent kingdoms in Asia Minor,—Cappadocia, Bithynia, Pontus, and Pergamos, of which the last two were the more notable. Pontus extended along the Euxine from the river Halys to Colchis, the land of the fabulous golden fleece. Pergamos corresponded to the country known as Mysia on the Ægean Sea.

Some time during the third century before the Christian era, Gallic tribes from Europe settled in the northeast of Asia Minor, within the bounds of the country then known as Phrygia. This region took from them the name Galatia, which was afterwards extended in its application to include the large Roman province of that name.

Antiochus the Great of Syria crossed the Hellespont and attempted the conquest of Greece. Here he was met by a Roman army, driven back into Asia, pursued, defeated, and shorn of all his territory in Asia Minor. The Roman Republic, not desiring to occupy the territory thus acquired, annexed it to the realm of its ally Eumenes, King of Pergamos (190 B. C.). About half a century later, King Attalus, the son of Eumenes, bequeathed his whole kingdom to Rome.

Pontus still remained an independent kingdom. In obtaining it the Romans had a hard struggle. Its king, Mithridates VI, was a great warrior, and for a long time he set Rome at defiance. Finally, however, he was thoroughly conquered by the Roman General Pompey, and his kingdom was annexed to the Roman Empire (66 B. C.).

**The People.**—The people of Asia Minor were of a mixed character. Besides the various native races, who formed the majority in the rural districts, there were many Greeks or people of Greek origin. Some of these were descendants of the old Ionians and other Greek colonists on the western coasts, and many others had come into the country after its conquest by Alexander the Great. This Greek colonization led to the introduction of Greek civilization and the use of the Greek language. The Jews also were numerous. Coming chiefly from Egpyt, Syria, and the more remote Babylonia, they had settled here during the Greek and Roman periods. Under the Roman rule the Jews enjoyed much liberty and freedom in the exercise of their religious customs. Many Romans also, especially of the official class, had been brought into the country by the Roman conquest. The Greeks, Romans, and Jews, resided chiefly in the cities, where they formed a large part of the population.

**Religion.**—Except the Jews and their converts all the inhabitants of Asia Minor were idolaters. They had many gods, and their worship was thus so divided that a new god or a new form of worship was a matter of small moment to them. Hence these idolaters were very tolerant of religions different from their own, and they permitted the Jews to erect synagogues and practice their religious rites undisturbed. Opposition to the Christian religion sometimes originated with the Jews, because Gentiles were admitted to the church;[1] at another time it had its origin with the idolaters on account of its interference with some established custom of the place, or with some trade or line of business. An example of such opposition is seen in the case of the wild riot at Ephesus.[2]

[1] Acts 13: 45; 14: 2, 19; 17: 5, 13.   [2] Acts 19: 23-41; 16: 16-23.

**The Great Roads.**—In the early times when Asia Minor formed a part of the Persian Empire, and perhaps still earlier, a great road used in the service of the king, and hence called the "Royal Road," extended from Susa in Persia to Ephesus by way of the Cilician Gates. In its course through Asia Minor this road was circuitous and difficult. Running northerly from the Cilician Gates it crossed the river Halys by a great bridge and probably passed through Pteria, Ancyra, and other important cities in that region. Thence by way of Sardis it ran to Ephesus. A road of later origin followed a more direct and easy path, south of the desert and through the valleys of the Lycos and the Meander, by way of the cities Colossæ and Laodicea.

**The Provinces.**—The Romans divided Asia Minor into several provinces. These provinces underwent frequent reconstruction with change of bounds and sometimes with change of name. To avoid confusion, readers of the New Testament need to keep this in mind. Old names, still in vogue but without political significance, were often used by New Testament writers. For example, at the time of Paul's journeyings, Lycaonia, Pisidia, and the eastern part of Phrygia formed a portion of the province of Galatia; Mysia, Lydia, Caria, and the western part of Phrygia had been incorporated into the province of Asia. At this time the peninsula comprised the following provinces,—Bithynia and Pontus, Cappadocia, Galatia, Cilicia, Pamphylia, Lycia, and Asia.

**Bithynia-pontus** lay on the north along the Euxine Sea. Little reference is made to this region in the New Testament. Peter in his first epistle addresses Christians resident in Bithynia and Pontus. For some reason Paul was not permitted to enter Bithynia.

**Cappadocia** was situated in the east of Asia Minor and was separated from Cilicia by the Taurus Mountains. The region is a cold, elevated table-land. Some of its Jewish residents were hearers of Peter on the day of Pentecost, and the apostle in his first epistle recognizes Christians in that province.

**Galatia** included Galatia proper or North Galatia, which was settled by the Gauls three hundred years before the country was visited by Paul, and South Galatia, which comprised Lycaonia, Pisidia, and the eastern part of Phrygia. The principal cities of the province were Ancyra, Tavium, and Pessinus in North Galatia, and Antioch, Iconium, Lystra, and Derbe in South Galatia.

**Ancyra,** the capital of the province, is now known by the name Angora in a district celebrated for its breed of goats.

**Antioch,** the chief city in South Galatia, was a Roman colony and the governing center for this region. There were several cities of this name, and to distinguish them this one was called "Antioch in Pisidia," or more accurately Antioch toward Pisidia, as the city was in Phrygia. At the time of Paul's visit, there was a large Jewish colony here, and also many Jewish proselytes.[1]

**Iconium,** sixty miles from Antioch, was situated on the route of travel between Ephesus and Tarsus, Antioch in Syria, and the cities of the Euphrates. The plains in the neighborhood, watered by irrigation, were covered with beautiful gardens and orchards.

**Lystra** was a city of Lycaonia, fifteen miles southwest of Iconium. It was at Lystra that the citizens, supposing Paul and Barnabas to be gods in the likeness of men, were with difficulty restrained from showing them divine honor.

**Derbe,** also in Lycaonia, twenty miles southeast of Lystra, was near the Cilician Gates.[2]

The name Galatia is ambiguous, sometimes meaning the Roman province, as above described, and sometimes the country of the Gauls, comprising only the northern part of that province. This double meaning of the term has given rise to much controversy in regard to the location of the churches addressed by Paul in his epistle to the Galatians. Many writers maintain that the epistle was specially intended for the churches in Ancyra and other cities of North Galatia. They hold that Paul visited these cities on his second missionary journey and probably also on his third journey. The supporters of this view, called "the Northern Galatia Theory," see grounds for their opinion in certain references in the epistle, implying inconstancy and fickleness, which are considered to be characteristic of the Gauls. The other view, known as "the South Galatia Theory," maintains that the epistle was written to the churches in Antioch, Iconium, Lystra, and Derbe. Prof. W. M. Ramsay, one of the strongest advocates of this view, holds that not only is there no evidence that Paul ever visited the cities of North Galatia, but that such a visit would be inconsistent with the narrative of his second journey through Galatia, as given in The Acts.

**Cilicia** was chiefly a coast country lying south of the Taurus range. It was separated from Syria by the Amanus Mountains. The eastern part consists of fertile plains and was called Cilicia Campestris, the western part is rugged and bore the name Cilicia Tracheia. The eastern trade route from Ephesus ran through Cilicia, crossing from Cappadocia by the Gates of Cilicia, thirty miles north of Tarsus, and entering Syria by the Gates of Syria.

**Tarsus,** the capital, situated on the Cydnus, was an important city and had fame as an educational center. It was also distinguished as the birthplace of the apostle Paul.

**Pamphylia** lay along the low coast country bordered on the north by

---

[1] Acts 13: 14–52.    [2] Acts 14: 1–21.

rugged mountains. The climate of the region is hot, humid, and unhealthy.

**Perga,** situated seven or eight miles inland, near the River Cestus, was the capital. **Attalia** was the principal port.

It has seemed remarkable that Paul on his first missionary journey made no stay in Pamphylia. Prof. W. M. Ramsay explains his action by the supposition that he was here seized with malarial fever which caused him to hasten to the highlands of the interior.

**Lycia** is a mountainous country, the Taurus range running near the coast and ending in massive promontories separated by deep bays. The country has a remarkable historic record. Many specimens of its antiquities are now in the British Museum. Lycia and Pamphylia were at one time united in one province.

**Myra,** the capital, stood near a navigable river three miles from the sea.[1] It has interesting architectural remains which indicate the former greatness of the city.

**Patara,** on a bold coast near the mouth of the River Xanthus, was an important commercial city. Its people were devoted to the worship of Apollo.[2]

**Asia** was probably the largest of the provinces of Asia Minor, and in historic interest it surpassed all others. It comprised the countries known as Mysia, Lydia, and Caria, together with the western portion of Phrygia. In the northwest was The Troad which included ancient Troy, and in the southwest were the Ionian and other Greek colonies. Among the noted places in this province were Ephesus, Smyrna, Pergamos, Thyatira, Sardis, Philadelphia, and Laodicea, the cities of "the seven churches of Asia," addressed by John in the book of the Revelation.[3]

**Ephesus,** the capital of the province, was in a fertile district and stood partly on lowland and partly on the hills near the mouth of the Cayster. It had a fine harbor so that at the beginning of the Christian era it was the emporium of that part of the peninsula north of the Taurus. During the ages, however, its harbor became filled up with earth brought down by the river, and its great trade passed over to Smyrna. Besides the two great roads that led easterly there were coast roads, one leading northerly to Smyrna, the other southerly to Miletus. Ephesus was the center of the worship of Diana, a goddess similar to the Greek Artemis, who was worshiped under different names throughout Asia Minor. The manufacture of shrines of silver, marble, and terra cotta, used in the worship of this deity, was a lucrative business in Ephesus.[4] Its temple of Diana was a grand specimen of Ionic architecture and was one of the "seven wonders of the world." The length of the building was 425 feet, the breadth

---

[1] Acts 27 : 5.  [2] Acts 21 : 1, 2; Horace, "Odes," Book III, 4, 64.
[3] Rev., chs. 2, 3.  [4] Acts 19 : 24–27.

220 feet, and its columns, of which there were 137, were sixty feet high, and six feet in diameter. The temple and its precincts were held most sacred and furnished safe asylum even to criminals. It was also used as a bank for the safekeeping of treasures. This great structure like other portions of Ephesus, is now a mass of ruins. Paul made Ephesus one of his chief centers of missionary enterprise. Paul himself did not probably visit all the cities of the surrounding country where churches were established, but directed the work carried on by his various associates. The apostle John is said to have spent the closing years of his life in Ephesus.

**Smyrna,** in a fertile district, once famous for its wines, is on the Ægean Sea forty miles north of Ephesus, with which it is now connected by rail. It was the seat of a temple for the worship of the god Nemesis. Among its deities was Dionysus the god of wine, of whose worship drunken revelry formed a conspicuous part. Olympian games were celebrated in Smyrna with great enthusiasm, and the various ceremonies connected with the worship of the gods were practiced here with nicest regard to pagan ritual. It was at Smyrna that Ignatius, Bishop of Antioch, was thrown to wild beasts in the amphitheater, and in the same city the aged Bishop Polycarp, a disciple of the apostle John, suffered martyrdom by burning at the stake. The present Smyrna, a flourishing city with a population of 200,000, is about two miles from the site of the ancient city.

**Pergamos** or **Pergamum,** about fifty miles northeast of Smyrna, is said to have been at one time the most splendid city of Asia Minor. Its ruins are still of great interest. The city was famous for its sculptures and other works of art, and also for a large manuscript library, most of which was removed to Alexandria. One of the leading features of the city was the temple grove Nicephorium in which were temples devoted to different gods, the temple of Aphrodite being the most splendid. Esculapius was one of the prominent gods of the city. In Roman times Pergamos was a famous seat of worship in honor of the emperor. Refusal to join in this worship brought severe persecution on the early Christians. In the museums of Berlin are preserved rich specimens of Pergamene art, among which are remarkable friezes which adorned the great altar of Zeus, representing war scenes of the fabulous ages.

**Thyatira,** on the road between Pergamos and Sardis, was founded by colonists from Macedonia after the conquest of Asia Minor by Alexander. It stood in a rich agricultural and grazing country, and was a prosperous manufacturing city. The dyeing of woolen goods was one of the leading industries, and it is supposed that Lydia whom Paul met at Philippi may have been connected with one of the dyer's guilds in Thyatira.[1] Apollo was the chief god of the city. Among the supersti-

[1] Acts 16 : 14.

tions of the place were the incantations of the sibyl Sambatha whose fane stood outside the walls.

**Sardis**, near the River Hermus and thirty miles south of Thyatira, was the capital of the ancient empire of Crœsus. Surrounded by a fertile country, the city was a great commercial center and an *entrepot* of dyed woolen manufactures. The temple of Cybele in Sardis was a massive structure, richly adorned with architectural skill, ruins of which still exist. In New Testament times Sardis in common with several other cities of this region was destroyed by pestilential fever. In consideration of this calamity imperial taxes were remitted for five years.

**Philadelphia**, about eighty miles east of Smyrna, was situated in a volcanic region on the lower slopes of Mount Tmolus, famous for its wines. In common with the whole surrounding country it was subject to violent earthquakes.

The neighboring cities **Laodicea, Colossæ,** and **Hierapolis,** situated in the rich and beautiful valley of the Lycos, a tributary of the Meander, were trade centers on the southern route between Ephesus and the East. So wealthy was Laodicea that after it had been nearly ruined by one of the earthquakes which were frequent in this region it refused help offered by the Roman emperor. The apostle Paul does not appear to have visited this district. In passing from Galatia westerly on his third missionary tour he took the more northerly and elevated route to Ephesus. The churches at Laodicea and Colossæ were probably founded by some of Paul's coworkers during the apostle's sojourn at Ephesus. Colossæ was the home of Philemon, Onesimus, Archippus, and Epaphras.[1] One of Paul's epistles was addressed to the church at Colossæ; the one he refers to as having been sent by him to the church at Laodicea has been the subject of much speculation.[2] Hierapolis was famous for its cave sacred to Pluto and for its hot springs. It was the birthplace of the stoic philosopher Epictetus.

**Miletus** was one of the leading Ionian cities. It was situated on the south side of a small bay near the mouth of the Meander. The distance from Ephesus, round the head of the bay, was twenty-five or thirty miles. The messengers sent by Paul may have taken the shorter water route across the bay.[3] This bay or harbor is now filled up by deposits from the river, so that the site of Miletus is ten miles from the shore.

**Halicarnassus** was a Dorian city and was famous for the mausoleum or tomb of Mausolus, one of "the seven wonders of the world." Bodrun is the modern name of the place.

**Cnidus** was an ancient Greek city situated on a promontory that runs out between the islands Cos and Rhodes on the southwest coast.[4] Among other interesting remains found here, showing the magnificence of the city, are those of the great theater.

[1] Col. 4: 16.  [2] Col. 4: 9, 12, 17.  [3] Acts 20: 17.  [4] Acts 21: 1.

## CHAPTER XIX
### GREECE

ANCIENT Greece or Hellas was partly continental and partly insular. Continental Greece occupied the peninsula in the southeast of Europe.

Greece is a mountainous country, and many of its peaks are made famous by their connection with fable and legend. Mount Olympus in Thessaly, supposed by the Greeks to be the highest mountain in the world (9,700 feet), was the fabled home of the gods. Parnassus and Helicon in Bœotia were the favorite haunts of Apollo, the muses, and the nymphs. The Vale of Tempe, in Thessaly between Mounts Olympus and Ossa, was noted for the wild grandeur of its scenery.

Peninsular Greece is deeply indented with bays and arms of the sea, adapting it to seafaring life. This feature also, together with the ruggedness of the country, developed hardihood and a spirit of independence in the people.

The Greeks, or Hellenes, as they called themselves, were divided into different tribes, as Ionians, Dorians, Achæans, and Æolians. Though these people had different governments, they regarded themselves as belonging to the same family, and considered all other races as their inferiors. All spoke the same language, though in different dialects.

The Greeks were a very religious people. They worshiped many gods, and lest they might unwittingly incur the resentment of some deity of whom they had not heard, they erected altars to "the unknown god." These Greek gods were imaginary beings in the form of men, having all the various human passions, as love, hatred, jealousy, and revenge. They differed in rank, beginning with Zeus the supreme deity and descending through the various grades to the nymphs and naiads of the groves and the rivers. Each god had his particular sphere of influence: Poseidon, like the Roman Neptune, ruled the sea; Phœbus or Apollo was the god of light, of prophecy, and of music; Hephæstus or Vulcan was the god of fire and the forger of thunderbolts; Hermes or Mercury was the messenger of the gods.

These old Greeks also believed in goddesses of different ranks and offices, as Pallas Athene, the goddess of wisdom; Artemis or Diana, the goddess of the chase and guardian against pestilence; Aphrodite or Venus, the goddess of love; and Hestia or Vesta, the guardian of the hearth and the home.

The gods revealed their will in various ways. In the earlier times they were said to have appeared to men personally. In later ages the oracle was a more common mode of communication. The god was supposed to speak through his priest or priestess at certain shrines or sacred places, which were usually in some dark forest or mountain glen. The most famous oracles were those of Apollo at Delphi in Phocis, and of Zeus at Dodone in Epirus.

The **National Games** formed an important bond of union among the Greeks. Of these there were four classes—the Olympian, the Isthmian, the Pythian, and the Nemean, of which the two first named were the most important. They consisted in running, leaping, boxing, wrestling, throwing the discus, chariot-racing, etc. The competitors underwent a period of training extending over several months. The contests took place in the presence of a vast concourse of spectators, and they were conducted under strict rules. The reward to the victor was a simple thing—a crown of pine or ivy leaves, and palm branches placed in their hands. The apostle Paul and other writers in the New Testament make frequent reference to these games.

The **Olympian Games** were held in honor of Zeus at Olympia, a valley in Elis in the Peloponnesus. Held once in four years they served as a measure of time. The valley was also famous as the seat of a celebrated sanctuary of Zeus, adorned with a great statue of this chief of the gods. This statue, made by the famous sculptor Phidias, was sixty-five feet high, and in its richness and beauty, seated on a throne inlaid with ivory and precious stones, probably surpassed anything of its kind ever fashioned by man. Important sculptures, architectural remains, and other antiquities have been discovered here by German and French explorers.

The **Isthmian Games** were celebrated every two years at a place near the eastern end of the modern canal across the isthmus, on the northeast of Corinth. Within the sacred grounds, inclosed by strong walls, were temples of Poseidon and of Palæmon. The stadium, where the games were held, was outside the walls.

**Greek Sages.**—Greece was famous for its wise men. A few of the many that could be named were Thales, Pythagoras, Anaxagoras, Empedocles, Socrates, Plato, Aristotle, Zeno, and Epicurus.

The **Stoics** and the **Epicureans** were noted schools of philosophy. The Stoics held that virtue, being the chief good, should be pursued for its own sake, regardless of any happiness that it may afford, that the world is governed by stern law imposed by an all-wise God, that men should be free from all passion whether of joy or grief, and submit without complaint to whatever befalls them, that their chief concern is to do their duty and bring their lives into harmony with the divine will. This sect was founded by Zeno about 300 B. C. The Epicureans, a sect founded by Epicurus about the same time, taught that nothing is brought about by supernatural interference, but that everything happens as the result of natural causes, that virtue is a means for the securing of happiness, which is the highest good. Thus the Stoics and the Epicureans were directly opposed to each other.

**Greek States.**—Greece in its early days comprised many small states, each having its own government and laws. The principal of these states were Thessaly and Epirus in the north; Ætolia, Doris, Phocis, Bœotia and Attica in the middle; and Achaia, Arcadia, Argolis, Messenia, and Laconia in the south. Each comprised a small district of country with a central city which exercised the chief governing power in the state. In fact in some cases the city was the state.

In the early period Athens, the chief city of Attica, and Sparta in Laconia were the leading and rival powers among the Greek states. The Athenians were noted for general culture, excelling in art, literature, and philosophy. The Spartans were of ruder type and were famous for physical culture and martial valor.

**Macedonia.**—In the later period of Grecian history there arose a new state called Macedon or Macedonia. It lay north of the Ægean Sea and of Thessaly. It had not been reckoned as a part of Greece. Its people, though of the Hellenic race, were rude and uncultured, but they were hardy and masterful. Toward the end of Greek supremacy, under their king, Philip of Macedon, the Macedonians secured the leadership of all Greece (338 B. C.).

Persia then ruled over all western Asia, and at different times her kings had attempted the conquest of Greece. In turn, Alexander the Great, Philip's son and successor, now waged war against the Persians. After gaining possession of Asia Minor, Tyre, Palestine, and Egypt, he marched easterly and defeated the king of Persia in the battle of Arbela, near the site of ancient Nineveh. Greece, in the person of Alexander, had now the mastery of the civilized world (331 B. C.).

Alexander's reign was short (336–323 B. C.), but it had momentous results. It led to an intermingling of races and a broadening of human sympathies before unknown in the history of the world. Throughout Western Asia and Northern Africa Alexander's conquests were followed by the establishment of Greek colonies, the introduction of Greek civilization, and an extensive use of the Greek language. In an important sense they prepared the way for the spread of the Christian religion. Thus it was that the New Testament came to be written in Greek.

**Greece Under Roman Power.**—On the death of Alexander (323 B. C.) his great empire was broken up into four principal divisions,—Egypt, Syria, Macedon, and Thrace, of which the two first named were the chief. While the small city-states in Greece proper, by forming leagues with one another, maintained a certain degree of independence, yet Macedonia was the dominant power. Finally, however, both the kingdom of Macedonia and the confederate republics were conquered by Rome and organized as Roman provinces (142 B. C.).

In New Testament times Greece formed two Roman provinces, Macedonia and Achaia. The province of Macedonia included Thessaly and portions of Thrace and Illyricum. As a portion of Paul's missionary field and the seat of the first Christian churches in Europe these provinces are specially interesting to the Bible student.

**The Province of Macedonia.**—It was to this province of Macedonia that the apostle Paul came first on crossing over from Troas in Asia.[1] Macedonia was a senatorial province, governed by a proconsul. Its chief cities were Thessalonica, Amphipolis, Philippi, Neapolis, Apollonia, and Berœa.

The cities of Macedonia, in Roman times, were connected with each other and with Rome by a great military road called Via Egnatia. This road, which was over 500 miles long, lay across the country between Dyrrachium on the Adriatic and Cypsela in Central Thrace. On the Italian side of the Adriatic it lay between Rome and Brundusium.

**Thessalonica**, situated on a bay of the Ægean Sea, called the Thermaic Gulf, had for its original name Therma and was called Thessalonica after the sister of Alexander the Great. It was the metropolis of Macedonia, and under the name Saloniki it ranks second among the cities of European Turkey at the present day. The emperor Augustus Cæsar made it a free city as a reward for aid given him by it during his war with the Roman Senate. From its position on the Via Egnatia and as a port it was an important trade center as well as a center of influence over the surrounding country.[2] Many Jews resided here in Apostolic times, and at the present day the Jews form a large proportion of the population.

**Amphipolis**, on the river Strymon three miles from its mouth, is said to have received its name from the fact that the river nearly encircles the city (*amphi*, around, and *polis*, city).

**Philippi** was situated on a small river eight or nine miles from the sea. Its site is marked only by ruins. Along the margin of the river may be traced the remains of the ancient walls of the city, with a gap supposed to mark the position of the gateway through which Paul passed on going out to the place of prayer by the riverside.[3] Philippi was a Roman colony having received this distinction in honor of a victory gained in the neighborhood by Augustus and Antony over Brutus and Cassius. Its magistrates thus had powers similar to those of magistrates of Rome, and they were attended by lictors bearing *fasces* as emblems of their authority. Philippi is spoken of in The Acts as the "chief city in that part of Macedonia."[4] Amphipolis, at that time, claimed this distinc-

[1] Acts 16:9-11.   [2] 1 Thes. 1:7, 8.   [3] Acts 16:3.   [4] Acts 16:12.

tion. Some prefer the translation the "first" city, that is, the first city the travelers visited; Neapolis as its seaport being regarded as a part of Philippi.

**Neapolis** (New City), now represented by Kavala, was situated on a high promontory. It was the port of Philippi, eight or nine miles distant.

**Apollonia** was on the Via Egnatia about halfway between Thessalonica and Amphipolis.

**Berœa**, now Veria, is about thirty-five miles south of Thessalonica.[1]

**The Province of Achaia.**—The Roman province of Achaia included peninsular Greece south of Macedonia and Illyricum, together with some of the adjacent islands. It was at first attached to the province of Macedonia, but it was afterwards made a separate province (27 B. C.). At the time of Paul's visits it was under the supervision of the Roman Senate, and hence its chief officer Gallio was styled proconsul.[2]

The southern part of the country, called the Peloponnesus, and in modern times the Morea, is nearly isolated by the Corinthian Gulf on the west and the Saronic Gulf on the east. The Isthmus of Corinth between these waters is at its narrowest part but four or five miles in breadth. The Peloponnesus is a mountainous country especially on its western side. The cities of Achaia referred to in the New Testament are Athens, Corinth, and Cenchreæ.

**Athens**, the most famous city of ancient Greece, is situated five miles from its seaport, Piræus on the Saronic Gulf. It was a city of images, statues, and sacred places. All the gods were honored,—Zeus, Bacchus, Apollo, Mercury, Ceres, and others,—each had a temple. The Agora or market place was crowded with statues and altars. Alleys, shaded by ornamental trees, and covered walks called *stoai* or porches, were delightful places of resort, where Zeno and other philosophers were wont to hold converse with their disciples.

On the south side of the Agora stood the rocky eminence called the Areopagus or Mars' Hill, on the summit of which was made a level platform surrounded by rock-hewn seats. This platform was reached by steps cut in the rock. Here was accustomed to meet a famous council or court also called "The Areopagus," which had jurisdiction in religious, educational, and other important matters. East of the Areopagus and separated from it by a slight depression stands another famous hill called the Acropolis. This precipitous rock rises about 240 feet above the city level, and is about 1,000 feet in length. Here stood that magnificent work of art the Parthenon, a temple of Pallas, the guardian goddess of Athens, and within the temple was the great statue of ivory and gold made by Phidias. In the earlier times Athens was the home of some of the most

[1] Acts 17:11.  [2] Acts 18:12.

distinguished Greeks, as Solon, Socrates, and Plato, but when it was visited by the apostle Paul it had no worthy representatives of these great men. It was, however, at this time the seat of certain famous schools of philosophy known as the Stoics and the Epicureans.

**Corinth**, situated in the middle of the Isthmus, with its two ports, Lechæum on the west and Cenchreæ on the east, thus being "the Door of the Peloponnesus" and "the Bridge of the Sea," became a great commercial and wealthy city. The Isthmian Games, which were celebrated in its neighborhood, also made it a center of life and influence.

During the wars with Rome Corinth was pillaged and utterly destroyed. For about one hundred years it lay in ruins. Then it was rebuilt, established as a Roman colony, became prosperous, and was made the capital of the province of Achaia and the residence of the proconsul. In Apostolic times there were many Romans and many Jews among its citizens. It had the ill-fame of being one of the most immoral cities in the world. The worship of Venus in this city was accompanied by licentiousness of the grossest character. At the time of his first visit Paul remained at Corinth for a year and a half, and two of his longest epistles were written to the church which he founded in this city.

## CHAPTER XX

## THE ISLANDS OF BIBLE STORY

Most of the following islands situated in the Ægean Sea and the Eastern Mediterranean are referred to in Bible Story,—Samothracia, Imbros, Lemnos, Lesbos, Chios, Samos, Patmos, Cos, Rhodes, Cyprus, Crete, and Malta.

**Samothracia,** now called Samothraki, is a small but conspicuous island, rising to the height of 5,250 feet in the northern part of the Ægean Sea. This island and the neighboring islands Imbros and Lemnos were centers for the worship of the deities known as the Cabiri.

**Lesbos,** sometimes called **Mytilene,** is a mountainous island in the Ægean Sea. Its chief town is Mytilene.

**Chios** is a fertile, mountainous island on the west of Smyrna, five miles from the coast. It is one of the many places spoken of as the birthplace of Homer.

**Samos** is an important island on the west of Miletus. The rocky ridge of the mainland opposite this island was called Trogyllium, from which the island was separated by a channel about a mile wide.[1] Pythagoras, sometimes called "The sage of Samos," was born on this island.

**Patmos,** about twenty miles south of Samos, is a bare, rugged island, belonging to a group called the Sporades. According to tradition the apostle John was exiled to Patmos, where, in a grotto, he is said to have received the Revelation.

**Cos,** having an area of about ninety-five square miles, was celebrated for its vineyards and its wines. It was the seat of a temple in honor of Æsculapius, with which was connected a school of medicine. This island was the birthplace of Apelles and Hippocrates.

**Rhodes,** having an area of 570 square miles, is a mountainous and very fertile island. It was the seat of three of the ancient Dorian Colonies, became noted as a center of art and oratory, and was prominent in commercial affairs. On the breaking up of the empire of Alexander it became the head of a confederation comprising the islands and cities on the coast of Asia Minor. Rhodes, the capital of the island, was famous for the Colossus, a gigantic statue 105 feet high, representing the sun-god **Helios.** This statue cost over $2,000,000, and was accounted one of "the seven wonders of the world."

[1] Acts 20: 6, 13.

**Cyprus,** situated on the south of Cilicia, is said to have derived its name from its rich copper mines (Gr. *Kupros,* copper). It is supposed to be the place spoken of in the Old Testament under the name Chittim.[1] It is a beautiful, fertile island having an area of 3,580 square miles. The favorite deity of the Cyprians was Aphrodite, who, according to a myth, had her origin in the sea-foam on the shores of the island. The chief cities were Salamis, Citium, Amathus, and Paphos. At the time of Paul's visit Cyprus was a senatorial province governed by a proconsul. Barnabas was a native of this island.

**Crete** or **Candia,** in the Ægean Sea sixty miles southeast of Greece, has an area of 3,300 square miles. It is mountainous with valleys of great fertility. Among its products are wheat, wine, and fruit. In Greek legend King Minos, a famous lawgiver of Crete, was by the gods made judge of the lower world. The character of the Cretans as given by Paul,[2] who quotes Epimenides, a famous poet, is confirmed by other writers. Crete is said to have had one hundred cities.[3] Of these the chief were Gnossus, Gortyna, Cydonia, and Lyctus. Many Jews were resident on the island, especially at Gortyna.[4] Titus had oversight of the church here.[5] The vessel in which Paul sailed to Rome was caught on the south of Crete by a violent wind that struck down from the mountains. Fair Havens at which the vessel touched afforded anchorage, but no secure harbor.

**Malta,** the ancient **Melita,** an island in the Mediterranean south of Italy, has an area of ninety-five square miles. Its products are cotton, corn, and tropical fruit. It is one of a group known as the Maltese Islands. The apostle Paul was shipwrecked here when on his way to Rome.[6] At this time the island was attached to the government of the Roman province of Sicily, and its chief officer was subordinate to the governor of that province.[7] The inhabitants are spoken of as "barbarous," by which is probably meant that they did not speak Greek.

---

[1] Isa. 23:12.
[2] Titus 1:12.
[3] Homer, "Iliad," II, 649; Virgil, "Æneid," III, 106.
[4] Acts 2:11.
[5] Titus 1:5.
[6] Acts 27:39-44.
[7] Acts 28:7.

## CHAPTER XXI
### ROME

The Roman Commonwealth like Babylonia and Assyria was a city-state. It began with the city of Rome, and in its development this city was not only the geographical center round which the empire grew, but it was the main source of its life and power. The first settlement or village, Rome, stood on an eminence called the Palatine Hill on the banks of the Tiber, fifteen miles from its mouth. As the population increased the bounds of the city were widened, until they included six other hills, and hence Rome has been called "The City of the Seven Hills." On one of these hills, called the Capitoline, was built a large temple, where, under the same roof, were the shrines of three great national deities, Jupiter, Juno, and Minerva. On the low ground between the Palatine and the Capitoline hills was the Forum or Market Place where justice was administered and where the people assembled on public occasions. Between the Palatine and another hill called the Aventine, was the Circus Maximus where the public games were celebrated.

In the early times the people of Rome comprised various distinct classes. The patricians, who claimed to be the original settlers, were the highest and ruling class, who alone at the first possessed political rights. The plebeians were "outlanders" who had come in from other places, seeking a home. They were allowed to hold land and other property, but they were excluded from share in the government. Later they rebelled and forced the patricians to admit them to the privileges of citizenship. The clients formed another class. They were attached to the patricians and did them service in return for their protection, the relation being similar to that between vassal and liege lord in the Feudal System. The largeness of a patrician's clientage was the measure of his rank and influence. There were slaves also, who for the most part were captives taken in war.

The early history of Rome is mixed with legendary and variant tradition. The earliest date assigned to the founding of the city is 753 B. C., which was a little before the time of Hezekiah, King of Judah. The first form of government was a monarchy, which lasted about 250 years. At the same time, acting as a judicial and advisory body, there was an assembly called the senate, which was composed of the fathers or the heads of families. Then there was a still larger body—a popular assembly (*comitia curiata*) which was composed of all the patricians who had come to years of manhood. This assembly made the laws and elected the king. In a later age the plebeians also were admitted to the popular assembly. The kings were so tyrannical that the people finally broke up the monarchy (509 B. C.).

**Religion.**—The religion of the Romans was similar to that of the Greeks. They had many gods and goddesses, each having his own function or presiding over a special sphere. Jupiter was the supreme deity. Juno, the wife of Jupiter, and Minerva, his daughter, the goddess of wisdom, shared with him the great temple on the Capitoline Hill. Mars was the god of war and was greatly revered. Janus, the god of the beginning and the ending of things, had two faces, looking before and behind. He was worshiped at the beginning and at the end of every enterprise. Vesta, nearly identical with the Greek Hestia, was the goddess of the hearth, and the fire on it was her symbol. Then as the Roman people regarded themselves as one great family, the temple of Vesta had its public hearth, on which the sacred fire, tended by the six vestal virgins, was kept ever burning. For any neglect of duty these virgins were severely punished. The Lares and Penates were household gods, and their images were placed at the entrance of the home. The Lares were the spirits of deceased ancestors who were supposed to remain hovering round their old homes to protect them from evil.

The Romans, like the Greeks, believed that the gods made known their will and the events of the future through oracles and certain phenomena of nature, as thunder and lightning, the flight of birds, and the entrails of animals slain in sacrifice. These phenomena were sought out and interpreted by priests, augurs, and soothsayers.

The College of Pontiffs superintended all religious affairs. One duty of this body was to keep in order the bridges leading to the temples. The Latin word bridge is *pons*, and the members of this body were called pontiffs (*pontifices*), that is bridge-makers. Under the later imperial government the emperor was at the head of the pontiffs, and was called Pontifex Maximus, chief pontiff.

The Romans resembled the Greeks also in having many religious festivals and games. They thought that their gods were pleased with these games, and they often made vows, promising the gods to honor them in this way in return for their favor and aid.

**The Roman Republic.**—The new government established on the removal of the kings was called a republic. Practically it was more like an oligarchy. At first the patricians alone had the management of affairs, and later a few leading spirits had control. In place of the kings two magistrates, called consuls, were elected for the term of one year. A consul was always attended by twelve officers called lictors, each carrying a bundle of rods (*fasces*) with an ax bound up in it—a symbol of the consul's power to punish by flogging or beheading.

During the period of the republic the domain of Rome was widely extended in all directions. Through conquest the whole of Southern and Central Europe, Northern Africa, and Western Asia were brought within its bounds. Foreign conquests had a demoralizing influence on the people, leading to luxury and vice. The government fell largely into the hands of ambitious and unscrupulous men who gained power through their influence with the army.

About the middle of the century preceding the Christian era the two most prominent public men in Rome were Caius Julius Cæsar and Cneius Pompeius. Cæsar possessed signal ability as a warrior, as a statesman, and as an author. Among his military achievements was the conquest of Gaul and Britain. Pompey was Cæsar's son-in-law. As a military officer he gained great renown. He captured the pirates who infested the Eastern Mediterranean; he conquered the great warrior Mithridates, King of Pontus, and drove him out of Asia Minor; he overturned the Syrian kingdom of the Seleucidæ; and he captured Jerusalem. At first Cæsar and Pompey planned to share the Roman world between them; but their ambition grew apace, and that great world was not large enough for both. The question of ownership was settled by appeal to arms. The two rivals with their forces met on the plains of Pharsalia in Thessaly. Pompey was defeated. He fled to Egypt, where, on his arrival, he was assassinated.

On his return to Rome Cæsar was accorded a triumph surpassing in brilliancy anything of its kind that the city had ever witnessed. He was master of Rome and that meant of the civilized world. His power was short-lived. As he sat in the senate chamber a band of conspirators rushed upon him and he fell pierced, it is said, by twenty-three wounds.

Three new aspirants to power now occupied the field, who were soon reduced to two—Mark Antony and Octavius, a grand nephew of Julius Cæsar. Like Pompey and Cæsar they would divide the Roman World between them. But the friends of the republic were not yet willing to submit to imperial rule. Led by Brutus and Cassius, who had taken active part in the plot against Cæsar, they made a final stand for their cause against Octavius and Antony near Philippi in Macedonia. They suffered disastrous defeat. Brutus and Cassius, unable to bear their ill fortune, committed suicide, and many others of their party followed their example.

Again, like Julius Cæsar and Pompey, Octavius and Mark Antony quarreled, and they decided the lot of empire between them by the naval battle of Actium fought off the coast of Greece. Octavius won the day.

Antony and his ally Cleopatra, Queen of Egypt, fled from the scene of conflict, and soon after Antony took his own life (31 B. C.).

**The Roman Empire.**—The empire might properly date its beginning with the battle of Actium, but it is sometimes regarded as beginning with the public investing of Octavian with imperial power (27 B. C.). The senate conferred on him the title Imperator and Pontifex Maximus, and, ranking him with the gods, gave him the name Augustus (Illustrious). Octavian or Augustus, as he is generally known, had now unlimited power, but his power was concealed as much as possible under old forms. The senate and the various officers of the republic still remained, but they were all creatures of the emperor whose hand was behind every movement.

The empire extended from the Atlantic to the River Euphrates, and from Central Europe to Central Africa. Its population was nearly 120,000,000. For the purposes of government it was divided into provinces, of which there were two classes—senatorial and imperial.

A senatorial province, that is one that was under the supervision of the senate, was supposed to have become so completely submissive to Roman authority, that it could be governed without military force. The chief officer over such a province was designated proconsul, in the New Testament called deputy,[1] and he held office for one year.

An imperial province required military force to keep it in order. It was placed under the direct supervision of the emperor, and its chief officer was styled legate or lieutenant, usually rendered governor in the Authorized Version of the New Testament.

**A Roman Colony.**—To aid in bringing newly-acquired countries under Roman influence, colonies were established in various places. A Roman colony consisted of a band of old soldiers or Roman citizens who with their families were transplanted into certain towns or districts. These citizens, who formed the ruling class in the community, were endowed with lands taken from the native inhabitants, and they were accounted citizens of Rome. Such a city or community represented Rome on a small scale. Its government was modeled after that of Rome, and its magistrates, called pretors, were accounted of higher rank than those of other cities. Corinth, Philippi, and Pisidian Antioch were Roman colonies.[2]

**Free Cities.**—Some cities within the empire were given special privileges as free cities. They chose their own magistrates and were in large measure independent of the government of the province in which they were situated. Athens, Ephesus, Antioch in Syria, and the cities of the Decapolis in Eastern Palestine belonged to this class.

**Roman Citizenship.**—Roman citizenship implied various rights and

[1] Acts 13: 7, 8, 12.  [2] Acts 16: 12.

privileges. A Roman citizen could not be punished by scourging,[1] and he had the right of appeal from the judgment of a provincial tribunal to the Roman emperor.[2] Such appeal stopped proceedings so that the prisoner could not be set at liberty without the authority of the emperor.[3] The right of citizenship came by birth when it was possessed by both parents; it could be obtained by purchase;[4] and it could be secured by military service or by special favor. Sometimes the right was conferred on whole cities.

**The Army.**—A large army was required to maintain order throughout the Roman Empire. A company of soldiers comprised one hundred men, and its captain was called a centurion. Several such officers are spoken of in the New Testament, all of whom appear to have been worthy men.[5] Six companies or centuries formed a cohort. Claudius Lysias, who rescued Paul from the Jewish mob, was commander of a cohort.[6] Ten of these cohorts formed a legion.

**Taxes.**—For the maintenance of its army, for the erection of public buildings, the construction of roads, and many other purposes, the Roman government required a large revenue. For this purpose taxes of various kinds were imposed, as poll tax, tax on property, duty on goods imported, and toll for traveling over the great roads. One of the roads lay between Damascus and the coast, passing through Capernaum. It is supposed that Matthew was a collector of tolls at Capernaum. In connection with the taxes an enrollment of the people was made, each person going to his family city for this purpose. Private persons often bargained with the government, agreeing to pay a lump sum for the taxes of a district or province. These persons then exacted exorbitant sums from the people. Hence, the collectors of taxes, called publicans, were held in reproach.

The inhabitants of the rural districts belonged chiefly to the nationality of the country in which they lived. In the cities the higher classes were Romans and Greeks. The Jews were numerous in all the great business centers. They had their synagogues and were generally left free to worship as they pleased. They made many proselytes from the idol-worshipers.

West of the Adriatic Latin was the general language. In the east the lower classes spoke the language of the country in which they lived; Greek was the language of literature, of educated people and business men.

The streets in the cities were narrow. The forum was the center to which people resorted to transact business. At meals they reclined on couches. Public baths were provided at great expense. Amusements

---

[1] Acts 16 : 37, 38 ; 22 : 25.  [2] Acts 25 : 10-12.  [3] Acts 26 : 32.
[4] Acts 22 : 28.  [5] Matt. 8 : 8, 10; 27 : 54; Acts 10 : 1, 2; 27 : 1.  [6] Acts 21 : 31 ; 22 : 26.

included the theater, chariot races, the various games of the circus, and baitings of wild animals. For these contests wild animals were brought from various places—bears and wolves from Northern Europe, lions and leopards from Africa, elephants and tigers from Asia. Convicts from the prisons were pitted against each other in deadly encounter, and even citizens of high rank made public spectacles of themselves in the arena to gratify a depraved public taste. A disabled gladiator was at the mercy of the spectators. According as they stretched out their hands with thumbs turned up or down, the victor understood that the people wished him to spare the life of his vanquished antagonist or to finish the work to the death.

The reign of Augustus was the golden age of Roman literature. Among the authors of the time were Virgil, Horace, Ovid, and Sallust. Above all in this reign came the fullness of time when the Saviour of the world should be manifested. It was during the reign of Tiberius that Jesus was crucified. Caligula and Claudius occupied the throne of the Cæsars during the Apostolic age.

The general moral condition of the empire at this time was low. Skepticism prevailed. Belief in the gods had lost its hold of thoughtful minds, and no higher faith had come in to take its place. Magic and superstition were rampant.

# CHAPTER XXII

## HISTORIC OUTLINE.—FROM THE CALL OF ABRAHAM TO THE DEATH OF MOSES

The Bible story goes back to the beginning of things when God created the heavens and the earth. Its chief concern is a revelation of God's will to man—"What man is to believe concerning God, and what duty God requires of man." Its history is incidental and relates mainly to the Hebrews whom God chose as the medium of his communication to the human family.

The great ancestor of the Hebrews was Abraham, the son of Terah, whose native place was "Ur of the Chaldees," an ancient city of Southern Babylonia. From this place Terah and his family migrated, journeying northerly up the Euphrates, having in view as their ultimate destination the land of Canaan.[1] They halted, however, at Haran in Mesopotamia, where Terah died. At the call of God, Abraham, accompanied by his nephew Lot, afterwards continued his journey by way of Damascus to Canaan.[2] Abraham's brother Nahor remained in Haran, where at a later period we find his descendants.[3] The date of Abraham's arrival in Canaan is supposed to have been about 2300 B. C.

For a short time Abraham dwelt in the Vale of Shechem between Mount Ebal and Mount Gerizim.[4] From this place he removed to a mountain between Hai and Bethel.[5] Then he journeyed southerly again by the watershed, along which ran the route of travel north and south. During a period of famine he sojourned in Egypt, from which he returned to Bethel.[6] Hitherto Abraham and Lot had kept together in their wanderings. Each had large herds and flocks, and their herdmen now began to quarrel over the pasture lands. This led to separation, Lot choosing the rich lands in the Jordan Valley, and Abraham going southerly into the highlands of Hebron.

At this time the inhabitants of Canaan included several different peoples, for the most part of Hamitic origin. At Hebron and in its neighborhood was a branch of that remarkable people called Hittites, the main portion of whom occupied territory north of Palestine. In the highlands round Hebron were also a people of gigantic stature called Anakim.[7] The Amorites occupied territory along the west of the Dead Sea and had their chief city at En-gedi. When the Israelites under Moses and Joshua

[1] Gen. 11 : 31.   [2] Gen. 12 : 1–5.   [3] Gen. 24 : 10; 28 : 1–5; 29 : 4.
[4] Gen. 12 : 6.   [5] Gen. 12 : 8.   [6] Gen. 12 : 10 to 13 : 4.   [7] Num. 13 : 33.

entered the Promised Land the Amorites had possession of a portion of the country on the east of the Dead Sea.[1] Then on the southern portion of the maritime plain dwelt the Philistines, who, though occupying but a small section of the land of Canaan, gave to the whole country the name by which at the present day it is commonly known. The Canaanites, again, were found on the coast plain of Sharon north of the Philistines, in the Plain of Esdraelon, and in the Jordan Valley. The Phœnicians or Zidonians occupied the coast plain north of Carmel and west of the Lebanons. The Hivites were on the south of Carmel, having their chief city at Shechem. The Jebusites lived in the highlands near Jerusalem. The Perizzites were probably on the northern portion of the Shephelah.

Palestine and the neighboring countries at this time formed part of the great Elamite Empire of Chedorlaomer. From the account given in Genesis of the western expedition of this monarch, it would appear that he had held the kings of the plain under his power for twelve years, when they rebelled. Thereupon, with his eastern vassals, he proceeded to chastise the rebels. Coming by way of Damascus, and marching southerly through the lands on the east of the Jordan, he defeated the Sepharvaim and other tribes as far as the Horites in Mount Seir. He then returned, passing northerly along the west side of the Dead Sea. Here he subdued the Amorites and then proceeded against the five rebellious kings of the cities of the plain. Having captured these kings and Abraham's nephew Lot, with his captives and his plunder he set out for home.[2]

The rescue of Lot and the captive kings by Abraham gives a fine illustration of the patriarch's valor and his promptness in action. It also shows us the strength of his household or retainers. "He armed his trained servants, born in his own house, three hundred and eighteen." If these servants had families of their own the total number would amount to a thousand or more.

Abraham left eight sons.[3] Of these Isaac, the child of promise, became the ancestor of the chosen people of Israel. From Ishmael, the son of Hagar the bondmaid, came the Ishmaelites. From Midian, one of the six sons of Keturah, sprang the Midianites, who inhabited the territory on the southwest of Palestine. Lot left two sons, Moab and Ben-ammi, whose descendants, the Moabites and the Ammonites, occupied territory on the east of the Dead Sea. Isaac left two sons, Jacob and Esau. Esau became the founder of a distinct people, called the Edomites or Idumæans.

For the double purpose of escaping the revenge of his angry brother, from whom by fraud he had taken his father's blessing, and of seeking a wife from his mother's kindred, Jacob went to Haran in Padan-aram. After twenty years' sojourn in this land, with his wives, eleven sons, one

---

[1] Num. 21 : 13, 26.   [2] Gen. 14 : 12.   [3] Gen. 25 : 1, 2.

daughter, and great possessions of flocks and herds he returned to Canaan. For a short period he dwelt in the fertile valley of Shechem, where Abraham had made his first home in Palestine. Then, moving southward, he visited Bethel, the scene of his wonderful vision many years before when he was on his way to Padan-aram. Going on southerly he came to Hebron where he found his aged father still living.

It would appear that Jacob now made his fixed residence at Hebron, or in that neighborhood, and that his sons, with the exception of Joseph and Benjamin, roamed far abroad wherever they could find pasturage for their flocks and herds. Among the places visited by them was the far-off valley of Dothan, one of the passes that lead out from Esdraelon through the highlands to the maritime plain. Here occurred that incident in the family life—the sale of Joseph by his brothers—an act sad enough in its origin, purpose, and carrying out, yet eventful and beneficent in its results.

What a wonderful story is this! Joseph, the favorite son of a fond father, the object of his brothers' envy, sold into slavery, falsely accused, thrust into a vile prison; then summoned to a royal court, the first counselor of a great king, the most powerful man next to the Pharaoh in all the land! All this reads like a tale of the Arabian Nights. And that picture of Jacob as he hears the tale: "It is enough; Joseph my son is yet alive: I will go and see him before I die." And yet with all his haste to see his long-lost son, he pauses at Beer-sheba to worship and ask counsel of God.

The sojourn of the Israelites in Egypt continued for over four hundred years. On the accession of a new dynasty, probably following the expulsion of the Hyksos, they were reduced to a state of bondage and toil under the lash. In this way they contributed their share of servile labor by which the Egyptian kings carried on their great public works—the building of temples, palaces, fortresses, treasure cities, the excavation of tombs, construction of canals, and obtaining material from the distant quarries.

**The Exodus** from Egypt is supposed to have taken place about 1490 B. C., though some authorities place the date fifty years later. The Egyptians were skilled in the making of linens, embroidery, ornaments of gold, silver, and precious stones and other lines of workmanship. During their stay among them the Israelites acquired much skill in these arts. Of this there is evidence in the tabernacle which they erected in the wilderness. Moses also was taught in all the wisdom of the Egyptian schools, which was not surpassed by that of any ancient civilization. That the spirit of independence and the religious tone of the people were of low type are shown by their conduct in the wilderness.[1]

[1] Ex. 16:3; 32:1; Num. 11:5; 14:2; 25:5.

The history of the Israelites in the Wilderness may be divided into five periods:—

1. **From Egypt to Mount Sinai.**—The chief events of this period, which comprised about two months, include the crossing of the Red Sea, the destruction of the Egyptian army,[1] the encampment at Marah, and at Elim,[2] the people fed with manna,[3] water brought from the rock,[4] the conflict with the Amalekites at Rephidim,[5] and the visit of Jethro, the priest of Midian.[6]

2. **The Encampment at Mount Sinai.**—This occupied about one year. The principal events here were the giving of the law,[7] the worship of the golden calf,[8] the building of the tabernacle,[9] the consecration of Aaron and his sons,[10] the numbering of the people,[11] and the organization of the tribes for encampment and marching.[12]

3. **The March From Sinai to Kadesh-barnea.**—The events during the journey included the murmurings of the people on account of the lack of flesh food,[13] the appointment of seventy elders to assist Moses,[14] the gift of quails,[15] and the sin of Miriam and Aaron.[16]

4. **The Encampment at Kadesh-barnea.**—While the twelve spies explored the land of Canaan from "the wilderness of Zinun to Rehob,"[17] for forty days the people remained at Kadesh.[18] How much longer they stayed here is not stated, but it would appear that they made this their headquarters for some time, and that they returned to Kadesh at the end of the forty years' wandering.[19] The evil report of the spies caused a great outburst of murmuring followed by repentance; and a willful and unsuccessful attempt, in opposition to the command of Moses, to take possession of the Promised Land.[20] The seditious conduct of Korah, Dathan, and Abiram, as well as their punishment probably took place at Kadesh.[21] Here also Miriam died.[22]

5. **The Circuitous March From Kadesh to the Arnon.**—Particulars of this long period of nearly thirty-eight years' wandering in the desert are scanty. It was during this time, when water failed, that Moses transgressed by smiting the rock instead of speaking to it to give forth water.[23] During these wanderings also, probably near their ending, Aaron died.[24] At some place also on this journey the people were bitten by serpents, and Moses erected the brazen serpent.

For some reason not explained the Israelites were to enter Canaan from the east. Edom lay between them and the country on the east side

[1] Ex. 14: 9-31.   [2] Ex. 15: 23-27.   [3] Ex. 16: 2-16.   [4] Ex. 17: 3-7.
[5] Ex. 17: 8-14.   [6] Ex. 18: 1.   [7] Ex., chs. 19-31.   [8] Ex. 32: 1-23.
[9] Ex., chs. 25-27.   [10] Ex., chs. 28, 29.   [11] Num., ch. 1.   [12] Num., ch. 2.
[13] Num. 11: 4.   [14] Num. 11: 11-30.   [15] Num. 11; 31-34.   [16] Num. 12: 1-15.
[17] Num. 13: 21.   [18] Num. 13: 25.   [19] Num. 20: 17.   [20] Num. 14: 1-45.
[21] Num. 16: 1-35.   [22] Num. 20: 1.   [23] Num. 20: 2-12.   [24] Num. 20: 23-29.

of the Jordan. Returning to Kadesh near the close of the forty years' wandering, Moses asked the king of that country for leave to pass through his territory. This was very decidedly and rudely refused. On account of this refusal the Israelites were compelled to make a circuit, passing down the west side of the Arabah, crossing over at the head of the Gulf of Akabah, and thence marching northerly along the east of Edom. They crossed the Land of Moab without opposition and arrived at the River Arnon, the dividing line between that country and the land which had recently been taken from Moab by the Amorites.

Moses now asked of Sihon, king of the Amorites, permission to cross his territory.[1] Refusal of this privilege led to war and the conquest of Sihon and also of Og, King of Bashan.[2] Balak, king of the Moabites, alarmed by these victories over his neighbors, in concert with the Midianites brought Balaam from his distant home in Mesopotamia to curse these warlike strangers who had come out of Egypt. In this hope he was disappointed, the curse sought for being turned into blessing.[3] But acting on the advice of this prophet, strangely compact of good and evil, the Moabites and Midianites wickedly seduced the children of Israel into grievous sin and thus brought on them the displeasure of Jehovah.[4] For this the Moabites were punished by the loss of their territory north of the Arnon, which the Israelites retained. The Midianites were more severely chastised by war, resulting in fearful slaughter, including their five kings and the wicked Balaam, and in the loss of many of their people who were taken captive by the Israelites, and of vast numbers of cattle, asses, and sheep.[5]

The division of the territory falling to the Israelites by the conquests on the east of the Jordan among the tribes of Reuben, Gad, and the half tribe of Manasseh was among the last public acts of Moses. Among his last words were his prophetic utterances respecting the different tribes. Afterwards from Pisgah's heights he viewed the goodly land beyond the Jordan, and then—he was not, for God took him.

---

[1] Num. 21 : 21–25.   [2] Num. 21 : 33–35.   [3] Num., chs. 22–24.
[4] Num. 25 : 2 ; 31 : 16.   [5] Num. 31 : 7–12, 32–40.

## CHAPTER XXIII

### HISTORIC SKETCH.—THE JUDGES

The Israelites crossed the Jordan about 1451 B. C. The conquest of Western Palestine occupied seven years, though some portions of the land were not secured until a much later period. Jerusalem remained in the hands of the Jebusites until the time of David.

At Gilgal near Jericho, to signalize the wonderful manner of crossing the Jordan, Joshua set up twelve memorial stones, taken from the dry bed of the river, and he made this place his headquarters during the period of conquest. Then followed the destruction of Jericho, the defeat at Ai, the final capture of this place, and the assembling of the people on Mounts Ebal and Gerizim.

An interesting diversion from the gruesome story of slaughter is the episode of the ruse practiced by the Gibeonites who, fearing the fate that had overtaken their neighbors, resorted to strategy. Clothing themselves in tattered garments and patched shoes, and filling their knapsacks with moldy bread, under pretense of having come from a very far country, they presented themselves before Joshua and the elders of Israel. In their distant home they had heard of the wonderful people of Israel and of the fame of their God, and they had been sent by their rulers to negotiate a treaty of peace. The treaty was made accordingly, and then it was discovered that these much-traveled delegates and their people lived hard by. But under the protection of a solemn covenant they could not be treated as enemies. They were made "hewers of wood and drawers of water" —servants of the sanctuary.

Alarmed by the speedy overthrow of the central states, five petty kings of Southern Canaan banded themselves together for offensive warfare. First they attacked the Gibeonites who had so unpatriotically formed an alliance with the foreign invaders. Prompt to the cry of the Gibeonites, Joshua, by a night march, hastened from Gilgal across the highlands to their aid. The battle was near the Beth-horons. The five kings fled down the Valley of Aijalon, with the forces of Israel in hot pursuit. And here occurred a wonderful phenomenon—the sun and the moon stood still at the command of Joshua to give him time to finish his day's work. Joshua followed up his victory by the capture of the leading cities of the south.[1] The conquest in this quarter was afterwards more fully completed by Caleb and Othniel.[2]

[1] Josh. 10 : 28-43.   [2] Josh. 15 : 13-19.

One more grand encounter with the heathen nations had Joshua in gaining possession of the Promised Land. The kings of the north—in Esdraelon, on the highlands beyond (afterwards Galilee), and round the foot of Mount Hermon—gathered their forces near Lake Merom, under Jabin, King of Hazor. It was a formidable army,—" even as the sand that is upon the sea shore in multitude, with horses and chariots very many." Again Joshua's victory was complete.

Having finished the work of conquest, Joshua removed the encampment from Gilgal to Shiloh, a place situated within the bounds of Ephraim on the east of the highway between Bethel and Shechem.[1] He then had the country surveyed and allotments made to those tribes that had not received their inheritance.

From this time until the building of the temple Shiloh was the religious center of Israel. Here the tabernacle, "The House of God," had its resting place, and here the great annual feasts were held. In Shiloh also the Ark of the Covenant remained until its capture by the Philistines in the days of Eli.[2]

When all the western tribes were settled in their appointed places, Joshua called to him the warriors of those tribes that had chosen their inheritance on the east of the Jordan, and having charged them to be faithful to their God, he sent them away to their homes.[3]

The well-rounded life of Joshua was now drawing to a close. No nobler Bible character is presented for our imitation. His principle of action—"As for me and my house, we will serve the Lord"—is well illustrated by the spirit of independence shown on that day when the ten spies gave their ill report and he and Caleb stood by themselves.[4] He was "strong and very courageous." When he had a work to do, he set about it promptly, and he did it thoroughly.

From the death of Joshua to the time of Saul—a period of over three hundred years—the Israelites were not bound together by any organized central government. Each tribe had its autonomy and was governed by its elders or assembly. This period is known as the time of the Judges. Except in the case of Samuel, the authority of the judge, so called, was local, extending over certain tribes only. Eli and Samson are supposed to have ruled at the same time.

The duties of the judge were not so much of a judicial as of a military character. He was not elected to office by the people or appointed in any authoritative way. Sometimes he was called to the office by the general popular voice at the time of an emergency; in some instances he was specially called of God, and his call was recognized by the people through

---

[1] Judg. 21:19; Josh. 18:1-10.   [2] 1 Sam. 4:3-11.
[3] Josh. 22:1-6.   [4] Num. 14:6-10.

his fitness for the service; and occasionally there was a tendency to hereditary succession.

Ephraim and Judah were the most prominent and self-assertive of the tribes. Ephraim especially was watchful of her rights and jealous of the supremacy of other tribes. After the disruption, the names Judah and Ephraim stood for the two divisions into which the nation was divided.[1]

During the period of the Judges the Israelites were harassed by various heathen tribes, including the Moabites, Ammonites, Midianites, Amalekites, Canaanites, and Philistines. The three first named were near of kin to the Israelites, but were none the less hostile. The lowland plains were most exposed to these invaders. The enemy usually entered the country by way of Esdraelon or by some pass between the maritime plain and the highlands. Thus the tribes bordering on these gateways were the greatest sufferers and were foremost in the development of martial spirit.

First the Israelites were oppressed for eight years by the king of Mesopotamia, and were set free by the judge Othniel.[2] Later, Eglon, King of Moab, in alliance with Ammon and Amalek, making Judah his base of operations, held supremacy until a deliverer arose in the person of Ehud.[3] Then the Canaanites made a final desperate effort to regain their lost possessions and were disastrously defeated along the Valley of the Kishon by Deborah and Barak.[4] Afterwards the Midianites, who overran the country bordering on Esdraelon, were repulsed with great slaughter by Gideon.[5] The tribes on the east of the Jordan, when attacked by the Ammonites, were delivered by Jephthah.[6]

The most warlike and troublesome of all Israel's neighbors at this time were the Philistines. Again and again they invaded the land. They were repulsed by Shamgar and harassed by Samson, but still they persisted in warfare until in the time of Eli they gained a great victory and carried off the Ark of the Covenant, the most sacred of all Israel's holy things. At the close of the period of the Judges so completely were the people under bondage to Philistia, that they were compelled to go to that country for the sharpening of their agricultural implements.

[1] Judg. 8: 1–3; 12: 1–6; Isa. 11: 13.  [2] Judg. 3: 7–11.
[3] Judg. 3: 12–30.   [4] Judg. 4: 1–24.   [5] Judg., chs. 6, 7.   [6] Judg. 11: 4–32.

## CHAPTER XXIV

### HISTORICAL SKETCH.—THE UNDIVIDED MONARCHY

In the history of the world, through revolutionary uprisings of the people, monarchical governments often give place to republics. Instances are rare in which, as the choice of a free people, monarchy has been adopted in exchange for some form of popular government. Such changes are generally brought about through the personal ambition and influence of great military leaders like Julius Cæsar or Napoleon. In the land of Israel the strange thing was that the people, who had been accustomed "to do every one that which was right in his own eyes," clamored for a king, while the most influential man in all the land set his face against the change.

Popular movements are contagious and spread from land to land. "Make us a king to judge us," said the Israelites to Samuel, "that we may be like all the nations."[1] Again they had marked the grand achievements of their heroic military judges, how they had led them to victory and given them rest from their enemies. Then the judge had demanded little from them for the maintenance of rank and power. The war in which he had figured being ended, he was a common man again like themselves. A king, thought they, would, in like manner, be unexacting, and yet a source of strength. In whatever way the desire of the people originated, it was not in accord with the mind of Samuel, nor was it pleasing to God. Possibly the offense was in the spirit of the asking rather than in the thing asked for.

**Saul** (1095–1055 B. C.).—Saul, the first king of Israel, was of the city Gibeah in the tribe of Benjamin. The story of his seeking the strayed asses and finding a kingdom is an interesting one. Chosen and anointed by Samuel in Ramah under the direction of the Spirit of God, the choice was confirmed by the sacred lot.[2] Of fine presence and noble character was the young king. Modest and retiring, he was in no haste to wear the kingly crown. When taunted with contemptuous words, "he held his peace," and went quietly home to look after his flocks and herds. Soon came the occasion for the vindication of his fitness for command.

A cry for speedy help came from Jabesh-gilead beyond the Jordan. The place was besieged by the Ammonites, and when the citizens offered to submit to the invaders, the reply of the haughty king of Ammon was— "On this condition will I make a covenant with you, that I may thrust out

---
[1] 1 Sam. 8: 4, 5.      [2] 1 Sam. 9: 10.

all your right eyes, and lay it for a reproach upon all Israel." With energy and promptness Saul played the king on this first occasion. "To-morrow, by that time the sun be hot, ye shall have help," was the word he sent back to the men of Jabesh-gilead. Three hundred and thirty thousand men were quickly on the move, and before the morrow had dawned the slaughter of the Ammonites had begun.[1]

The battle of Michmash was one of the noted events of the reign. The Philistines held fortified posts at Geba, Bethel, and other places near Gibeah, Saul's capital, in the very heart of the country. The Israelites had been disarmed. Not a sword or a spear was found with any man, save Saul and Jonathan. The smiths had been banished that there might be no one to furnish instruments of war. By a daring act Jonathan assaulted the Philistine camp at Geba. It was like stirring up a hornet's nest. The whole horde of the Philistines poured over the highlands— thousands of chariots, horsemen, and footmen—and encamped at Michmash. Paralyzed with fear the Israelites "hid themselves in caves, and in thickets, and in rocks, and in high places, and in pits."

Samuel had promised to come at a certain time to offer sacrifice before the battle began. He did not arrive at the appointed time. Saul's men were deserting, and he had but six hundred remaining. At last, contrary to commandment, he himself offered the sacrifice. Scarcely had the service ended when Samuel arrived. He was greatly displeased, chided the king for his rashness, and told him that on account of his disobedience the throne should not continue in his family.

The battle that followed resulted in a great victory for Israel. Jonathan especially gained great distinction for his valor.[2]

Once again was Saul tested. When the Israelites were journeying in the wilderness, they were treated most unkindly by the Amalekites. And now Saul was commanded of the Lord through Samuel to destroy this people utterly, to save nothing alive either man or beast. Saul returned to Gilgal bringing with him Agag, the king of Amalek, and also as spoil the best of the sheep and oxen.[3] When reproved by Samuel for his disobedience, he pleaded that the people had spared the animals for sacrifice to Jehovah. The prophet's memorable answer was, "To obey is better than sacrifice. . . . Because thou hast rejected the word of the Lord, he hath also rejected thee from being king."[4]

Again there was war with the Philistines, and now it was on the borders of Judah, in the Valley of Elah that runs down from the highlands through the shephelah. It was here that the youthful David met and slew the haughty Goliath as he shouted insult and defiance to the Israelites and their God.[5]

[1] 1 Sam., ch. 11.   [2] 1 Sam., chs. 13, 14.   [3] 1 Sam. 15:8, 9.
[4] 1 Sam. 15:13–28.   [5] 1 Sam. 17:1–58.

Meanwhile David had been anointed by Samuel as Saul's successor. Already, too, Saul had been stricken by his malady, and ever and anon the evil spirit, usurping the throne of reason, "troubled him." Doubtless it came upon him through brooding over those fateful words of Samuel, "The Lord hath rent the kingdom of Israel from thee this day, and hath given it to a neighbor of thine, that is better than thou."

Though apparently not recognized by Saul, David was no stranger at court, where his skill as a player on the harp had been sought after to drive away the evil spirit that disturbed the disordered mind of the king. He now became an officer in the army and stood high in royal favor. But the king's love soon turned into malignant hatred. Jealousy was the baneful influence that wrought the change. The killing of the giant had made the young man famous. And now as Saul and his retinue passed along, joyous bands of women came out of the cities, playing on instruments of music, dancing, and singing,—"Saul hath slain his thousands, and David his ten thousands."[1]

The evil spirit could no longer be exorcised by the sweet music of the harp. David's life was in danger. Twice, as he played, the infuriated king hurled at him his javelin to pin him to the wall.[2] David sought safety with Samuel at Ramah. Then he made his home in the cave of Adullam supposed by some to be in the Valley of Elah where he slew the giant.[3] He fled to the wilderness south of Hebron, and then to the wilderness of En-gedi. Everywhere he was hunted as a bird upon the mountains. Twice he could have slain the man who thus sought his life. Saul entered a cave where David was hiding, and came so near that David cut off the skirt of his robe.[4] Again, while the monarch slept and his faithless guards lay slumbering round him, David went to his encampment and carried off his spear which stood at his head.[5] Finally David went to the king of Gath in Philistia and received from him the city of Ziklag which he made his home.[6]

Saul had a long though not a prosperous reign of forty years. He left matters worse than he found them. The Philistines dominated the land. Saul's last encounter with this people resulted in disastrous defeat, in his own death, and that of his three sons.[7]

No sketch of his reign would be complete without at least some reference to the love of Jonathan and David, which, like the glintings of the diamond in the night, by its touches of sweet light here and there relieves some of the deepest shadows of the dark picture.

**David** (1055–1015 B. C.).—Having his capital at Hebron, for seven and a half years David ruled over Judah. During the first two years of this period, Ish-bosheth, the only surviving son of Saul, was the nominal

[1] 1 Sam. 18:7.   [2] 1 Sam. 18:11; 19:10.   [3] 1 Sam. 22:1.   [4] 1 Sam. 24:4.
[5] 1 Sam. 26:12.   [6] 1 Sam. 27:6.   [7] 1 Sam. 31:6.

ruler of the other tribes. For some time an indecisive war was carried on between the two kingdoms. Ish-bosheth was a man of little force of character, and the stability of his throne was dependent on Abner, the able commander of his army. This high-spirited officer, taking offense at some interference on the part of Ish-bosheth, abruptly abandoned him and went over to David, to whom he pledged his allegiance. Shortly after, both Ish-bosheth and Abner were assassinated, the former by two of his courtiers, the latter by Joab, the commander of David's army.[1] A few years later the two divisions were reunited into one kingdom under David.

David's reign was a series of trials and triumphs. War, waged chiefly for securing hitherto unpossessed portions of the Promised Land, continued throughout the greater part of the time. Men liable for service in war were enrolled in twelve divisions of 24,000 each, the divisions serving in turn for one month.

Jebus, in the very heart of the kingdom, had up to this time been held by the native heathen. Its citizens deemed their fortress impregnable and sent David a taunting message that the blind and the lame within it were an effective defense against his attacks. This city he captured, changed its name to Jerusalem, and made it the national capital. He also brought the Ark of the Covenant to Jerusalem, thus making the city the religious center of the kingdom.[2]

Those old and troublesome foes of Israel, the Philistines, David drove out of their strongholds in the highlands, pursued them to their own country, and took from them the city of Gath. He also conquered Damascus, Zobah, Moab, Ammon, and Edom. Through these conquests David's territory extended from the Mediterranean to the Euphrates, and embraced an area ten times greater than that over which Saul ruled.

One of the most prolonged wars of the reign was that conducted by Joab against the Ammonites. This clever general, having gained possession of the reservoirs for the water supply of Rabbah, the capital of Ammon, sent for David that he might by his presence at the capture of the city have the personal honor arising from the victory. It was while this war was in progress that David's sinful conduct in the matter of Uriah took place.[3]

David's greatest troubles, which were, in large measure, the outcome of polygamy, were caused by his own sons. Amnon's shameful misconduct, followed by his death, instigated by Absalom, and this again followed by Absalom's conspiracy, rebellion, and death, weighed heavily upon him. Then, in quick succession, came the rebellion of the northern tribes led by Sheba.[4]

[1] 2 Sam. 3: 30; 4: 7.
[2] 2 Sam. 5: 6-9.
[3] 2 Sam. 11: 1-17; 12: 26-31.
[4] 2 Sam. 13: 1-14, 28, 29; 15; 18.

The story of David's hasty flight from Jerusalem over Olivet and across the Jordan to escape from Absalom, is touchingly sad. "And David went up by the ascent of mount Olivet, and wept as he went up, and had his head covered, and he went barefoot." Then what a picture of paternal love, which the basest filial ingratitude could not quench, is that of David mourning the death of Absalom,—"The king was much moved, and he went up to the chamber over the gate, and wept: and as he went, thus he said, O my son Absalom, my son, my son Absalom! would God I had died for thee, O Absalom, my son, my son!"

The closing days of David's life were embittered by Adonijah's attempt to seize the throne. This movement, which had the coöperation of Joab, was thwarted by the prompt action of the prophet Nathan, and the succession was secured to Solomon.

**Solomon** (1015–975 B. C.).—Solomon's reign of forty years was on the whole peaceful and prosperous, and it may be regarded as the golden age of the Hebrew nation. At this time the kingdom, extending from the borders of Egypt to the Euphrates, had its widest limits. The chief features of the reign comprised the founding and fortifying of cities, the building of temples, and enlarged intercourse with foreign nations.

Solomon's greatest work was the Temple at Jerusalem. This famous structure, for which David had prepared much material, planned after the pattern of the Tabernacle, was seven years in building. It was not remarkable for its great size, but it was adorned with lavish expenditure of gold, and other costly material. Timber was obtained from Mount Lebanon within the territory of Hiram, King of Tyre. It was floated in great rafts to Joppa and thence carried across the rugged country thirty-five miles to Jerusalem. Skilled artisans also were brought from Tyre. In compensation Solomon gave Hiram wheat and olive oil, and also presented to him twenty cities of northern Galilee—a gift which Hiram little appreciated.[1]

The dedication of the temple took place on the occasion of the annual festival known as the Feast of Tabernacles. Amid great national rejoicing and with a grand procession of the heads of the various tribes, the Ark of the Covenant was removed to the Most Holy Place within the veil of the temple.

The Ark at this time still contained the Two Tables of the Law. No mention is made of Aaron's rod, the Pot of Manna, or the Brazen Serpent, though this last-named was in existence down to the time of Hezekiah.

Solomon extended the walls of Jerusalem, added to their height, and built ramparts upon them for the defense of the city. Huge blocks of stone thirty feet in length are still to be seen in the wall. Excavations

[1] I Kings 5: 1–12; 9: 10–14.

were made beneath the city so as to form great reservoirs for water which was brought to them by aqueducts from beyond Bethlehem.

Solomon's wisdom exceeded that of all the wise men of his time. He was skilled in natural history. In his three thousand proverbs was crystallized the experience of the ages. Among his literary accomplishments, too, was the divine gift of poetry which he exercised in his songs numbering a thousand and five.

Not the Queen of Sheba alone, but kings of far-off countries, "sought the presence of Solomon, to hear his wisdom, that God had put in his heart," and in admiration of his greatness they bestowed on him rich presents of gold and other things of value.

Solomon derived large revenue from his traffic which, in alliance with Hiram, he carried on with distant lands beyond the seas. Once in three years came his ships to Ezion-geber, laden with gold, silver, precious stones, ivory, spices, and other products of Arabia and India.

The glory of Solomon's kingdom was short-lived. It dazzled for a brief space, like the blaze of a meteor, and then vanished away. Even in his own day there were clouds in the horizon that foreboded evil to come.

Polygamy and alliance with heathen nations wrought the downfall of the kingdom. Solomon had many wives,—from Egypt, Moab, Ammon, Edom, and other lands. These women led him astray, so that if he did not himself become a worshiper of idols, he erected temples in their honor and encouraged idolatry. The prophets of the day warned him but without effect.

In the tribe of Ephraim was a young man named Jeroboam, active, industrious, enterprising. Solomon took him into his service and gave him high position. The prophet Ahijah met Jeroboam on the highway, took him aside in the field, and by symbolic act stirred within him ambitious thoughts of empire. The young man, unable to wait God's time, as did David, assumed regal airs and aroused the suspicions of the king. To save his life he fled to Egypt where he was taken into favor and remained until after the death of Solomon.

**The Disruption.**—The line of cleavage between North and South—always visible, at times threatening—now, on the death of Solomon widened into disruption. Magnificent structures, costly equipage, and a luxurious court, however much it added to national glory, meant heavy taxes and oppression of the people.

Rehoboam, Solomon's son and successor, evidently hoping to conciliate the proud Ephraimites by honoring that ancient center within their bounds, chose Shechem as the place for his coronation. Here, with Jeroboam at their head, the discontented tribes demanded redress of grievances. Receiving a haughty reply from their ill-advised king, with the national cry of dissent—"To your tents, O Israel—" they declared their independence of the House of David. The central, northern, and eastern tribes withdrew their allegiance from the House of David and formed a separate state known as the Kingdom of Israel. There remained to Rehoboam only the tribes of Judah, part of Benjamin, and the weak tribe of Simeon. The usually accepted date of the division is 975 B. C., but some recent investigators make it 937 B. C.

The division line between the two kingdoms was somewhat variable according as the one or the other prevailed. In the main, on the western side the Valley of Aijalon and on the eastern side Wady Suweinit formed the boundary. Bethel was generally in the northern kingdom, though it sometimes fell to the southern.[1] "From Geba to Beer-sheba" was the proverbial expression of the limits of Judah.

[1] 2 Chron. 13: 19; 16: 6.

## CHAPTER XXV

### THE KINGDOM OF ISRAEL

THE Kingdom of Israel had a brief existence of about two hundred and fifty years. During this period there were nineteen kings, belonging to nine different dynasties, usually ending with conspiracy and the murder of the king. Throughout the history of the kingdom, plot succeeded plot, and one adventurer after another seized the throne. The army was often made the instrument of carrying out the change from one dynasty to another. It was thus that Zimri gained the throne, and thus was it that he in turn was overcome by Omri. To save himself from capture Zimri shut himself up in his palace, set it on fire, and perished in the flames. In like manner Jehu secured the throne. The most prominent of the kings were Jeroboam, Omri, Ahab, Jehu, and Jeroboam II.

The following is the complete list of kings with the usually accepted date of accession:—

| | | | |
|---|---|---|---|
| Jeroboam | 975 B. C. | Jehu | 884 B. C. |
| Nadab | 954 | Jehoahaz | 856 |
| Baasha | 953 | Joash | 840 |
| Elah | 930 | Jeroboam II | 825 |
| Zimri | 929 | Zechariah | 773 |
| Omri | 929 | Shallum | 772 |
| Ahab | 918 | Menahem | 772 |
| Ahaziah | 898 | Pekahiah | 761 |
| Jehoram | 896 | Pekah | 759 |
| | | Hoshea | 730* |

Shechem was the first capital, but during the reign of Jeroboam it was changed for Tirzah. Later, Omri built the strongly-fortified city of Samaria and made it the permanent capital.

Jeroboam, fearing that if his people went to Jerusalem to worship they might be drawn back to their old allegiance to the House of David, established two religious centers—one at Dan in the extreme north, and the other at Bethel on the southern border. Probably in imitation of Egyptian custom, he placed in each a golden calf as representative of deity. Then in place of the festivals provided for by the Mosaic law, he established a festival of his own devising, to be held at Bethel. In this way he laid the foundation of that idolatry which characterized the

---

* Some chronologists suppose an interregnum between Jeroboam II and Zechariah, and another interregnum between Pekah and Hoshea.

northern kingdom throughout its whole history and gained for himself the bad distinction "Jeroboam, who made Israel to sin."[1]

A memorable incident occurred at Bethel on the occasion of one of these festivals. While Jeroboam, as priest, was sacrificing to the golden calf, a prophet from the land of Judah appeared on the scene. After watching the proceedings for a little, in solemn imprecation he declared that the time would come when a prince of the House of David would slay the priests of the high places on the altar at Bethel and burn upon it human bones. Then as a sign of his divine authority to make this prediction, he said the altar would be rent and the ashes poured out, which immediately took place.[2]

Ahab's reign was signalized for unexampled religious declension. This wicked and weak king, the pliant tool of his infamous and stronger-minded Zidonian wife Jezebel, established Baal-worship in Israel and persecuted the worshipers of Jehovah.

In the reigns of Ahab, Ahaz, and Jehoram, lived that remarkable man Elijah, with whose mission are connected many interesting incidents of Bible story. The picture one would form of this man is that of a restless wanderer, long-haired, lithe and agile, clad in rough attire. Thus of rude exterior, he was uncourtly and austere in manner, of nervous temperament, unconventional, calling things by their right names. His disciple and successor Elisha lived during the reigns of Jehu and Jehoash. Jonah, Amos, and Hosea, prophets of the northern kingdom, lived in the reigns of Jeroboam II and Menahem.

Wars prevailed throughout the greater part of the nation's existence. Israel and Judah, sometimes allies, were often at war with each other. Damascus, which became independent on the death of Solomon, was a formidable enemy during the reigns of Ahab and several of his successors. Benhadad of Damascus, with thirty-two petty kings as allies, probably his vassals, besieged Samaria. Ahab readily submitted to the payment of tribute but refused further demands. This refusal led to renewed hostilities in which Benhadad was defeated.[3] Later, however, while attempting to recover Ramoth-gilead, Ahab was defeated and slain.[4] Again came reverse to the Syrians at a siege of Samaria, when, panic-stricken, they fled, leaving their store of provisions and vast treasures behind them.[5] But during the reign of Jehu, Hazael overran the whole of his territory on the east of the Jordan.[6] And yet again Israel was victorious in the reign of Jeroboam II.[7]

Moab, long a vassal state, paying the king of Israel large tribute in sheep and wool, having rebelled on the death of Ahab, was laid waste by an allied army of Israel and Judah, led by Joram and Jehoshaphat.

---

[1] 1 Kings 12: 26-33.    [2] 1 Kings 13: 1-32.    [3] 1 Kings, ch. 20.    [4] 1 Kings 22: 1-40.
[5] 2 Kings 6: 24 to 7: 1-20.    [6] 2 Kings 10: 32, 33.    [7] 2 Kings 14: 25.

During the siege of Kir-hareseth, a city near the south end of the Dead Sea, Mesha, King of Moab, reduced to straits, offered his eldest son for a burnt offering on the city wall in sight of the Hebrew army. The allied kings were so horrified by the deed that they raised the siege and withdrew to their own land.[1]

In 1868 French explorers discovered at Dibon, the ancient capital of Moab, a *stele* or slab of black basalt, with an inscription upon it by Mesha, referring to this event of Bible history. The inscription contains thirty-four lines in the Moabite dialect, which differs little from Hebrew. Before the stone could be removed it was badly broken by rival Arabs. The fragments are now in the Louvre in Paris.

About fifty years before its fall, during the reign of Menahem, Israel was invaded by Pul, King of Assyria, and was compelled to pay a tribute equal to nearly $2,000,000.[2] Thirty years later, during the reign of Pekah, Tiglath-pileser of Assyria conquered the country and carried off captive the inhabitants of Galilee and Gilead.[3] Hoshea, Pekah's successor, submitted and paid tribute to the king of Assyria, thus for the time saving the remnant of his kingdom. But at a later date, during the reign of Shalmaneser IV, trusting to Egypt for assistance, he threw off his allegiance. Shalmaneser then invaded the country and laid siege to Samaria. For three years the city held out, but finally, reduced by famine, it was compelled to yield.[4] Sargon, who had in the meantime succeeded to the throne of Assyria, carried away captive the king and principal inhabitants of the land. The country was afterwards settled by people deported from the east by the king of Assyria.[5] Through their intermarriage with the Israelites who remained in the land, there sprang a mixed race known in later times as Samaritans.

[1] 2 Kings 3 : 4-27.   [2] 2 Kings 15 : 19.   [3] 2 Kings 15 : 29.
[4] 2 Kings 17 : 1-6.   [5] 2 Kings 17 : 24.

## CHAPTER XXVI

## THE KINGDOM OF JUDAH

AFTER the disruption the southern section, known as the Kingdom of Judah, continued until the captivity to be ruled by the descendants of David without change of dynasty. There were in all nineteen kings and one queen, of whom the most distinguished were Asa, Jehoshaphat, Joash, Amaziah, Jotham, Hezekiah, and Josiah.

The following is the complete list of rulers with the date of accession: —

| Rehoboam | 975 B. C. | Jotham | 758 B. C. |
| Abijah | 951 | Ahaz | 741 |
| Asa | 955 | Hezekiah | 725 |
| Jehoshaphat | 914 | Manasseh | 696 |
| Jehoram | 889 | Amon | 641 |
| Ahaziah | 885 | Josiah | 639 |
| Athaliah | 884 | Jehoahaz | 609 |
| Joash | 878 | Jehoiakim | 609 |
| Amaziah | 838 | Jehoiachin | 598 |
| Uzziah (or Azariah) | 809 | Zedekiah | 598 |

Rehoboam was not willing that the revolting tribes should cut themselves loose, and he gathered a large army for the recovery of their allegiance; but, accepting the counsel of the prophet Shemaiah, he abandoned the enterprise. There were, however, large accessions of priests, Levites, and others from the northern kingdom, who left their old homes on account of the idol-worship which Jeroboam had established. The most important event of the reign was the invasion of the country with the plundering of the temple by Shishak, King of Egypt. The chief feature of Abijah's short reign was a great victory over Jeroboam with the capture of Bethel and other border towns.

Asa was noted as a religious reformer. He also added to the military strength of the kingdom by building fortresses and gathering a large army. Alarmed by the threatening attitude of the king of Israel, Asa formed an alliance with the king of Damascus, giving him the temple treasures as the price of his support.[1]

Jehoshaphat had a long and prosperous reign. Various neighboring states, by the payment of tribute, recognized his supremacy. He carried out important religious reforms and adopted vigorous measures for instructing his people in the law. He built a line of forts along his northern frontier and strengthened the army.[2] During this reign the

[1] 2 Chron. 16 : 1–6.  
[2] 2 Chron. 17 : 1–19.

Moabites, Ammonites, and Edomites invaded the land. Marching round the south end of the Dead Sea and along its western shore, they came up to the highlands by the pass of En-gedi and thence advanced to the wilderness of Tekoa. Jehoshaphat and his people, alarmed by the presence of such a formidable foe, betook themselves to prayer. The answer soon came. The allied forces of the enemy quarreled among themselves and destroyed each other, leaving for Jehoshaphat no other task than the gathering up of the spoil.[1]

Among the mistakes of Jehoshaphat were his alliances with the idolatrous kings of Israel. He allowed his son and successor Jehoram to marry Athaliah, the daughter of Ahab and Jezebel, thus bringing untold evil to Judah. He joined Ahab in war against Syria for the recovery of Ramoth-gilead. He entered into commercial relations with Ahaziah for traffic over the Red Sea—an enterprise which resulted in total failure. Later he joined Jehoram in an expedition against Mesha, King of Moab.[2]

Jehoram began his reign by the murder of all his brothers. Then, influenced by his wife Athaliah, he established the worship of Baal, and his whole reign, though short, was one of wickedness and disaster. The Edomites, who had been subject to Israel since the time of David, revolted; the Philistines and Arabians invaded the country and carried away captive all the king's sons except Azariah.[3]

Azariah, guided by the counsel of his mother Athaliah, was pursuing the evil course of the House of Ahab when his reign was cut short. While he was on a visit to Joram, King of Israel, the revolt under Jehu took place, and he fell with other victims of Jehu's zeal.

Athaliah, hearing of her son's death, with monstrous wickedness put to death, as she supposed, all the princes of the House of David. One of her grandsons, however, Joash, then about a year old, stolen away by his aunt, escaped the cruel slaughter.[4] Hidden in one of the chambers of the temple, the young prince was cared for by this aunt's husband, the priest Jehoiada.[5] When he was seven years old, by a well-laid scheme devised by the good priest, Joash was presented to the assembled people and crowned king amid their joyful acclaim. Athaliah, while shouting "Treason, Treason," paid the just penalty of her deeds in being speedily put to death.[6]

The early part of the reign of Joash was noted for a great religious revival led by Jehoiada. The worship of Baal was abolished and the temple of Jehovah repaired. After the death of Jehoiada, Joash fell into idolatry and even commanded this faithful friend's son Zechariah to be stoned to death, because of his warning against idol-worship. The last words of the dying martyr—"The Lord look upon it, and require it"

[1] 2 Chron. 20: 1–30.    [2] 2 Chron. 21: 5, 6; 22; 20: 35–37; 2 Kings 3: 4–27.
[3] 2 Chron. 21: 8–20.    [4] 2 Chron. 22: 10, 11.    [5] 2 Chron. 22: 12.    [6] 2 Chron. 23: 1–15.

—were in strange contrast with those of him who was the first to suffer the same form of death under the Christian dispensation.[1] This long reign ended in disaster and violence. A Syrian army invaded the country and carried away the treasures of the temple and of the king's palace. Rescued from the general massacre of princes in his infancy, Joash fell at last by the hand of the assassin.[2]

Amaziah waged successful war against the Edomites and brought away many captives. Joash, King of Israel, afterwards defeated him, broke down the walls of Jerusalem, and carried away much plunder.[3]

Uzziah, who reigned fifty-two years, was famous as a warrior and maintained a large army. He is also spoken of as a lover of husbandry, and as having great wealth in cattle and vineyards. Elated by his successful enterprises, he entered the temple and assumed the priests' functions of burning incense. For this he was smitten with leprosy.[4]

Jotham was a worshiper of the true God. He was also famous as a builder of cities, castles, and towers. He carried on successful wars against the Ammonites and compelled them to pay him large tribute.[5]

Ahaz was a gross idolater, worshiping images of Baal and sacrificing even his own sons in burnt offering to his false gods.

Unable to withstand the combined forces of Pekah, King of Israel, and Rezin, King of Damascus, he asked aid from Tiglath-pileser, King of Assyria, at the same time sending him a rich present which he made up in part from the temple treasure. The Assyrian monarch, well pleased over the opportunity of taking part in western affairs, marched to Damascus, captured the city, and sent away captive many of its inhabitants. Ahaz met the conqueror in Damascus, but he gained little for the gold he had sent him.

While at Damascus Ahaz saw a heathen altar the fashion of which pleased him. He at once sent a model of it to Jerusalem ordering an altar made after the same gattern. On his return he commanded that this new altar be used in place of the one before the temple.[6]

Hezekiah's reign was a remarkable reformation period. This good king removed idols from the land, restored the worship of Jehovah, and enriched the temple service. The brazen serpent which Moses made in the wilderness, having become an object of worship, Hezekiah had the courage to call it "a piece of brass" and to break it in pieces.[7] Having determined on a grand celebration of the passover feast he sent messengers all through the land, calling on the people to be present. He even sent letters to the remnant from the captivity in the northern kingdom, urging them to join in keeping the festival. Some accepted the invitation, but others

[1] 2 Chron. 24 : 15–22; Acts 7 : 60.  [2] 2 Chron. 24 : 23–26.  [3] 2 Chron., ch. 25.
[4] 2 Chron., ch. 26.  [5] 2 Chron. 27 : 1–9.  [6] 2 Kings 16 : 10–16.
[7] 2 Kings 18 : 4 ; 2 Chron., ch. 29.

mocked the postmen and laughed them to scorn.[1] Hezekiah also greatly improved the water supply for Jerusalem.

One of the chief events of the reign was an invasion of the country by Sennacherib of Assyria. Hezekiah, to secure peace, agreed to pay tribute, stripping the temple of its gold to obtain the means of discharging his obligations.[2] Not satisfied with this, Sennacherib renewed his demands and threatened the same fate to Judah as had befallen the northern kingdom. Hezekiah, filled with alarm, gave himself to prayer. In Isaiah, the greatest of the prophets, the distressed king found a comforter and a counselor. Isaiah came to him with a message from Jehovah, bidding him not to fear, for He would defend him from the insolent foe. And so it came to pass. Sennacherib's vast army was destroyed by a messenger of the Lord, whether it was by a sudden visitation of plague or otherwise can only be a matter of conjecture. The haughty Assyrian got him hastily back to Nineveh.[3]

The lengthening of Hezekiah's life in answer to his prayer is also one of the interesting events of the reign.[4]

Manasseh, who succeeded Hezekiah, not only reëstablished idolatry, but cruelly put to death the worshipers of Jehovah. Chastised by a period of captivity in Babylon, he came back to his kingdom a better man and made some amends for his former wickedness. His son Amon, during a reign of two years, followed the evil example of his father's earlier life.

Josiah succeeded to the throne when he was but a child of eight years. He had good advisers, among whom was the prophetess Huldah, a woman of great ability and influence. Thus encouraged, Josiah repaired the temple, purified the land from its idolatry, and restored the ancient worship. While working in the temple, the priests found a copy of the law of the Lord as given through Moses, which had long lain hidden during the years of idol-worship. Josiah read it with care and enforced its commands. His reign was thus noteworthy as a period of reform rather than for the strength of its foreign policy. Josiah visited Bethel, the headquarters of Jeroboam's idol-worship. Taking the bones from the ancient sepulchers in the neighborhood, he burned them on Jeroboam's altar; he also slew on it the priests of the high places; then he utterly destroyed it and burned the idol grove. In this literal fashion he fulfilled a long-forgotten prediction.[5]

Meanwhile the supremacy in the far East had passed over from Nineveh to Babylon. Then followed the struggle between Babylonia and

---

[1] 2 Chron. 30: 1-11; 32: 30.　　　　　　　　[2] 2 Kings 18: 13-16.
[3] 2 Kings 18: 17-37; 19: 1-37; 2 Chron. 32: 1-22.
[4] 2 Chron. 32: 24; Isa., ch. 38.
[5] 1 Kings 13: 1-3; 2 Kings 23: 15-20.

Egypt, and the little kingdom of Judah, lying in the pathway of these great powers, was now the victim of the one and now of the other. Josiah held himself as a vassal of the king of Babylon. Accordingly when Pharaoh-necho with a large army was marching northerly along the coast plain of Palestine to make war against his eastern rival, Josiah felt called on to oppose his progress. Meeting the king of Egypt at the entrance of Esdraelon, near Megiddo, he was defeated and slain.[1]

The good prophet Jeremiah began his ministry during this reign. He was greatly affected by the death of Josiah and mourned his loss as a national calamity. The prophets Zephaniah and Nahum also lived at this time.

Matters were now in a wretched state and so continued until the final overthrow of the kingdom. The so-called kings held their position simply as vassals either of Egypt or of Babylon. Idolatry prevailed and the prophets of Jehovah were persecuted.

Jehoahaz, son of Josiah, reigned but three months. On his return from the north Pharaoh-necho exacted heavy indemnity, sent Jehoahaz captive to Egypt, and placed on the throne his brother Eliakim, changing his name to Jehoiakim.[2] Nebuchadnezzar, in his turn, dethroned Jehoiakim, and made Jehoiachin, his son, king in his stead. Again at the end of three months, distrusting the loyalty of Jehoiachin, he sent him in chains to Babylon and raised to the throne Josiah's youngest son Eliakim. At the same time Nebuchadnezzar plundered the temple of its furniture and deported to Babylon ten thousand of the principal inhabitants, including nobles, officials, artisans, and warriors. Among the captives was the prophet Ezekiel; Daniel also and his three friends were taken away at this time, or as some think at an earlier date (597 B. C.).[3]

At this crisis of affairs there was division and strife among the citizens. A strong party, including the king's advisers, hoping to gain help from Egypt, favored revolt from the king of Babylon. The prophet Jeremiah strongly denounced this course, thereby bringing on himself the fierce hostility of that party. Charged with treason against his country and with working in the interests of Babylon, he was thrust into a vile dungeon where he suffered greatly.[4]

Zedekiah disapproved of the ill treatment to which Jeremiah was subjected, but he lacked strength of will, and was so completely under the influence of his courtiers that he failed to assert his authority. Thus, against his better judgment and regardless of his oath of fealty to the king of Babylon, moving on to the ruin of himself and his kingdom, he formed an alliance with Egypt.

The day of reckoning came. The Babylonian army overran the

---

[1] 2 Kings 23 : 28–30 ; 2 Chron. 35 : 20–27.   [2] 2 Kings 23 : 31–37 ; 2 Chron. 36 : 1–4.
[3] 2 Kings 24 : 1–17 ; 2 Chron. 36 : 9, 10.   [4] Jer. 32 : 1–5 ; chs. 36, 37, 38.

country and invested Jerusalem. Pharaoh sent a strong force to aid the besieged, affording brief respite and awakening false hope. Nebuchadnezzar having repulsed the Egyptians resumed the siege. Many were killed in the conflict, but more died of famine and pestilence. Crazed by hunger, women ate the flesh of their own children, and persons of high station were compelled to use the vilest refuse for food. For sixteen months the siege went on, when the walls gave way, and at the midnight hour the enemy rushed into the city. The walls, the temple, the whole city were leveled to the ground and burned.[1]

Many of the inhabitants had already fled to neighboring countries; others had escaped to the wilderness or had hidden in caves. The number of men carried to Babylon at this time is given as 832, but including women and children it would be from 3,000 to 4,000.[2]

Zedekiah with his wives and children sought safety in flight. By the same route that David fled from Absalom, he hastened over Olivet toward the Jordan Valley. He was captured on the way and taken to Riblah, thirty-five miles north of Baalbec, where Nebuchadnezzar had his headquarters. After reproaching him for his lack of fidelity, Nebuchadnezzar ordered his sons to be slain in his presence, and then his eyes to be put out. Bound with fetters Zedekiah was then taken to Babylon.[3] Thus were literally fulfilled the two seemingly contradictory predictions of Jeremiah and Ezekiel. The one had foretold that he should be taken to Babylon; the other that he should not see it.[4] Two of Judah's kings were now held captive in Babylon. After being kept in prison thirty-seven years Jehoiachin was set free and highly honored by the king then occupying the throne.[5]

Jerusalem was now a mass of ruins, forsaken and desolate. Many of the poorer class of people still remained in the villages and smaller towns. A few also of the higher classes, whose loyalty could be depended on, were left in the land. No doubt most of those who had fled during the war returned after the Babylonians had withdrawn. Jeremiah was taken out of prison by Nebuzaradan, the commander of the Babylonian army, and told that he was free to go to Babylon or remain in Judæa. He chose to remain.[6]

Gedaliah was made governor of the impoverished people that remained in Judæa. He had his headquarters at Mizpah, to which place gathered many of those who had escaped captivity, among whom was Jeremiah. Soon also those who had fled to neighboring countries began to return to the home-land. Gedaliah's rule was short. A certain man named Ishmael of the House of David, with a small band of associates,

[1] 2 Kings 25: 1–17; 2 Chron. 36: 11–21.  [2] Jer. 52: 29.
[3] 2 Kings 25: 1–11; 2 Chron. 36: 11–20.  [4] Jer. 32:4; Ezek. 12:13.
[5] 2 Kings 25: 27–30.  [6] Jer. 39: 11–14.

came to him, and, under guise of friendship, treacherously killed him together with many of the people at Mizpah. Ishmael then fled to the Ammonites. Fearing that the king of Babylon would hold them responsible for the murder of Gedaliah, many of those who had been living at Mizpah sought safety in Egypt, taking Jeremiah with them. They made their homes in the border towns of Tahpanhes and Migdol.[1] A third deportation from Judæa to Babylon followed, probably as punishment for the killing of the governor. It comprised 745 men or including women and children about 2,500[2] (582 B. C.).

[1] 2 Kings 25: 22–26; Jer., chs. 40, 41, 42, 43.   [2] Jer. 52: 30.

## CHAPTER XXVII

### THE BABYLONIAN PERIOD

The system of deportation of the inhabitants of conquered lands to some distant country was common with the Assyrians and Babylonians. No doubt the chief object was to break up the national existence of a troublesome people and place them under such conditions as would afford guarantee against rebellion. In the case of the Jews it was desirable to remove them beyond the reach of Egyptian influence.

The Babylonian exiles, especially those of the first deportation, included the best of the Jewish people and such as would naturally be leaders in any national movement. While some of the more troublesome were put to death, imprisoned, or sold into slavery, the great majority were placed in communities by themselves and given the privilege of their own local government with their own officers, laws, and religion. One of their important colonies was by the "River" Chebar, which has been identified by recent explorers as the Chebar Canal near ancient Nippur.[1] The exiles of the later deportations, having been more persistent in their rebellion, were probably treated with greater severity.

Some of the exiles in Babylon had earnest longings for the home-land, and they were greatly cheered by the hope held out by the prophets that, if not themselves, their children would return to the land of their forefathers.[2] In the monotonous plains of Babylonia they would miss the varied scenery, the mountains and the valleys, the rugged hills and deep glens which gave charm to their own Judæan land.

But most of them would soon become accustomed to the new conditions. It was a fruitful land, this land of exile to which they had come, far surpassing that home-land which they had left beyond the great desert. The Chaldæans round them were of kindred stock, for this was the native land of Abraham, the great progenitor of the Hebrew people. The language of these people, known as the Aramaic, was similar to their own; and so they engaged in the business of the country, mingled with its inhabitants, and adopted many of its customs. Some of them, as Daniel and his three friends, rose to positions of trust and honor in the government of the great empire.

There was danger in this land of plenty and of many gods, of their forgetting the land and the religion of their forefathers. And some of

---

[1] Ezek. 1 ; 3.  
[2] Ps. 137.

them did forget. Thus they had need of faithful teachers, like the prophet Ezekiel, to instruct them and warn them against declension.

New conditions would, in some respects, lead to modifications of old-time worship. There was no temple service; the great national festivals were discontinued. Instead, the Sabbath came to be observed more as a day when little communities would gather together for reading the Scriptures and for prayer. Thus probably originated the synagogue service which in later times became so marked a feature in the religious life of Palestine.

The development of scribism was an important feature of the captivity period. The name scribe indeed occurs in the early history of the Hebrew kingdom, but it then designated a royal secretary or officer who wrote the king's letters and decrees and kept his accounts.[1] The scribe's functions gradually changed. Even before the captivity they involved the study and classifying of the sacred writings. Now, during the exile, the scribes had charge of these books. It was their business to transcribe them when new copies were required, to read them on the Sabbath to the little assemblies of the people, to explain anything that was obscure, and, as new conditions arose, to show how precepts and laws applied to cases not specifically stated in the text. Still later when the Hebrew language was falling into disuse, the scribes translated what they read into the Aramaic tongue.[2]

Their work thus involving very responsible duties, the scribes became a distinct class, for admission to which candidates underwent special training.[3] This training, said to have begun at a very early age, was carried on under some rabbi who was skilled in sacred lore.

It is impossible to trace the development of scribism through the different stages of its history. The expansion went on gradually during the Persian and Grecian periods until, at the beginning of the Christian era, the scribe was the most important functionary in the Jewish economy.

At some period, just when may not be certainly known, it fell to the scribes to discriminate between the writings that were to be accepted as of divine authority and those that were of mere human origin, of selecting and compiling the scattered fragments or *excerpta* into books, and of classifying and arranging these books according to some principle of order, as the Law, the Prophets, and the Hagiographa. Tradition attributes this work to Ezra who is described as "a ready scribe in the law of Moses" and as "a scribe of the law of the God of heaven."[4]

In connection with the synagogue service, which was designed mainly for instruction, the scribe was a teacher, whose duty it was "to give the sense" of the sacred writings, citing the comments or unwritten

---

[1] 2 Sam. 8:17; 20:25; 1 Kings 4:3; 2 Kings 12:10.  
[2] Neh. 8:8-13.  
[3] 1 Chron. 2:55.  
[4] Ezra 7:6, 12.

law, handed down orally, as it was believed, from the time of Moses, and perhaps also giving his own interpretation of these traditions.

In their work of transcribing the Scriptures the scribes were exceedingly scrupulous to have everything exactly as it was in the text from which they copied, even counting the letters and making every letter like that in the original. In giving the meaning and application of the text it became their custom in later times to descend into nice points of casuistry, and into many details of the most trifling character, often giving these trivialities an importance beyond the weightier matters of the law. Their minute attention to these little things is illustrated in the questionings of the scribes and Pharisees in regard to the conduct of Jesus and his disciples in the matter of defilement and of keeping the Sabbath.[1] The scribes determined the line of duty by what "was said by them of old time"; Jesus "taught as one having authority."[2]

The teaching of the scribes was based on the belief that in the first instance God gave Moses certain explanations of the law, or addenda to it, which were passed down orally through responsible persons from generation to generation. It was held also that, in adaptation to the needs of the different ages, these original traditions were expanded by additional comments given through divinely-inspired interpreters, which were in like manner handed down orally from one age to another. During the second century of the Christian era the original traditions were compiled in a book known as the Mishna; the comments on these traditions formed another book called the Gemara; while the Mishna and the Gemara together formed the Talmud.

[1] Matt. 15:1-9; 23:1-7.  [2] Matt. 7:28, 29.

## CHAPTER XXVIII
## THE MEDO-PERSIAN PERIOD

The conquest of Babylon by Cyrus brought the Jews under Medo-Persian rule. By royal edict the captives were permitted to return to Palestine and rebuild their ruined city and temple. There was, however, little enthusiasm among the exiles to undertake this wearisome and dangerous march of seven or eight hundred miles across the vast desert. A little band was all that could be mustered for the journey.

Just how many there were in the first company is a matter of conjecture. Close examination shows that the number given by Ezra is the grand total of those who returned to Jerusalem under various leaders at different times.[1] Between the time of Sheshbazzar and that of Nehemiah, who are included in the list of leaders, nearly 100 years elapsed (538–445 B. C.).

Cyrus appointed Sheshbazzar governor of Judah, and gave into his charge the sacred vessels of the temple which Nebuchadnezzar had carried away. He also authorized him to collect funds for rebuilding the temple from all who were willing to help on the work.[2] Zerubbabel very shortly succeeded Sheshbazzar as governor, and under him and Joshua the high priest the temple was built and its service set in order.

Some scholars suppose that Sheshbazzar was the Chaldee name of Zerubbabel; while others, probably more correctly, consider that two different persons are spoken of, Sheshbazzar being a son of the captive King Jehoiachin and uncle of Zerubbabel.[3]

Within a few months of his arrival in Jerusalem Zerubbabel arranged for obtaining timber for the temple from Mount Lebanon, according to the grant of Cyrus, bringing it to Joppa, as had been done in the building of Solomon's temple. The altar of burnt offering was set up on its old site, the regular sacrifices were offered, and the festivals were observed as in the olden time. The foundations of the temple were laid with due ceremonial as had been provided for. But here the work ceased and nothing more was done for about seventeen years.

This delay in building the temple was in part due to opposition from the people of the surrounding country, especially from those of mixed Hebrew and heathen descent who occupied the territory of the northern kingdom of Israel. At first these people asked permission to join in building the temple and in the worship of Jehovah; but Zerubbabel and

---

[1] Ezra 2: 64, 65.  [2] Ezra, ch. 1.  [3] 1 Chron. 3: 16–19.

Joshua very decidedly refused to allow them any share in such service. This may seem like a hard and unjustifiable exclusion, but the conditions are too imperfectly known to warrant any severe judgment. The outcome of the refusal was opposition to the work and that undying hatred between Jews and Samaritans which was handed down through the ages.[1]

The delay in building the temple, however, was, in large measure, perhaps chiefly, due to the apathy of the Jews themselves. While they erected fine dwellings for their own use, possibly using materials that had been provided for the temple, they solaced themselves and excused their inaction by the specious plea that the time for building the Lord's house had not come.

It was not until about 520 B. C. that the building of the temple was resumed. Cyrus had been dead several years, two of his successors had also passed away, and the throne of Persia was now occupied by Darius I. The apathetic people of Jerusalem were awakened and aroused to action by the stirring appeals of Haggai and Zechariah, two zealous prophets who had returned from the captivity.[2] The work was then taken up again and carried forward with alacrity.

The builders were watched. Reports were sent to the king that these restless Jews should be looked after. Darius, who had already had trouble enough with insurrections, ordered search of the records at Ecbatana to ascertain if the Jews had been authorized by Cyrus, as they asserted, to carry on the work in which they were engaged. The edict was found. Whereupon the king commanded his officers in the western province to aid the building of the temple with funds from the royal treasury and threatened with severe punishment any persons who obstructed its progress.[3] Accordingly the work prospered and was brought to successful completion in the sixth year of Darius's reign (518 B. C.).[4]

Of the events which took place in Palestine during nearly three fourths of the century that followed the completion of the temple, both historian and chronicler make little mention. Meanwhile the great world-powers of the age were busy. Within this period Greece was invaded by Darius and Xerxes, and there were fought the battles of Marathon, Thermopylæ, and Salamis. This same Xerxes, as some suppose, was the Ahasuerus who put away his wife Vashti and took in her place the beautiful Jewess Esther, and at whose court figured in different capacities Haman and Mordecai.[5]

When next the curtain rises on Jewish affairs the scene opens at Ecbatana in far-off Persia. It is the twentieth year of the reign of Artaxerxes Longimanus, in the year 445 B. C. The new character presented is Nehemiah, a Jew, a man of strong personality, wealthy, high in

---

[1] Ezra 4 : 1-4.   [2] Hag., ch. 1 ; Zech., ch. 8.   [3] Ezra 4 : 1-24 ; 5 : 3-17 ; 6 ; 1-12.
[4] Ezra 6 : 13-15.   [5] Esther 1 : 10-22 ; chs. 2-10.

the king's favor, whom he serves as cup-bearer.  The story of how this clever and noble-minded man learned the state of Jerusalem, of his grief over its defenseless condition, of how he gained from the king leave of absence, with a royal commission as governor of Judah and possessed of authority to rebuild the walls of Jerusalem, is a graphic and beautiful pen-picture.[1]

Of the period of silence between the finishing of the temple and the appearance of Nehemiah, enough is told to show that in Jerusalem it was a time of social and religious declension, of oppression of the weak by the strong, and of mockery in the service of God.  Not indeed of idol-worship, for of this the Jews had been weaned during the Captivity; but it was a grudging service that was given to Jehovah and a placing on his altar of such things only as could be turned to little account for selfish ends.[2]

In tracing the narrative of events as given in the books of Ezra and Nehemiah a difficulty presents itself in regard to the priority in point of time of these two workers.  Ezra's visit to Jerusalem is said to have been the earlier of the two; whereas internal evidence would reverse the order.  Ezra's strict measures in the matter of intermarriage with the heathen, which were generally adopted by the people, if they had preceded the coming of Nehemiah, must have made the condition of matters in this regard found by the latter, to say the least, very improbable.  The practice of such intermarriage seems to have been going on without restriction when Nehemiah came upon the scene.  Again, Ezra's prayer indicates that the walls of Jerusalem were then completed, which was the special work of Nehemiah.  It has been suggested that the date of Ezra's visit should read thirty-seventh year of Artaxerxes in place of "seventh year," which would make the date 427 B. C. instead of 457 B. C.  Others again find an explanation in supposing that Ezra's visit was in the seventh year of Artaxerxes II, that is in the year 398 B. C.[3]

Nehemiah's mission was specially for the building of the walls of Jerusalem.  On his arrival he set about his work in a systematic way and carried it through with surprising dispatch.  He encountered great obstacles—enough to have discouraged and baffled a man of less courage and energy.  Sanballat, the governor of Samaria, Tobiah, the Ammonite, and Geshem, the Arabian, with great persistency, by ridicule, open hostility, and ingenious stratagem, sought to frustrate the enterprise.  They stirred up the neighboring peoples—Arabians, Ammonites, and Philistines—to attack the workmen engaged in building the wall.  To meet this hostility Nehemiah divided his men into two companies—one for labor and one for defense.  Even the laborers kept their weapons by their

---

[1] Neh. 1:1–11; 2:1–8.  [2] Mal. 3:5; Neh. 5:1–5; Mal. 1:7, 8.
[3] See "History of the Jewish People," by Professor Kent, pp. 196–200.

side. Trumpeters were stationed at various places to summon the guard to any point where an attack might be made.[1]

Nehemiah's office of governor was to him a source of little personal gain. Seeing that the people were oppressed by heavy taxes, he refused, during the twelve years of his rule, to add to their burdens by exacting the salary attached to his position. His liberal hospitality shows that he was possessed of a large heart as well as of great wealth.[2] He seems to have gone back to Persia at the end of his twelve years' leave of absence and to have returned later to Jerusalem for another term.[3]

Nehemiah's vigor was as pronounced in his capacity of ruler as it was in that of builder. This is marked in his dealing with the question of Sabbath observance, and with that of intermarriage with the heathen.[4]

Ezra was accompanied to Jerusalem by about 6,000 of his people. He also received much gold and silver and many vessels for the temple service from others who preferred remaining in the land of captivity. King Ahasuerus, too, whether the first or the second Persian ruler of that name may not be certainly known, and the officers of his court gave him liberal aid. The total value of the contributions from all sources is estimated at over $4,000,000. The journey occupied about four and a half months.[5]

Ezra's chief work in Jerusalem was in the line of religious and social reform. It consisted in repairing the temple, organizing the temple service, instructing the people in the law, and in breaking up the practice of intermarriage with the heathen. He assembled the people in a wide open space in front of the water gate of the city, and mounting a high platform he read to them from the Book of the Law from early morning until midday. As he read, the Levites present explained the meaning to the people. Nehemiah also being present aided in the work. This was kept up from day to day for a week. The service was accompanied with prayer, rehearsing of God's mercies, and confession of sin, and was followed by great religious revival.[6]

After their exclusion from partnership in building the temple at Jerusalem and from worship with the Jews, the Samaritans erected a temple of their own on Mount Gerizim overlooking the ancient city of Shechem. For high priest in the service here they chose Manasseh, grandson of the Jewish high priest Eliashib, who had been expelled from Jerusalem because he refused to put away his wife, the daughter of Sanballat. The temple on Gerizim stood for 150 years, when it was destroyed by John Hyrcanus.

The enmity between Jews and Samaritans continued down through the centuries, and it was still in full vigor in the time of our Saviour. The

---

[1] Neh. 4 : 1–23; 6 : 1–19.  [2] Neh. 5 : 14–18.  [3] Neh. 13 : 6, 7.  [4] Neh. 13 ; 15–28.
[5] Ezra 7 : 8.  [6] Neh., chs. 8 , 9, 13 ; Ezra, chs. 9, 10.

direct road between Galilee and Judæa lay through Samaria, passing near the base of Gerizim, and Jews journeying to the feasts at Jerusalem were on the way subjected to serious outrage. Hence they were accustomed to take the longer route along the east side of the Jordan.

Down to the present day the Samaritans, now few in number, occupying a separate quarter in Nablus, hold their three great annual festivals on Mount Gerizim. They regard themselves as the true children of Jacob, having for their Bible only the Pentateuch and the Book of Joshua.

Jewish territory in the time of Ezra and Nehemiah was very small, not exceeding 400 square miles. Following the reforms of these great leaders there came a period of prosperity and expansion. Many Jews of the dispersion were attracted to the old home land, and the bounds of the little province were somewhat widened, especially on the north. Then, probably as the result of Jewish sympathy with revolt against Persian rule in Phœnicia and Egypt, there followed under Artaxerxes III a period of oppression. The account given by historians of these times, however, is very meager.

After Nehemiah the office of civil ruler seems to have become extinct, and the local government to have fallen under a hierarchy of which the high priest was the chief officer, and his associates formed a priestly aristocracy. The activity and influence of the scribes as religious teachers became more and more pronounced.

The synagogue, probably a product of the exile, was largely matured during the Persian period. Its first irregular stages may have existed in the time of the monarchy, but during the exile the Jews, deprived of temple service, would naturally hold meetings in the various localities where they were living. References that seem to imply this are found in the book of Ezekiel.[1] The prominence of the scribes after the return to Palestine would tend to establish the custom; while Ezra and Nehemiah had the qualifications required for giving it regular system. Later, during the Greek and Roman supremacy, when the Jews became widely dispersed, the influence of the synagogue on their character and life can scarcely be overestimated.

[1] Ezek. 8:1; 14:1; 20:1; 33:31; 11:15, 16.

# CHAPTER XXIX

## THE GREEK PERIOD.—333-168 B. C.

THE Greek Period of Jewish history dates from the conquests of Alexander the Great in Asia to the time of the Maccabees. While Alexander was carrying on the siege of Tyre, the Samaritans hastened to tender him their allegiance. The Jews moved more slowly. Jaddua, the high priest at Jerusalem, restrained by obligations to the king of Persia, at first refused submission. But after Tyre and Gaza had fallen, he reconsidered the matter and was ready to pledge loyalty to the great conqueror. Alexander made no show of resentment for this tardiness, but ever after treated the Jews with much consideration.

Alexander's aim was to build up out of the various peoples he had conquered one vast homogeneous empire. He would have all speaking the same language, observing the same laws, and professing the same religion. In carrying this purpose into effect, wherever he went he founded Greek cities and established Greek colonists, that they might be centers of influence for the working out of the assimilating process he had planned.

On the death of Alexander the two great divisions of his empire that gave continuity to the thread of history were Egypt and Syria. It was with the affairs of these two empires mainly that for the succeeding century and a half Jewish history was connected. In both of these empires the great conqueror's plans were adopted. Greek civilization was the ideal sought after. The rulers of Egypt during this period are known as the Ptolemies; those of Syria as the Seleucids or Seleucidæ. The new capital of Egypt was Alexandria, founded by Alexander; that of Syria was Antioch, founded by Seleucus, the first of the Seleucids.

Palestine geographically was more closely related to Syria, but for 125 years it, as well as Phœnicia, was held by Egypt. The Seleucid kings from time to time asserted their right to the country, and there were frequent contests between the two rivals over the disputed territory; Palestine, lying in the road between the contestants, was overrun by the opposing armies and often made the battle field. Then, as both countries claimed its allegiance, it was sure to be punished by one or the other for disloyalty.

For the most part the Jews were well treated by the Ptolemies, and were encouraged to settle in Alexandria and other cities of Egypt. The taxes demanded from them were moderate and they were allowed a measure of self-government. The high priest was at the head of civil as well as religious affairs, in the management of which he was aided by a council of scribes and elders. Meanwhile, also, the Jews were granted such privilege by the kings of Syria that many of them were induced to settle in Antioch and in various cities of Asia Minor.

The period is not lacking in interesting features. The Greek version of the Old Testament Scriptures known as the Septuagint was begun under the direction of Ptolemy Philadelphus for the Greek-speaking Jews of Alexandria. The work is said to have been done by seventy learned Jews and thus got the name Septuagint from the Greek word for seventy.

The battle of Banias, fought near Mount Hermon between Syria and Egypt, secured to Syria permanent possession of Palestine. While the war was going on the Jews suffered greatly. Their country was plundered, and many of the people were seized and sold into slavery, while others sought safety in flight.

The Jews were shown much favor by Antiochus the Great, who ruled over Syria at the time of the conquest. Those who had been sold as slaves were brought back, taxes were remitted until the country recovered from the effects of the war, the temple service was provided for, and Jewish law was enforced. So much confidence had Antiochus in the fidelity of the Jews that he brought 2,000 Jewish families from Babylon and placed them in the provinces of Asia Minor to counteract the disloyalty that prevailed in that part of his empire.

There were in Judæa at this time two strong opposing influences which have been described under the names Judaism and Hellenism. The first named was an intense devotion to external observance of the law of Moses as interpreted and expanded through the traditions of the scribes. Hellenism meant conformity to Greek custom and the adoption of Greek institutions. Both systems had gradations from the border land of indifference through the various degrees of partiality to intense devotion. With extreme Judaists righteousness consisted more in sacrifice, fasting, ablutions, and such like externals than in love to God and justice to one's neighbors. The thoroughgoing Hellenist would discard the whole system of Jehovah-worship for Greek games, the gymnasium, and sacrifices to the Greek gods. Unprincipled men, ambitious of preferment, of good standing at the Syrian court, or of social standing, were ready to become active instruments in uprooting the religion of their fathers and putting heathen worship in its place.

Antiochus, surnamed Epiphanes ("Illustrious") succeeded Antiochus the Great. Energetic, passionate, and unscrupulous, he set about establishing Hellenism throughout his dominion. No measures were too extreme for his purpose. Onias III, a zealous supporter of the faith of his fathers, was high priest. His brother Jason was the leader of the Hellenists in Jerusalem. Through bribery Jason persuaded Antiochus to depose

Onias and make him high priest in his brother's stead. He then proceeded along the most radical lines to carry out the schemes of his party. Among other things he established in Jerusalem a gymnasium where young men were taught to renounce their religion and to disown their nationality. In token that he meant no half measures he sent to Tyre a large sum of money, taken from the public treasury, in aid of a sacrificial festival to the god Hercules.

Soon there appeared a new rival for the office of high priest. A certain Menelaus, who was not even of the priestly tribe, by outbidding Jason in the promise of gold, was put in his place by Antiochus. He began his career by plundering the temple to obtain the price of his office, and by the murder of the former high priest Onias for charging him with sacrilege.

A false report that Antiochus was dead led to revolt in Jerusalem. Jason was restored to the high priesthood, while Menelaus took refuge in the citadel. But Antiochus soon gave ample proof that he was not dead. He made a furious attack on Jerusalem, drove Jason into exile, restored Menelaus to office, slaughtered the inhabitants—men, women and children —and sold thousands into slavery. Two years later, in his most malignant mood, Antiochus ordered that every trace of the old Jewish religion should be effaced; there should be no more keeping of the Sabbath, no more sacrificing to Jehovah, no more circumcision. Any one found having a copy of the Jewish Scriptures in his possession should be put to death.

The Syrian general Apollonius, with an army of 50,000 men, came to Jerusalem to enforce the king's commands. Taking advantage of the Sabbath, when the Jews would offer no resistance, he began his work of spoliation and outrage. The walls of the city were torn down, houses were plundered and set on fire, men, women and children were sold into slavery. The altar of burnt offering where sacrifice had for ages been offered to Jehovah, was converted into a heathen shrine, and upon it was offered swine's flesh in honor of Olympian Zeus. Jews who held fast to their religion fled from the city—some to foreign lands, some to hiding places in the wilderness. It was not in Jerusalem alone that such things were done. Officers were sent through the land of Judah to see that all were yielding compliance with the king's orders.

The city of Modin, situated a few miles northwest of Jerusalem, near the Beth-horons, is memorable as the place where one brave man dared to stand out against the oppressor. Here dwelt an aged priest Mattathias and his five sons, John, Simon, Judas, Eleazar, and Jonathan. The heathen altar had been erected and the king's officer had called upon the assembled people to do it honor. Mattathias calmly looked on until a Jew proceeded to the altar to offer sacrifice, when he rushed forward and slew the idolater. Then he and his sons slew the officer, and, fleeing to the mountains, hid themselves in caves where they were soon joined by a band of followers of like spirit with themselves.

Mattathias lived but a short time after the affair at Modin. He left behind him five stalwart sons whose heroic exploits rank among the most remarkable events of Jewish history. Judas, surnamed the Maccabæus, ("the hammer"), took the lead, and from him the whole family received the name Maccabees. Sometimes also they were called Hasmonæans from their grandfather Hasmon.

Under the leadership of Judas, the Maccabees began a course of aggressive warfare against the Syrians and apostate Jews. At first they made their attacks at night and lay concealed through the day. Success gave them courage. To prevent the enemy taking advantage of them, they had to give up their scruples against fighting on the Sabbath. Though opposed by forces much larger than their own, the Maccabees gained two splendid victories.

Antiochus, finding the Maccabees, though few in number, were foes that needed to be seriously reckoned with, sent against them an army of nearly 50,000 men under three generals of tried skill. The forces of the Maccabees were encamped at Mizpah, a place famous in the annals of Jewish history.[1] The Syrians took their position at Emmaus, and so certain were they of victory that they were accompanied by Phœnician slave-traders for the purpose of buying Jewish captives. By a well-planned maneuver Judas gained here his third battle, not only routing the enemy, but gaining possession of the camp with all its rich supply of gold, food, and weapons (166 B. C.). Yet a fourth victory did Judas gain. This time it was in the south near Hebron. Sixty thousand Syrians under Lysias were defeated and put to flight, leaving five thousand dead on the field.

Judas now took possession of Jerusalem, with the exception of the citadel of Acra which was held by a Syrian garrison. His first great work was to repair and cleanse the temple, which was sadly dilapidated and for three years had been polluted by heathen worship. The stones of the defiled altar were removed, a new altar was built, and new vessels were procured for the temple service. Then, amid great rejoicings and songs of praise, the worship of Jehovah was resumed by a happy people. For eight days they kept holiday, and, in memory of the great event, they established a new festival known as the Feast of Dedication or The Feast of Lights (165 B. C.).

[1] 1 Sam. 7 : 5–13.

## CHAPTER XXX

### THE MACCABÆAN PERIOD

The exact date which determines the beginning of the Maccabæan Period is to some extent arbitrary. Perhaps the restoration of the temple service as an outcome of the struggle may suitably mark the introduction of the era. Some historians place it three years earlier when Mattathias began at Modin the great work of the Maccabæan family; it might be placed twenty-two years later when to religious liberty there was added to the Jewish people independence in civil affairs.

Judas now found time to chastise the Idumæans, the Ammonites, and other neighboring people who were giving annoyance. No sooner had he returned from these excursions in the south than a call came for aid to the Jews in Galilee and in Gilead beyond the Jordan. Forces were speedily dispatched thither, the enemy was overcome, and in due time filling the air with triumphant songs as they marched, all the Jews of those outlying regions were conducted to Judæa.

There seemed now to be promise of rest, especially when tidings came that the "mad man," Antiochus Epiphanes, had died in the Far East. To Judas it seemed a good time to complete the work now so far advanced. The citadel of Acra, a menace to the temple, was still held by a Syrian garrison, and he at once set about its capture.

This enterprise was soon arrested. A great Syrian army of 100,000 footmen, 20,000 horsemen, and thirty-two war-trained elephants, under the skilled general Lysias, accompanied by the young king Antiochus V, having marched along the coast plain, was now advancing toward Jerusalem by way of Hebron. Nothing daunted, Judas abandoned the siege of the citadel and hastened with his little army to meet the foe. He was soon compelled, however, to retreat to Jerusalem, closely followed by the Syrian army. The destruction of the city and of Jewish hope now seemed inevitable. God interposed. Tidings came that a rival for the throne threatened disturbance at Antioch. Making a compromise with the Jews, Lysias with his great army hastened home. At the same time Antiochus removed Menelaus from the office of high priest and appointed Alcimus, of the house of Aaron, but a pronounced Hellenist, in his place.

Alcimus, finding himself powerless to resist the opposition of Judas to his schemes, soon retired to Antioch, where he appealed to Demetrius who had succeeded to the throne of Syria. The new king espoused his cause and sent him back with a strong force under Nicanor to establish him in the high priesthood. Judas met the Syrian army and with a much smaller force inflicted on it terrible defeat. Nicanor was killed, and the whole Valley of Aijalon, where thirteen hundred years before Joshua wrought such havoc with the Amorites, was strewn with the dead bodies of Syrian soldiers.

Judas knew well that this victory would be avenged, and he resolved on seeking help from abroad. He accordingly sent embassadors to Rome, asking its interference on behalf of his people. The Roman Senate promised assistance and commanded Demetrius to desist from persecuting the Jews. But before the messengers returned a large Syrian army under Bacchides had invaded the country, and a great battle had been fought near Beth-horon in which the Jews were defeated and Judas was slain.

The death of Judas was a severe blow to the Maccabæan party. To add to their loss his brother John also was killed shortly after. Eleazar, another brother, had met a singular death during the invasion of Lysias. Rushing forward under a great elephant which he thought bore the king, he stabbed the animal and was crushed to death by its fall. Jonathan, who with Simon alone of the five brothers now survived, became the leader of the party. As a warrior he was not equal to Judas, but he was more skilled in strategy and diplomacy.

The high priest Alcimus now for a short time ruled as he pleased. His policy was to break down all distinction between Jew and Greek, and he removed the wall that separated the outer court of the temple, admitting Gentiles to the sacred inclosure from which they had been excluded. But while the Judaists were viewing his acts with horror, Alcimus was removed by death. Soon after Jonathan and Bacchides agreed on terms of peace.

Jonathan and his party were now aided by the weakening of Syrian power through the strife of rival claimants for the throne. Both parties courted his support and vied with each other in showing him favors. Honors came thick upon him. He was appointed high priest, raised to the dignity of prince, invested with purple, and entitled to wear a crown of gold. He was made governor of Judæa and his territory was enlarged. In the midst of all this prosperity Jonathan fell the victim of treachery. Tryphon, a new claimant to the throne of Syria, found him in his way. By fair promises he got him in his power and then put him to death.

Simon alone remained of the sons of Mattathias. He was modest and retiring, willing for others to lead when they possessed the ability, but a noble, capable man and ready to command in time of need. Chosen as leader, he entered into a compact with Demetrius II, Tryphon's rival, offering him his support in return for full recognition of freedom for the Jews.

Judæa was now practically independent. So long wasted by war, it now assumed a brighter aspect, its industries flourished, and its people were relieved from taxes. Simon was high priest and civil ruler. He possessed the sovereign right of coining money, and it is said that silver shekels of his coinage are still extant. His first care was to secure possession of the citadel in Jerusalem and other strongholds in the land. His measures against the Hellenists were severe. Those of this party who would neither leave the country nor quietly accept the new order of things he put to death. Imitating the example of his brothers, he sent embassadors to Rome, bearing a great shield of gold as a gift to the Roman Senate.

Simon's reign was not free from trouble. An attempt made by a new occupant of the Syrian throne he successfully resisted. His end, like that of his brothers, was tragic. While at a banquet given by his son-in-law, Ptolemy, he and his two sons were treacherously murdered. Ptolemy's hope of securing favor with the king of Syria was the probable motive.

John Hyrcanus, Simon's son, succeeded as ruler of the Jews. On the whole his long reign of thirty years was peaceful and prosperous. He made war against the Samaritans, destroyed their temple on Mount Gerizim, laid the city of Samaria in ruins, and annexed the country to his realm. He also conquered the Idumæans and compelled them to adopt the distinctive rites of the Jews.

The union of religious and secular functions in the office of the high priest had for some time been a matter of concern to a party of zealots who in the time of Jonathan took the name Pharisees. As political interests broadened out under the later Maccabæan rulers, and came to be regarded as the more important concern of the high priest's office, the "separatists," for such is the meaning of the word Pharisees, became more pronounced in their dissent. Then the fact that one not in the direct line of Aaronic descent was holding the office of high priest was to them a gross outrage.

As an outcome of scribism, it was now in the reign of Hyrcanus that the Pharisees became a prominent and organized force in Jewish affairs. Their tenets were religious and led them into politics only to guard the interests of religion. Rigid observance of the law was the focal point in which their distinctive features centered, yet not the written law of Moses, but that law as it was explained and enlarged by the traditions. Holiness for them consisted in the doing of certain things and in the avoiding of other things. Among their chief duties were fastings, formal prayers, repetition of Scripture texts, ablutions, washing of hands and cups, and in the keeping of certain rules of Sabbath observance. They were careful to avoid all defilement, including association with unclean persons, that is, persons not of their sect. Their attitude toward outsiders was "Stand by thyself, come not near to me; for I am holier than thou."

The Pharisees believed in the spirit world, in the resurrection of the body, and in future rewards and punishments. While they believed in man's responsibility, they also held that ultimate human destiny is dependent on divine will.

Contemporaneous with the Pharisees was the sect called Sadducees. They were of high social rank, wealthy, and ambitious. Being worldly in their aspirations, they were disposed to magnify the importance of the secular side of the high priest's office. They were supporters of the Hasmonæan dynasty. As to religious views, they respected the teachings of the Pentateuch, but refused to accept the traditions. The doctrine of the Resurrection and that of future rewards and punishments they rejected, because they found for them no support in the Pentateuch.

There was also in Judæa at this time a brotherhood called the Essenes. In some of their views in regard to holiness they resembled the Pharisees —only they were more rigid. They formed a strictly religious order. All the members dressed in white. They carefully observed the Mosaic law, ceremonial purity, celibacy, communism, and meditation. Avoiding intercourse with the world, they lived chiefly in retired places.

Hyrcanus made his wife his successor in the civil government and his son Aristobulus in the office of high priest. Aristobulus seized the government for himself and threw his mother into prison. He took the title of king, and during his short reign of one year he adopted many Greek customs, destroying much of the good that had been done by his predecessors, for which he was surnamed "Phil-Hellene." He was succeeded by Alexander Jannæus the third son of Hyrcanus.

Alexander Jannæus on coming to the throne married Alexandra, the widow of Aristobulus. His reign was one of almost constant war, of internal trouble, and rebellion. For six years civil war prevailed. The Pharisees opposed his rule and so aroused his anger that he had 800 of them crucified, having first ordered their wives and children to be slaughtered before their eyes. As the result of conquests he added considerably to Jewish territory.

Alexandra succeeded her husband in the government, while Hyrcanus, his eldest son, became high priest. Alexandra reversed the policy of her husband in showing favor to the Pharisees, and it was said that "while she governed other people, the Pharisees governed her." Her brother Simon ben Shetach, a leader of the Pharisees, took prominent part in restoring ceremonial observances and laws of ritual that had fallen into disuse. The Sadducees, in their turn, were the victims of persecution. During the reign the Sanhedrin, now the highest judicial and religious tribunal, was reconstructed, admitting the scribe to its membership and widening the influence of the Pharisees. A law was also promulgated imposing a temple tax of half a shekel on every Jew over twenty years of age.

On the death of Alexandra a struggle for the chief power ensued (69 B. C.). The right of succession belonged to Hyrcanus II, but this weak prince was forced to yield his claims to both high priesthood and kingship to his more energetic brother Aristobulus II. This change of ruler meant much for the Sadducees, for Aristobulus, like his father, was their friend.

The story of Jewish history here reaches an important epoch. Independent rule is about to come to an end, and the Jews to come under a new mistress—Rome in place of Antioch. Coincident with these changes in Palestine and taking prominent part in bringing them about, comes into notice the family of the Herods. The founder of this noted family, that for a century held conspicuous place in the history of Palestine, was Antipater, governor of Idumæa. Ambitious of taking part in Jewish affairs and finding a tool suited to his purpose in the pliant Hyrcanus, he persuaded him to renew the struggle for the throne. Aretas, King of Arabia, was induced to aid the enterprise with an army of fifty thousand men. Aristobulus was defeated and forced to take refuge in the temple mount of Jerusalem.

The Roman general Pompey had just completed his conquests in Asia Minor, and it pleased him to take a hand in the business going on at Jerusalem. At first he sent one of his officers and later he came himself. Aristobulus, having placed himself in his power and failing to carry out certain terms agreed on, was thrown into prison. The citizens of Jerusalem opened its gates to Pompey, but the friends of Aristobulus refused to admit him to the citadel. For three months Pompey strove in vain to force an entrance, and then, seizing his opportunity on the day of Pentecost, on which the Jews would not fight, he made himself master of the stronghold. Fearful slaughter ensued. Priests were slain at the altar, and 12,000 citizens were massacred. Pompey and his officers profaned the temple by entering the Holy of Holies, but they refrained from plundering the temple of its treasures.

Pompey introduced great changes. Judæa was made a Roman province and placed under tribute. Hyrcanus was reinstated as high priest and civil ruler under the guidance of Antipater. Samaria and other territory were annexed to the province of Syria. Taking with him Aristobulus and his sons Alexander and Antigonus to grace his triumphal march through the streets of the great capital, Pompey proceeded to Rome.

This was a transition period with Rome also—the passing of the Republic and the birth struggle of the Empire—and the successive steps of this transition were reflected in the working out of the new order of things in Judæa. The leading characters Pompey, Crassus, Cassius, Julius Cæsar, Mark Antony, and Octavian, that figured in the great drama at Rome, played their parts also in the changing scenes in Judæa.

# CHAPTER XXXI

## THE ROMAN PERIOD

The loss of independence was borne differently by different classes of Jews. Some were patient under the yoke and waited hopefully for the coming of the Messiah "who would restore all things"; but others, who were more restless, taking the matter into their own hands, sought restoration by rebellion against the Roman power. Leaders of these last were Aristobulus and his sons Alexander and Antigonus, who had regained their liberty. The rebels were defeated, and Aristobulus was sent again prisoner to Rome.

During the contest for supremacy at Rome between Julius Cæsar and Pompey, Antipater supported the latter; but when he found that he was not on the winning side, he hastened to make amends by rendering such service to the victor as to gain his favor. Thereupon Julius Cæsar confirmed Hyrcanus in his offices of priest and chief ruler of Judæa with Antipater as his adviser. He also bestowed many favors on the Jews, including relief from tribute and from the support of the Roman garrisons in Judæa. Hyrcanus was nominal ruler, but Antipater wielded the power and in carrying out his ambitious aims had his eldest son made governor of Jerusalem and his second son Herod governor of Galilee.

Herod, the last-named son, known in history as Herod the Great, was destined to a remarkable career in the affairs of Palestine. This career, however, he came very near spoiling of its fulfillment by an act of daring at the outset. In ridding Galilee of a band of robbers he put their leaders to death. The power of capital punishment was at this time vested in the Sanhedrin, and that body, jealous of its prerogative, summoned Herod to Jerusalem to answer for his conduct. Though he came invested in purple robes and surrounded by a bodyguard, he escaped condemnation only by speedy departure from the city. Herod was astute in his plans as well as bold in action. To insure popularity with the Jews and to strengthen his position as ruler, he at an early stage formed an alliance with the favorite Hasmonæan family by becoming betrothed to Mariamne, granddaughter of the high priest Hyrcanus.

At the height of his power, when all his schemes seemed to be prospering, Antipater fell, the victim of a plot. While attending a feast given by Hyrcanus he died of poison which the butler was hired by an assassin to administer.

During the period of disturbance at Rome which followed the assassination of Julius Cæsar, Antigonus thought the opportunity favorable for securing the throne of Judæa. For this enterprise he gained the aid of the Parthians, a warlike people who inhabited a country near the Caspian Sea. Many of the Jews who disliked the rule of Herod and Phasael joined his standard. Arriving at Jerusalem Antigonus, by means of a plot, made prisoners of Hyrcanus and Phasael. Hyrcanus was mutilated by having his ears cut off to disqualify him for the office of high priest, and was then carried off to Babylon by the Parthians. To escape a worse fate, Phasael committed suicide.

The capture of Herod also formed part of the lot, but by no device could the wary governor of Galilee be got into the trap. He sought safety in flight. The strong fortress of Masada on the west coast of the Dead Sea offered an asylum. Here he placed his betrothed wife Mariamne with other friends, and leaving them to the care of his brother Joseph, he went to Egypt and thence hastened to Rome (40 B. C.).

At Rome Herod was received with every mark of confidence and favor. Octavian and Antony promised him their aid, and the Senate passed a decree making him king of Judæa. Elated by this turn of fortune Herod returned to Palestine to take possession of his kingdom.

Meanwhile Antigonus had been king and high priest of Jerusalem, but he had done little to establish his power. Much time and means he had vainly expended to gain possession of Masada, a work in which he was still engaged when Herod returned. The people, plundered by the Parthians whom he had brought into the country, were tired of his rule, and as Herod passed along his forces were continually augmented by those who desired change.

Herod's first concern was to relieve Masada. This done he proceeded against Jerusalem, but failing to gain expected help he had in the meantime to abandon the enterprise. In the spring of 37 B. C., aided by a large Roman force, he resumed the siege. At the end of five months the ramparts gave way and the city was captured. The Roman soldiers were maddened by long resistance, and fearful slaughter ensued. Antigonus, in abject submission, threw himself at the feet of the conqueror and pleaded for mercy. The Roman general, looking on him with contempt, called him Antigona (the feminine form of Antigonus). The wretched prince was taken to Antioch, where after being cruelly scourged he was beheaded (37 B. C.).

Herod was king. A singular compound of good and bad—mostly bad—was this King Herod. Jealous, vindictive, cruel and relentless, he could be restrained by no tie of friendship or of love from yielding to the raging tiger within him. He began his reign by the slaughter of forty-five leading Sadducees of the Sanhedrin, who had opposed his entrance into Jerusalem. Yielding to the importunities of Alexandra, Mariamne's mother, he appointed her son Aristobulus IV high priest in place of Ananel to whom he had at first given the office. Aristobulus, a youth of seventeen years, handsome, of commanding stature, and of graceful demeanor, called forth expressions of admiration from the people. Herod's jealousy was aroused, and he contrived a scheme for getting rid of his supposed rival. At a feast given by Alexandra at Jericho Aristobulus was plunged into a fish-pool, as if in sport, by men hired for the purpose, and kept there until he was drowned.

The aged high priest Hyrcanus, now by mutilation disqualified for office, Herod brought back to Jerusalem and for a short time treated him kindly. But even this inoffensive old man was not exempt from cruel suspicion, and, accused of plotting against Herod, he was put to death.

Mariamne also became the object of Herod's torturing jealousy. Again and again he determined on her death, but relented. His evil surmisings were intensified by the false tales of his sister Salome, a woman capable of the blackest wickedness. At Salome's instigation Herod's cupbearer brought him a love-potion which he said was sent to him by his wife. It proved to be poison, and Mariamne was condemned and executed. For this deed Herod is said to have been ever after haunted by the keenest remorse.

Other victims followed. Among them were Alexandra, and Mariamne's sons Alexander and Aristobulus. Tall and of princely bearing, educated by the best instructors at Rome, these young men were prominent figures at Herod's court. The Jews were proud of them as promising scions of Hasmonæan stock. But Salome, finding them in the way of her purposes, traduced them as plotting revenge on account of their mother's death. Yet, five days before he died, Herod put to death another son, Antipater, who was indeed a despicable traitor, deserving of his fate.

Amid scenes such as these, in the last year of Herod's reign, there was born in Bethlehem, Jesus the Saviour of the world. Rumor spread abroad that the Messiah, the long-expected king of the Jews had come. It reached the ever-attentive ears of Herod, and "he was troubled."[1] After all his efforts to guard his throne, was there yet another rival? He would crush that new-born king ere he had left the cradle. It may seem strange that a deed so monstrous as that massacre of the babes of Bethlehem should find no record on the pages of history save in the Gospel of Matthew. But in the dark shadow of Herod's other monstrous deeds, the taking off of a few children in a small town could easily escape notice.

By a chronological error the year of the birth of our Lord is placed four years too late. Thus Anno Domini I should have been Anno Domini 5, and so on down to the present time four years must always be added to the date to give the true "year of our Lord."[2]

[1] Matt. 2: 1–23.   [2] See Davis's Bible Dictionary under Jesus Christ.

Herod the Great was famous as a builder of fortresses, palaces, and cities. The temple-fort in Jerusalem he rebuilt and named it Antonia in honor of his patron Mark Antony. For himself, partly as a residence and partly as a fort to protect him from the Jews indignant over his heathen innovations, he built a splendid palace in Jerusalem. He tore down the temple which had been erected after the return from the Captivity and erected in its place a much grander edifice. Of the cities built by him the most noted was Cæsarea with its great breakwater and its temple with a colossal statue of Augustus. He rebuilt Samaria and renamed it Sebaste, the Greek for Augusta. The principal street of Antioch he adorned with colonnades, and in various other cities he erected temples, gymnasia, and market places.

Herod's kingdom embraced the whole land of Palestine on both sides of the Jordan. At his death it was divided among his three sons: to Archelaus, with the title of king, fell Idumæa, Judæa, and Samaria;[1] to Herod Antipas, Galilee and the territory between the Yarmuk and the Arnon called Peræa; and to Philip, the territory on the north of the river Yarmuk, embracing the small districts Ituræa, Trachonitis, Auranitis, Gaulanatis, and Batanea.[2]

Archelaus had a troubled and inglorious reign of ten years, at the end of which on complaint of the Jews he was banished to Gaul. Judæa was then formed into a Roman province governed by a procurator.

Procurators were for the most part appointed only in imperial provinces governed by a legate of the emperor. The duty of the procurator in such cases consisted in collecting the revenue and in judging in causes appertaining to fiscal affairs. The procurator of Judæa, however, had a wider range of duties. There being no legate in the province he was charged with the general government and was invested with military and judicial authority. In some matters he was subordinate to the legate of Syria. He usually resided at Cæsarea, but went to Jerusalem at the time of the feasts, taking with him a strong military force.

The taxes were of two kinds—a direct tax collected by imperial officers under the control of the procurator, and an impost tax which was farmed out to the highest bidder and again sold out to collectors. These collectors or publicans were of low social and moral standing and were looked upon with contempt.[3]

The Sanhedrin, comprising seventy members—priests, scribes, and elders—possessed large powers as a legislative and judicial body. The power of life and death, once vested in the Sanhedrin, now belonged to the procurator. The high priest, who was appointed by the procurator, was president of the Sanhedrin.[4]

[1] Matt. 2: 22.  
[2] Luke 3: 1.  
[3] Matt. 11: 19; 21: 31.  
[4] John 18: 31.

Pilate, fifth in succession of the procurators in Judæa, ruled during the active ministry of our Lord. His term of office lasted about ten years (A. D. 26-36). Very early in his reign he excited violent opposition. The Jews were now very scrupulous in the matter of images. Jewish coins had no head impressed upon them. Pilate sent Roman soldiers into Jerusalem with standards bearing on them the image of the emperor. This and other innovations held by the Jews to be idolatrous, led to serious riots.

Pilate's treatment of his subjects was so tyrannical that he was at last sent to Rome by the legate of Syria to answer their accusations before the emperor. He is said to have ended his life by suicide.

Philip II, with the title of tetrarch, had a long reign of thirty years, during which he maintained order and held the good will of his subjects. The capital of his tetrarchy was at Paneas which he rebuilt and named Cæsarea Philippi. His wife was his niece Salome, daughter of Philip I and Herodias, and she that asked for the head of John the Baptist.

Herod Antipas, the tetrarch of Galilee, was he whom our Saviour designated "that fox," a term aptly descriptive of his cunning nature. He is brought to notice in the New Testament as the Herod who beheaded John the Baptist, and he who declined to take any part in the condemnation of Jesus when Pilate sought to be rid of the responsibility of this act. Like his father Herod the Great he was famous as a builder. Among his works was the city of Tiberias on the west coast of the Sea of Galilee. His palace in this city was noted for its splendor. Herod Antipas divorced his first wife, the daughter of Aretas, King of Arabia, and married Herodias, the wife of his half-brother, Philip I. This brought about a war with Aretas, in which Herod suffered disastrous defeat. After a long reign he was accused of disloyalty to the Roman emperor and was banished by him to Gaul.

Of all the Herods none had a more varied and romantic career than Herod Agrippa. He was the son of Aristobulus and grandson of Herod the Great and Mariamne. Educated at Rome he acquired the polished address of high social life and at the same time habits of extravagance. He became involved in debts which he could not pay. At one time so hopeless were his fortunes that he was about to commit suicide. His sister, the Herodias of ill-fame, interceded in his behalf with her husband, Herod Antipas, who appointed him to the ignoble position of overseer of the markets in Tiberias. Losing this position through a quarrel with Herod Antipas, he found his way back to Rome. Here, through unguarded speech, he so incurred the resentment of the emperor Tiberius that he was thrown into prison. Caligula, on his accession to the throne, set him free and made him ruler over the tetrarchy of Philip with the title of king (A. D. 37); and he afterwards added Galilee and Peræa to his kingdom (A. D. 40). Still later the emperor Claudius, to whom he had rendered important service, bestowed on him the government of Judæa and Samaria (A. D. 41). Thus for a short time was all Palestine brought again under one ruler.

Herod Agrippa, as far as it related to external form, was a thoroughgoing Jew. He made his home in Jerusalem, was careful in observing the law, and regular in offering the daily sacrifice. He sought in every way to please the Jews, and to this end he persecuted the Christians. It was he who killed the apostle James, and "because he saw it pleased the Jews," with the same purpose in view, imprisoned "Peter also."[1]

Herod's death is briefly described in The Acts of the apostles. The occasion of his visit to Cæsarea is said to have been the celebration of games in honor of the Roman emperor. The Tyrians and Zidonians, whose country, bordering on Galilee, lay outside the bounds of Herod's kingdom, had in some way offended the king. They were dependent on Galilee for grain and other food material, and they feared that in his irritation Herod might cut off their supplies. They accordingly availed themselves of this opportunity to appease his wrath. On the second day of the festival, seated on his throne and arrayed in a robe of silver tinsel, that glittered in the sunlight, the vain king made an oration to the people. With ready use of his susceptibility to flattery, they cried out: "The voice of a god! The voice of a god!" Suddenly smitten with a fatal and loathsome disease, Herod was borne hastily from his throne to the couch of death.[2]

[1] Acts 12: 1–5.   [2] Acts 12: 20–23.

# PRONOUNCING INDEX

AA′ RON, 125
Ab′ a-na, or Ab′ a-nah, 79, 80
A-bi′ jah, 36, 140
Ab′ ner, 133
A′ bra-ham, 31, 33, 36, 43, 46, 69, 122–124
Ab′ sa-lom, 133, 134
A′ bun-cis, 89
A′ bu–Sim′ bel, 89
Ac′ cho, 85, 86
A-cel′ da-ma, 43
A-cha′ ia, 110
      Province of, 112
Ach′ me-tha, 70
Ac′ ra, 44, 158
A′ cre, 28
A-crop′ o-lis, 112
Ac′ ti-um, 119
Ad-o-ni′ jah, 134
A-dul′ lam, Cave of, 23
Æ′ sop, 101
Æ-to′ li-a, 110
Af′ ri-ca, 12
A-ga′ de, 71, 72
A′ gag, 131
Ag′ o-ra, The, 112
A′ hab, 62, 73, 80, 82, 83, 84, 137, 138, 141
A-has-u-e′ rus, 78, 151
A′ haz, 140, 142
A-ha-zi′ ah, 137, 140
A-hi′ jah, 135
Ah′ ri-man, 77
A-hu′ ra-maz′ da, 77
A′ i, 39, 127
Ai′ ja-lon, or A′ ja-lon, 22, 31, 39, 46, 127, 136
A-ka-bah′, 94
Al′ ci-mus, 159, 160
Al-ex-an′ der, Jan-næ′ us, 162
Al-ex-an′ der (son of Ar-is-to-bu′ lus II), 163, 164
Al-ex-an′ der (son of Her′ od the Great), 166
Al-ex-an′ der, the Great, 78, 85, 101, 110, 155
Al-ex-an′ dra, 162
Al-ex-an′ dra (Mother of Ma′ ri-am′ ne), 165, 166
Al-ex-an′ dri-a, 88, 90, 155
Am′ a-lek, 29, 96
Am′ a-lek-ites, 98, 129, 131
Am′ a-nus Mountains, 79, 99, 104
Am′ a-thus, 115
Am-a-zi′ ah, 140, 142
A-men-ho′ tep, 89

Am′ mon, 61, 133, 143
Am′ mon-ites, 42, 60, 63, 130, 133, 141, 152
Am′ non, 133
A′ mon, 140, 143
Am′ o-rites, 22, 60, 122, 123, 126
A′ mos, 138
Am-phip′ o-lis, 111
Am′ ra-phel, 70, 72
An′ a-kim, 122
An′ a-nel, 166
An-cy′ ra, 103
An-go′ ra, 103
An′ no Dom′ i-ni, 166
An-tig′ o-nus, 163, 164, 165
An′ ti Leb′ a-non, 15
An′ ti-och (in Pi-sid′ i-a), 103
An′ ti-och (in Syr′ i-a), 81, 82, 155
An-ti′ o-chus E-piph′ a-nes, 156–159
An-ti′ o-chus the Great, 102, 156
An-ti′ o-chus V, 159
An-tip′ a-ter, 163, 164
An′ ti Tau′ rus, 99
An′ to-ny, Mark, 118, 119
Aph′ ro-di′ te, 106
A-pol′ lo, 100, 108
Ap-ol-lo′ ni-a, 112
Ap-ol-lo′ ni-us, 157
Ar′ a-bah, The, 48, 97
A-ra′ bi-ans, 141, 152
A-ra′ bi-a, 61
A-ra′ bi-a Pe-træ′-a, 98
A′ ram-na-ha-ra′ im, 65
Ar′ a-rat, 12
Ar-be′ la, 110
Ar-ca′ di-a, 110
Ar-che-la′ us, 167
Ar-chip′ pus (-Kip-), 107
Ar-e-op′ a-gus, 112
Ar′ e-tas, 98, 163
Ar′ gob, 58
Ar′ go-lis, 110
Ar-is-to-bu′ lus II, 163, 164
Ar-is-to-bu′ lus IV, 166
Ar-is-to-bu′ lus, son of Herod the Great, 166
Ar-is-to-bu′ lus (son of John Hyrcanus), 162
Ark of the Covenant, captured by Philistines, 128
      Brought to Jerusalem, 133
      Moved to the temple, 134
Ar-ma-ged′ don, 30
Ar′ non, 54, 57, 126
Ar′ o-er, 62

Ar-tax-erx′ es Lon-gim′ a-nus, 78, 151
Ar-tax-erx′ es II, 78
Ar′ te-mis, 105
Ar′ vad, 85, 86
A′ sa, 82, 140
Ash′ dod, 20, 21
Ash′ er, 18, 86
Ash′ ke-lon, 20, 74
Ash′ to-reth, 85
Ash′ ur, 73
Ash′ ur-ban′ i-pal, 73, 75
A-shur-na′ sir-pal, 73
A′ si-a (Province), 105
A′ si-a Mi′ nor, 99, 107
    Description of, 99
    Historical sketch of, 102
    People of, 102
    Religion of, 102
    Great roads of, 103
    Provinces of, 103
As-syr′ i-a, 65–77
    A. proper, 69
    Historic sketch of, 71–76
    Religion of, 73
    Ancient cities of, 66, 67, 69
    Explorers in, 66
    " Finds " in excavated cities, 67
    Temples and palaces of, 67
    Character of people, 73
As-ty′ a-ges, 76
Ath-a-li′ ah, 140, 141
Ath′ ens, 110, 112
At-ta-li′ a, 105
At′ ta-lus, 102
At′ ti-ca, 110
Au-gus′ tus Cæ′ sar, 111, 119
Au-ra-ni′ tis, 61
Az-a-ri′ ah, 141
A-zo′ tus, 21

Ba′ al, 85
Ba′ al-bec′, 79, 81
Ba′ al-gad, 49
Ba′ al-ha′ zor, 32, 33
Ba′ a-sha, 137
Bab′ y-lon, 67
    Description of, 68
    Destroyed by Sennacherib, 74
    Taken by Cyrus, 76, 77
Bab-y-lo′-ni-a, description of, 65, 66, 68
    Cities of, 66, 69
    Explorers in, 66
    Libraries of ruined cities in, 67
    " Finds " in excavated cities, 67
    Its mode of dealing with conquered states, 71
    Religion of, 72
    City–States of, 72
    History of, 71, 76
    Old Babylonia, 72
    New Babylonian Empire, 76
Bag′ dad, 68
Ba′ laam, 59, 62, 126

Ba′ lak, 126
Ba′ ni-as, 156
Ba-ra′ da, 79
Ba′ rak, 26, 129
Bar′ ley Vale, 34
Bar′ na-bas, 100, 115
Ba′ shan, 57, 58, 126
Ba-ta-ne′ a, 61
Bau′ cis, 100
Be′ er-she′ ba, 38, 43, 46, 136
Be-his-tun′, 68
Bei-rut′, 80, 86
Beit Jib′ rim, 24
Bel′ ka, 59, 61
Bel-shaz′ zar, 77
Ben-am′ mi, 123
Ben-ha′ dad, 73, 80, 82, 138
Ben-ha′ dad III, 83
Ben′ ja-min, 18, 39, 136
Ben′ ja-min, Heights of, 39
Ben′ ja-mites, 36
Be-re′ a or Be-rœ′ a, 112
Beth′ a-ny, 45
Beth-ba′ rah, 29
Beth′ el, 35, 36, 124, 131, 136, 138
Beth-ho′ ron, 22, 39, 127, 157
Beth′ le-hem, 45
Beth-sa′ i-da, 51
Beth′ shan or Beth-she′ an, 34, 62
Beth-she′ mesh, 23
Be-ze′ tha, 44
Bi′ ble, 11, 12
Bi′ ble lands, 12
Birs Nim′ rud, 68
Bi-thyn′ i-a, 101
Bi-thyn′ i-a–Pon′ tus, 103
Black Ob′ e-lisk, 67, 70, 73
Bœ-o′ ti-a, 110
Bo′ ghaz Ke′ ui (Bo′ gaz Ke′ e), 100
Book of the Dead, 92
Bor-sip′ pa, 67, 68, 69
Boz′ rah, 97
Brun-du′ si-um, 111
Bu-ka′ a, 15

Cæ′ sar Au-gus′ tus, 111, 119
Cæs-a-re′ a, 20, 167
Cæs-a-re′ a Phi-lip′ pi, 49, 168
Cæ′ sar, Ju′ li-us, 118
Cai′ ro, 88
Ca′ lah, 66, 67, 69, 70, 73
Ca′ leb, 127
Ca-lig′ u-la, 121, 168
Cal-lir′ho-e, 57
Cam-by′ ses, 78, 89, 93
Ca′ na, 27
Ca′ naan-ites, 123, 129
Can′ di-a, 115
Ca-per′ na-um, 51
Cap-pa-do′ ci-a, 101, 103
Car′ che-mish, 75, 80, 81, 93
Ca′ ri-a, 103
Car′ mel, 25, 32

Cas′ si-us, 118
Cave of Mach-pe′ lah, 46
Ca-ys′ ter, 99, 105
Cen′ chre-æ or Cen′ chre-a, 112, 113
Chal-de′ an Em′ pire, 76
Che′ bar, 69, 147
Ched-or-la′ o-mer, 123
Che′ ops (Ke′ ops), 92
Chin′ ne-reth, 50
Chi′ os, 114
Chit′ tim, 115
Cho-ra′ zin, 51
Ci-li′ ci-a, 104
Ci-li′ ci-an Gates, 99, 103, 104
Cities of the Plain, 54, 55
Cit′ i-um, 115
Clau′ di-us, 121
Cle-o-pa′ tra, 119
Cni′ dus, 107
Cœl′ e-syr′ i-a, 15, 61
    Routes of travel in, 79
Col′ chis, 101
Co-los′ sæ, 107
Cor′ inth, 112, 113
Cos or Co′ os, 107, 114
Cras′ sus, 163
Crete, 115
Crœ′ sus, 77, 101
Croc′ o-dile, River, 19
Cy-ax′ a-res, 75, 76
Cyd′ nus, 104
Cy-do′ ni-a, 115
Cy′ prus, 115
Cyp′ se-la, 111
Cy′ rus, 76, 77, 150, 151

Da-mas′ cus, 62, 80, 81, 133
Da′ mi-eh Ford, 34, 56, 59
Dan, 18, 23, 37, 49
Dan′ iel, 66, 144
Daph′ ne, 82
Da-ri′ us I, 78, 151
Da-ri′ us III, 78
Da′ vid, kills Goliath, 23
    In Adullam, 23
    Flees from Absalom, 38
    Spares soul's life, 40
    Captures Rabbah, 62
    Wages war against Moab, 63
    Defeats King of Zobah, 81
    Captures Damascus, 82
    Alliance with Hiram, 85
    Other references, 131–134
Daw′ son, Sir Wm., 55
Dead Sea, 53, 54
Deb′ o-rah, 29, 129
De-cap′ o-lis, 62, 63
De-me′ tri-us, 160
Der′ be, 104
Der-el–Be′ ha-ri, 89
Di-a′ na, 105
Di′ bon, 139
Di′ on, 62

Di-o-ny′ sus, 106
Dis-ci′ ples, The, 26
Divisions of Palestine in New Testament times, 18
Do′ ris, 110
Do′ than, Vale of, 28, 32, 34
Dur-shar-ru′ kin, 66, 70, 74
Dyr-ra′ chi-um, 111

Ea, 72
East′ ern Pal′ es-tine, 57–64
    Physical features of, 57
    Rivers of, 57
    Divisions of, 57, 58
    Conquest of, 60
    Tribes in, 60
    Social condition of, 61
    In time of our Lord, 61
    Routes of travel in, 62
E′ bal, 32, 33, 127
Ec-bat′ a-na, 70, 151
E′ dom, 97, 98, 133
E′ dom-ites, 98, 141
Ed′ re-i, 58
Eg′ lon, 129
E′ gypt, 87–93
    Description of, 87
    Religion of, 91
    History, 91
E′ hud, 129
Ek′ ron, 20, 21, 74
E′ lah, 137
E′ lah, Vale of, 23, 131
E′ lam, 70
E′ lath, 94, 97
El-az-ir-i′ yeh, 45
E-le-a′ zar, the Mac′ ca-bee, 160
E-leu′ the-rop′ o-lis, 24
E′ li, 128
E-li′ a-kim, 144
E-li′ a-shib, 153
E-li′ jah, 138
E′ lim′ e-lech, 63
E-li′ sha, 138
El′ la-sar, 67, 69
El Li′ san, 54
Em-balm′ ing, 90
En′ dor, 25, 26, 29
En-gan′ nim, 28, 34, 35
En-ge′ di, 41
Ep′ a-phras, 107
Eph′ e-sus, 101, 105
E′ phra-im, location of, 18
    Name of Northern Kingdom, 129
Ep′ ic-te′ tus, 107
Ep-i-cu-re′ ans, 109
E-pi′ rus, 110
E′ rek or U′ rek, 67, 69
E′ ri-du, 67, 68
E′ sar-had′ don, 73, 75
E′ sau, 123
Es-cu-la′ pi-us, 106

Es-dra-e′lon or Es-dra′e-lon, description of, 28, 29, 30
    A highway, 29
    A gateway, 28
    A battle-field, 29, 30
    Soil of, 29
    Gideon's victory in, 29
    Saul's defeat in, 29
    Deborah's victory in, 29
    Josiah's death in, 30
Es-senes′, The, 162
Es′ther, 151
Eu′me-nes, 102
Eu-phra′tes, 65, 66
Ex′o-dus, The, 124
E-ze′ki-el, vision of, 66
    Other references, 93, 144, 145, 148
E′zi-on-ge′ber, 94, 97
Ez′ra, 78, 148, 150, 152
    Character of his work, 153

Fair Ha′vens, 115
Falconer, Principal, Introductory Note, 5-8
Farah, 52
Farah, wady es, 34
Feast of Dedication, 158
Feast of Lights, 158
Free cities in Roman Empire, 119
Funeral Ceremonies, 90

Gad, 18, 60
Gad′a-ra, 51, 62
Ga-la′tia, 102, 103
    Ambiguity of name, 104
Gal′i-lee, 18
    Tribes settled in, 18
    Description, divisions, bounds of, and people of, 25
    Cities of, given to Hiram, 25
    Cities of, 26
    Fertility of, 26
    Character of people, 26
    Roads of, 27
    References to, in New Testament, 26
Gal′i-lee, Sea of, 50, 51
Gath, 20
    Description of, 21
Gau-la-ni′tis, 61
Gauls, 101, 102
Ga′za, 20, 21, 74
Ge′ba, 38, 39, 131
Ge′bal, 85, 86
Ged-a-li′ah, 145, 146
Ge-ma′ra, 149
Gen-nes′a-ret or Gen-nes′a-reth, Lake of, 50
Ger′a-sa, 62
Ger′i-zim, 32, 33
    Temple on, destroyed, 127, 153
    Festivals on, 154
Ge′shem, 152
Ge′shur, 58
Geth-sem′a-ne, 38

Ge′zer, 23, 93
Ghor, The, 51
Gib′e-a, 39
Gib′e-on, 39
Gib′e-on-ites, 40, 127
Gid′e-on, 29, 129
Gil-bo′a, 29, 32
Gil′e-ad, 58, 59
Gil′gal, 127
Gnos′sus, 115
Go-li′ath, 23, 131
Gor′di-an Knot, 101
Gor′di-um, 101
Gor′di-us, 101
Gor-ty′na, 115
Go′shen, 88
Greece, 108-113
    General features of, 108
    People of, 108
    Games of, 109
    Sages of, 109
    States of, 110
    Under the Romans, 110
    In New Testament Times, 111
    Invaded by Darius and Xerxes, 151

Hag′ga-i, 151
Hal-i-car-nas′sus, 101, 107
Hall of Col′umns, 89
Ha′man, 151
Ha′math, 79, 80, 81
Ha′mor, 33
Ha′ran, 122
Ha′rod, 29, 34
Has-mo-næ′ans, 158
Hau′ran, 58
Haz′a-el or Ha′za-el, 73, 83
Haz-a-zon-ta′mar, 41
Ha′zor, 128
He′ber, 29
He′bron, 46
Heights of Ben′ja-min, 39
He′li-op′o-lis, 88
Hel′len-ism, 156
Her′mon, description of, 15, 49
Her′ods, The, 163
Her′od A-grip′pa, 168, 169
Her′od, Phil′ip, 49, 167, 168
Her′od An′ti-pas, 167, 168
Her′od Family, 163
Her′od the Great, rebuilt Samaria, 35
    At Masada, 42
    Various incidents in his career, 165-167
    Favored by Roman Senate, 165
    Governor of Galilee, 164
    Builds temple at Banias, 49
    Takes Jerusalem and is made king of Judæa, 165
    Slays his sons and the babes of Bethlehem, 166
    Death of, 53
He-ro′di-as, 168
He-rod′o-tus, 92

Hesh′ bon, 57
Hez-e-ki′ ah, 73, 74, 140, 142, 143
Hi-e-rap′ o-lis, 107
Hi′ er-o-glyph′ ics, 91
Hill of Mo′ reh, 25
Hin′ nom, 43
Hip′ pos, 62
Hi′ ram, 85, 134
Hit′ tites, 100, 122
Hi′ vites, 123
Hor, 97
Ho′ ram, 23
Ho′ reb, 95
Ho′ rus, 91
Ho-se′ a, 93, 138
Ho-she′ a, 137
Hul′ dah, 143
Hu′ leh, 49
Hyk′ sos, 92, 93, 124
Hyr-ca′ nus, John, destroys Samaritan temple, 153
    Destroys temple on Gerizim, 161
    Ruler of Judæa, 161
    Succeeded by wife and son, 162
Hyr-ca′ nus II, supported by Antipater, 163
    Seized and mutilated by Antigonus, 165
    Put to death by Herod, 166

I-co′ ni-um, 104
Id-u-me′ a or Id-u-mæ′ a, 97
Ig-na′ ti-us, 106
Im′ bros, 114
I-o′ ni-a, 101
Ip-sam′ bul or A-bu-Sim′ bal, 88, 89
I′ saac, 46, 123
I-sa′ iah, 74, 93
Ish-bo′ sheth, 133
Ish′ ma-el, 123
Ish′ tar, 75
I′ sis, 91
Is′ ra-el, Kingdom of, 18, 137–139
Is′ ra-el-ites, 11
    From Joshua to Saul, 127–129
    In Egypt, 124
    In the wilderness, 125
    At Kadesh-Barnea, 125
    Period of undivided monarchy, 130–136
Is′ sa-char, 18
Isth′ mi-an Games, 109

Jab′ bok, 51, 57
Ja-besh-gil′ e-ad, 61
Ja′ bin, 128
Ja′ cob, 31, 33, 46
    At Padan-aram, 123
    At Shechem, 124
    At Hebron, 124
    Route of funeral cortège, 90
Ja′ cob's Well, 33
Jad-du′ a, 155

Ja′ el, 29
Jaf′ fa, 20
Ja′ lud, 51
Ja′ son, 156, 157
Jau′ lan, 58
Je′ bel Mu′ sa, 95
Je′ bus, 133
Je-ho′ a-haz, 137, 140, 144
Je-hoi′ a-da, 141
Je-hoi′ a-chin, 140, 144, 150
Je-hoi′ a-kim, 76, 140, 144
Je-ho′ ram, 83, 137, 140, 141
Je-hosh′ a-phat, 63, 64, 140, 141
Je′ hu, 30, 34, 62, 73, 137
Je′ nin, 21, 28
Jeph′ thah, 129
Jer-e-mi′ ah, his lamentation for Josiah, 30
    Other references, 93, 144, 145
Jer′ i-cho, 53
    Siege of, by Joshua, 53
    In time of our Lord, 53
    Destruction of, 127
Jer-o-bo′ am, 35, 135, 137, 138
Jer-o-bo′ am II, 81, 83, 137, 138
Je-ru′ sa-lem, description of, 43–45
    Defended by ravines, 44
    Historic note of, 45
    Destroyed by Nebuchadnezzar, 76, 127, 145
    Condition when visited by Nehemiah, 152
Jesh′ i-mon, description of, 40
Je′ sus, 50, 166
Je′ thro, 125
Jews, in Asia Minor, 102
    During Babylonian period, 147–149
    Return from Babylon, 150
    Delay building the temple, 150, 151
    Their territory in time of Ezra, 154
    Under Ptolemies and Seleucidæ, 155–158
    In time of Maccabees, 159–163
    Under Roman rule, 164–169
Jez′ e-bel, 34, 138
Jez′ re-el, 34
    Valley of, 28, 29, 34
Jo′ ab, 133
Jo′ ash, 137, 141
John, The Apostle, 106
John, the Baptist, 40
John, the Maccabee, 160
Jo′ nah, 138
Jon′ a-than, bravery at Gibeah, 40, 131
Jon′ a-than, the Maccabee, 160
Jop′ pa, 20
Jor′ dan, River, 48–53
    Sources of, 48
    Affluents of, 51
    Fords of, 52
    Of no commercial value, 52
    Associations of, 52
    Crossed by Israelites, 55, 56
Jor′ dan, Valley of, 48–56

Jor′ dan, Description of, 48
    Wonderful depression of, 48
    Origin of, 48
    Why it had no cities, 53
Jo′ seph, 124
Josh′ u-a, at Gerizim and Ebal, 33, 40
    Victory at Aijalon, 127
    Victory near Lake Meron, 128
    Death of, 128
Josh′ u-a, the High Priest, 151
Jo-si′ ah, slain by Pharaoh-necho, 30, 75
    Lamented by Jeremiah, 30, 140, 143, 144
Jo′ tham, 33, 140, 142
Ju-dæ′ a, 37–47
    Boundary of, 37
    Historic note, 37
    Size, 38
    Physical features of, 38
    Battles in, 40
    Fertile districts of, 41
    Ruins in, 41
    Routes of travel in, 46
    Under Simon the Maccabee, 160, 161
    A Roman province, 163
    Under Procurators, 167
Ju′ dah, location of tribe, 18
    Name of Southern Kingdom, 18, 129
    History of kingdom, 140–146
Ju-dæ′ ism, 156
Ju′ das Mac-ca-bæ′ us, 158–160
Judg′ es, how chosen and their duties, 128
Ju′ li-us Cæ′ sar, 118
Ju′ pi-ter, 100

KA-DESH-BAR′ NE-A, 125, 126
Ka′ nah, 34
Ka-na′ tha, 58, 62
Kan′ a-wat, 58
Kar′ nak, 89, 93
Ke′ desh, 26
Ke′ rak, 64
Ke-tu′ rah, 123
Kham-mu-ra′ bi, 68, 70, 72
Kid′ ron, 43, 56
Kir-har′ a-seth or Kir-har′ e-seth or Kir-ha′-resh, 64, 139
Kir-jath-ar′ ba or Kir-i-ath-ar′ ba, 46
Ki′ shon or Ki′ son, 28, 29
Kiz′ il Ir-mak′, 99

LA′ CHISH, 24, 67, 74
La-co′ ni-a, 110
La′ ish, 49, 85
Land of the Twin Rivers, 65
Land, The, a commentary on the Bible, 11
Lands of the Euphrates and the Tigris, 65–78
    Physical features, 65
    Explorers in, 66
    Excavated cities, 66
    Temples and palaces, 67
    Libraries, 67
La-od-i-ce′ a, 107

Lar′ sam, 69
Le′ ah, 46
Leb′ a-non, description of, 15
Led′ dan, 49
Lej′ jan, 58
Les′ bos, 114
Lib′ nah, 74
Lit′ a-ny, 79
Lit′ tle Her′ mon, 25
Lot, 122
Lux′ or, Temple of, 88
Lyc-a-o′ ni-a, 103
Ly′ ci-a, 105
Lyc′ tus, 115
Lyd′ da, 20, 21
Lyd′ i-a, 101, 103
Lyd′ i-a (Paul's convert), 106
Lyd′ i-ans, 101
Ly′ si-as, 158, 159
Lys′ tra, 104

MA′ A-CHAH or Ma′ a-cah, 58
Mac-ca-bæ′ an Period, 159–163
Mac′ ca-bees, The, 42, 158
Mac′ e-don, 110
Mac-e-do′ ni-a, 110
    Province of, 111
Ma-chæ′ rus, 57
Mach-pe′ lah, Cave of, 46
Ma-ha-na′ im, 62
Mal′ ta, 115
Mam′ re, 46
Ma-nas′ seh, tribe, 18, 60, 126
Ma-nas′ seh, Samaritan high priest, 153
Ma-nas′ seh, King, 75, 140, 143
Ma-neph′ ta, 93
Man′ e-tho, 92
Ma′ rah, 94
Mar′ a-thon, battle of, 151
Mar′ duk, 72
    Priests of, 77
Ma′ ri-am′ ne, 164, 166
Mar′ i-time Plain, 19
    Roads and passes of, 21
Mark An′ to-ny, 118, 119
Mar′ on-ites, 15
Mar Sa′ ba, 40
Mars' Hill, 112
Mar′ sy-as, 100
Mas′ pe-ro, 89
Mas-a′ da, description of, 42, 165
Mat-ta-thi′ as, 157, 158
Mat′ thew, 27
Ma′ zor, 87
Me-an′ der, 99, 107
Med′ e-ba, 59
Medes, 75, 76
Me′ di-a, 70, 76
Me′ do-Per′ si-a, 76, 77, 78, 150
Me-gid′ do, 29, 30, 34, 75
Mel′ i-ta, 115
Mem′ phis, 88, 92
Men′ a-hem, 137, 139

Men′ e-la′ us, 157, 159
Me′ nes, 92
Mer′ cu-ry, 100
Mer′ o-dach-bal′ a-dan, 73, 74
Me′ rom, 49
Me′ sha, 64, 139
Mes-o-po-ta′ mi-a, 65
Mes-se′ ni-a, 110
Mich′ mash or Mich′ mas, 39, 40, 46, 131
Mi′ das, 101
Mid′ i-an, 29, 123
Mid′ i-an-ites, 126, 129
Mig′ dol, 90, 146
Mi-le′ tus, 101, 107
Mi ner′ va, 117
Mish′ na, 149
Mi′ shor, 59, 60
Mith′ ri-da′ tes, 102
Miz′ pah, 38, 145, 158
Miz′ ra-im, 87
Mo′ ab (Lot's son), 123
Mo′ ab, 63, 64, 133, 138
Mo′ ab-ites, 42, 59, 61, 63, 64, 126, 129, 141
Mo′ ab-ite Stone, 139
Mo′ din, 157
Mon′ u-men′ tal Stones, 60
Mor′ de-cai, 70, 151
Mo-re′ a, 112
Mo′ reh, 25, 29
Mo-ri′ ah, Mount, 44
Mo′ ses, 59, 124, 126
Mosque of Omar, 45
Mount Car′ mel, 32
Mount E′ bal, 32
Mount Ger′ i-zim, 32
Mount Gil-bo′ a, 32
Mount Her′ mon, 15
Mount Hor, 97
Mount Mo-ri′ ah, 44
Mount Ne′ bo, 59
Mount of Ol′ ives, 38
Mount Se′ ir, 97, 98
Mount Ser′ bal, 95
Mount St. Cath′ er-ine, 95
Mount Ta′ bor, 25
Mount of Trans-fig′ u-ra′ tion, 15, 49
Mount Zi′ on, 43
Mu′ gheir, 69
My′ ra, 105
My′ si-a, 103
Myt-i-le′ ne, 114

NA′ A-MAN, 80
Nab-a-thæ′ ans, 98
Nab-lus′, 35
Na-bop-a-las′ sar, 75, 76
Nab-u-na′ id or Nab-o-ni′ dus, 76
Na′ dab, 137
Na-ha′ li-el, 57
Nahr (river), Ban′ i-as, 49
Nahr ez Zer′ ka, 19
Nahr, Jal′ ud, 28, 34
Nahr, Ru′ bin, 19

Na′ hum, 144
Na′ in, 26, 27
Na-o′ mi, 63
Naph′ ta-li, 18
Nar′ am Sin, 76
Na′ than, 134
Naz′ a-reth, Hills of, 26, 27
Ne-ap′ o-lis, 35, 112
Ne′ bo, 59
Neb-u-chad-nez′ zar, 75, 76, 81, 144, 145
Neb-u-zar-a′ dan, 145
Ne′ by Sam′ wil, 38
Neg′ eb, description of, 42
Ne-he-mi′ ah, 150–153
Ne′ me-an Games, 109
Nem′ e-sis, 106
Ni-ca′ nor, 159, 160
Ni′ ce-pho′ ri-um, 106
Nile, 87
Nim′ rud, 73
Nin′ e-veh, 66, 75
Nip-pur′, 67, 69
North Galatian Theory, 104

OC-TA′ VI-AN, 118, 119, 163
Og, 58, 60
Ol′ ives, Mount of, 43, 46
O-lym′ pi-an games, 109
O′ mar, Mosque of, 45
Om′ ri, 35, 82, 137
On, 88
O-nes′ i-mus, 107
O-ni′ as, 156, 157
O′ phel, 44
Or′ mazd, 77
O-ron′ tes, 79
O-si′ ris, 91, 92
Oth′ ni-el, 127, 129

PA-DAN-A′ RAM, 31
Pal′ es-tine, isolation of, 12
 On world's highway, 12
 Diversity of, 13
 Names, 14
 Physical features of, 16
 Divisions of, 15, 18
 Climates, 16, 17
 Its dependence on Mediterranean, 17
 Harbors of, 19
 Roads in, 21, 27, 39, 43, 46
 Between two fires, 155
Pal-my′ ra, 81
Pam-phyl′ i-a, 104
Pa′ ne-as, 49, 168
Pa′ phos, 115
Pa′ ran, 94
Pat′ a-ra, 105
Path′ ros, 87
Pat′ mos, 114
Paul, 20, 81, 100, 103, 106, 107, 111, 112, 113, 115
Pe′ kah, 137, 142

Pek-a-hi′ah, 137
Pel′la, 62
Pel′o-pon-ne′sus, 112
Pe-lu′si-um, 88, 89
Pe-ni′el, 62
Pe-ræ′a, 18, 61
Per′ga, 105
Per′ga-mos, 101, 106
Per′ga-mum, 106
Per′iz-zites, 123
Per-sep′o-lis, ruins of, 70
Per′si-a, 70, 76
Pe′ter, 20
Pe′tra, 97
Pha′raoh-ne′cho, 30, 75, 76, 81, 144
Phar′i-sees, 149, 161, 162
Phar′par, 80
Pha′sa-el, 165
Phil-a-del′phia, 62, 107
Phi-le′mon, 100, 107
Phil′ip (Herod), 49, 61, 168
Phi-lip′pi, 111
Phi-lis′ti-a, 20
Phi-lis′tines, 40, 123, 131, 152
Pho′cis, 110
Phœ-ni′ci-a, description of, 19, 84–86
Phœ-ni′ci-ans, 123
Phryg′i-a, 101, 103
Phryg′i-ans, 101
Pi′late, 168
Pis′gah, 59
Pi-sid′i-a, 103
Pi′thom, 88, 89
Plain of Do′than, 34
Pol′y-carp, 106
Pom′pey, 118, 163
Pon′tus, 101, 102
Pool of Si-lo′am, 44
Proc′u-ra-tors, 167
Promised Land, The, 14
Provinces, Ro′man; senatorial and imperial, 119
Pte′ri-a, 103
Ptol-e-ma′is, 86
Ptol′e-mies, The, 155
Ptol′e-my Phil-a-del′phus, 156
Pul, 139
Pyr′a-mids, 88, 90
Pyth′i-an games, 109

RA, 88, 91
Rab′bah or Rab′bath, 61
  Captured by David, 62
Ra′hab, 87
Ra′hah, 95
Ram′e-ses, 88
Ram′e-ses II, 89, 93
Ram′leh, 20, 21
Ra-moth-gil′e-ad, 62, 83, 141
Ram′say, Prof., 104, 105
Raph′a-na, 62
Râs-es–Sufsâfeh, 95
Re-ho-bo′am, 35, 135, 140

Reph′i-dim, 96
Reu′ben, 18, 60
Re′zin, 142
Rhodes, 114
Rib′lah, 81, 145
Ro′man Em′pire, 119
Ro′man Tax′es, 120, 167
Rome, 116, 121, 163
Ro-set′ta Stone, 91
Ruth, 63

SAD′DU-CEES, The, 162, 163
Sa′fed, 26
Sa-kà-ri′a, 99
Sal′a-mis, 115
  Battle of, 151
Sa-lo′me, 166
Sa-ma′ri-a (City), 35, 73, 82, 138
  The woman of, 33
Sa-ma′ri-a (Country), tribes in, 18
  Bounds of, 31
  Physical features, 31, 32
  Roads, 36
  Valleys and plains, 33, 34, 36
  Repopulated by Esorhaddon, 75
  How regarded in New Testament times, 18, 31
Sa-mar′i-tans, 18, 33
  Their origin, 139
  At present time, 154
  Their Bible, 154
  Excluded from part in building temple, 150, 151
  Build temple in Gerizim, 153
  Enmity between them and Jews, 153
  Submit to Alexander the Great, 155
Sa′mos, 114
Sam-o-thra′ci-a, 114
Sam′son, 23, 128
Sam′u-el, 130
San-bal′lat, 152
San′he-drin, 162, 167
Sar′a-bat, 99
Sa′rah, 46
Sar′dis, 101, 107
Sar′gon, 71, 72, 73, 74, 139
Saul, the King, 29, 40, 61, 130, 131
Sayce, Prof., 44
Scribes, 148, 149
Scrib′ism, 148, 161
Scy-thop′o-lis, 34, 62
Sea of Gal′i-lee, 50
Se′ir, Mount, 97, 98
Se′lah, 97, 98
Se-leu′ci-a, 82
Se-leu′ci-dæ, The, 155
Sen-nach′e-rib, 67, 69, 73, 74, 75, 143
Seph-ar-va′im, 123
Sep′tu-a-gint, The, 156
Ser′a-pe′um, 88
Ser-bal′, Mount, 95
Set I, 89, 93
Shal′lum, 137

Shal-ma-ne′ ser I, 73
Shal-ma-ne′ ser II, 67, 73, 80
Shal-ma-ne′ ser IV, 73, 139
Sham′ gar, 129
Shar′ on, 19
    Cities of, 20
She′ ba, 133
She′ chem, town, description of, 35, 137
She′ chem, Valley of, 33
She-ma′ iah, 140
Sheph′ e-lah or Sheph′ e-la, 22, 24
Shesh-baz′ zar, 150
Shi′ loh, 36, 128
Shi′ shak, 93
Shu′ nem, 26, 28
Shur, wilderness of, 94
Shu′ shan, 67
Si′ don or Zi′ don, 19, 85
Si′ hon, 60, 126
Si-lo′ am, Pool of, 44
Sim′ e-on, 18
Si′ mon, the Mac′ ca-bee, 160, 161
Si′ mon ben–Shit′ tach, 162
Sin, 72
Si′ nai, 95
Si-na-it′ ic, Co′ dex, 95
Sis′ e-ra, 29
Smyr′ na, 101, 105
Sod′ om, 54, 55
Sol′ o-mon, 85, 93, 134, 135
So′ lon, 101
So′ rek, 23
South Galatian Theory, 104
Spar′ ta, 110
Sphinx, 90
Sto′ ics, 109
Stones used in worship, 59, 60
Suc′ coth, 62
Su′ rar, 23
Su′ sa, 67, 70
Su-wein′ it, Wady, 31, 39
Sy′ char, 35
Syn′ a-gogue, when established, 148
    Origin and development of its service, 154
Syr′ i-a, 79–83
Syr′ i-an Gates, 99

TA′ BOR, MOUNT, 25
Tad′ mor, 81
Tah′ pan-hes, 88, 89, 145
Tal′ mud, 149
Ta′ nis, 89
Tan′ tu-rah, 19
Tar′ i-che′ æ, 50, 51
Tar′ sus, 104
Tau′ rus Mountains, 99
Te-ko′ a, 42, 64, 141
Tel-el–A-mar′ na Tablets, 91
Tell-el–Ka-di, 49
Tell-el–Ka-sis, 28
Tell Kei′ mun, 21
Tem′ ple tax, 162

Tem′ ple (The Second), 150, 151
Thebes, 88, 92
Ther-mop′ y-læ, battle of, 151
Thes-sa-lo-ni′ ca, 111
Thes′ sa-ly, 110
Thoth′ mes, III, 93
Thy-a-ti′ ra, 106
Ti-be′ ri-as, 50, 168
Ti-be′ ri-as (Lake), 49
Ti-be′ ri-us, 121
Tig-lath-pi-le′ ser I, 73, 83
Tig-lath-pi-le′ ser III, 73
Tim′ nath, 23
Tir′ zah, 35, 137
To-bi′ ah, 152
Trach-o-ni′ tis, 58, 61
Trip′ o-lis, 85, 86
Tro′ ad, The, 105
Try′ phon, 160
Tyre, 19, 76, 85
Ty-ro-pœ′ an, 43, 44

UMM KEIS, 51
Um Sho′ mer, 95
Ur, 67, 69
U′ rek, 69
Uz-zi′ ah, 140, 142

VALE OF E′ LAH, 23
Vale of So′ rek, 23
Vash′ ti, 151
Vi′ a Eg-na′ ti-a, 111

WAD′ Y EL AFRANJ, 24
Wad′ y el He′ sy, 24
Wad′ y en Nar, 56
Wad′ y es Sur, 23
Wad′ y es Sur′ ar, 23, 46
Wad′ y Far′ ah, 34
Wad′ y Hesh′ bon, 57, 59
Wad′ y Kelt, 39
Wad′ y Ke′ rak, 63
Wad′ y Nar, 21
Wad′ y Su-wein′ it, 31, 39
Warren, Sir Charles, 44
Well of Ha′ rod, 29, 34
Wil′ der-ness of E′ tham, 94
Wil′ der-ness of Ju-dæ′ a, 40
Wil′ der-ness of Ju′ dah, 40
Wil′ der-ness of Pa′ ran, 94
Wil′ der-ness of Shur, 94
Wil′ der-ness of Sin, 94
Wil′ der-ness of Si′ nai, 94, 95
Wil′ der-ness of the Wan′ der-ing, 93–96

XERX′ ES, 78, 151

YAF′ FA, 20
Yar′ muk, 51, 57

ZAR′ E-PHATH, 85, 86
Zeb′ u-lun, 18
Zech-a-ri′ ah (Prophet), encourages building of the temple, 151
Zech-a-ri′ ah (King), 137

Zech-a-ri' ah (Priest), 141
Zed-e-ki' ah, 140, 144, 145
Ze' no, 109
Zeph-a-ni' ah, 144
Zer' ka, Maa' in, 57
Ze-rub' ba-bel, 150
Zi' don, 19, 85

Zig' gu-rat, 67
Zim' ri, 35, 137
Zi' on, 43
Zo' an, 88, 89
Zo' bah, 81, 133
Zor, description of, 52
Zo' rah, 23

# LIST OF MAPS.

| | MAPS |
|---|---|
| THE ASSYRIAN AND BABYLONIAN POWERS | I |
| LANDS OF THE SOJOURN AND WANDERING | II |
| PALESTINE AS DIVIDED AMONG THE TWELVE TRIBES | III |
| THE DOMINIONS OF DAVID AND SOLOMON | IV |
| THE KINGDOMS OF JUDAH AND ISRAEL | V |
| PALESTINE IN THE TIME OF CHRIST | VI |
| HILL COUNTRY OF EASTERN JUDÆA AND BENJAMIN | VII |
| LOWER GALILEE AND ESDRAELON | VIII |
| THE SHEPHELAH OR LOW COUNTRY, PHILISTIA AND SHARON | IX |
| PALESTINE AND ADJACENT COUNTRIES, ILLUSTRATING MACCABÆAN AND EARLY APOSTOLIC HISTORY | X |
| THE WORLD AS KNOWN IN THE APOSTOLIC AGE | XI |
| ST. PAUL'S FIRST AND SECOND JOURNEYS | XII |
| ST. PAUL'S THIRD JOURNEY AND JOURNEY TO ROME | XIII |
| PLAN OF JERUSALEM, WITH ADJACENT TERRITORY | XIV |

THE
ASSYRIAN AND BABYLONIAN
POWERS.
Red tint shows extent of Assyria proper,
Red outline shows Assyrian Power, at the time of Israel's deportation, 722 B. C.,
Purple tint shows Israel at the time of deportation by Sargon, 722 B. C.,
Yellow tint shows extent of Babylonia proper,
Yellow outline shows Babylonian Power, about 600 B. C.,
Green tint shows Judah, carried to Babylonia by Nebuchadnezzar, 587 B. C.,
SCALE OF MILES.
0 50 100 200 300
The M.-N. Co.
E Longitude 42° East F from 44° Greenwich G
CASPIAN SEA
MEDITERRANEAN SEA
(THE GREAT SEA)
PERSIAN GULF
ARMENIA
ASSYRIA
MESOPOTAMIA
BABYLONIA
MEDIA
SUSIANA
(ELAM)
PERSIA
SYRIA
ARAM
CILICIA
SHINAR
CHALDAEA
Syrian Desert
Sinai Peninsula
Desert
Mt. Ararat
Niphates Mt.
Taurus Mts.
Zagros Mts.
Mt. Orontes
Mt. Hermon
Mt. Carmel
Mt. Hor (of Tradition)
Nineveh
Babylon (Babel)
Assur (Asshur)
Calah (Nimrud)
Arbela
Dur Sharrukin
Carchemish
Haran
Edessa
Damascus
Tyre
Sidon
Jerusalem
Samaria
ISRAEL
JUDAH
Ur
Erech (Warka)
Eridu
Susa (Shushan)
Agbatana (Ecbatana)
Tadmor (Palmyra)
Euphrates
Tigris
Halys
Araxes
Red Sea
Gulf of Akabah

Map II

## LANDS of the SOJOURN and WANDERING.

PALESTINE
as divided among the
Twelve Tribes.
SCALE OF MILES.
0 5 10 15 20 25 30
• Boundary Towns.
○ Interior Towns.
◉ Cities of Refuge.
Reference to Coloring,
Showing Elevations and Depressions.
Below Sea Level
Sea Level to 500 ft. above
500 ft. to 1,000 ft. above
1,000 ft. to 2,000 ft. "
2,000 ft. to 3,000 ft. "
3,000 ft. to 5,000 ft. "
Above 5,000 ft.
34°30°
35°
35°30°
36°
Longitude 35° East from 35°30° Greenwich
MEDITERRANEAN SEA
Sidon or Zidon
Zarephath
Tyre
Achzib
Accho
R. Kishon
Mt. Carmel
Dor
Jokneam
Plain of Sharon
Nahr el-'Aujah
Japho or Joppa
Jabneel
Ashdod
Ashkelon
Gaza
Gerar
Lebanon Mts.
Mt. Hermon
Ijon
Dan or Laish
DAMASCUS
River Pharpar
Migdal-el
Kanah
Kedesh
Iron
Waters of Merom
Ramah
Cabul
Jefat
Rimmon
Golan
Sea of Chinnereth
Ashtaroth
Rakkath
Hammath
Aphek
Bethlehem
Daberath
Chesulloth
Mt. Tabor
Megiddo
Mt. Gilboa
Edrei
Bethshean
Engannim
Dothan
Jabesh Gilead
Mahanaim ?
Asher
Mt. Ebal
Mt. Gerizim
Shechem
Taanath-shiloh
Janoah
W. Kanah
River Jabbok
River Jordan
Mt. Gilead
Ramoth Gilead
Shiloh
Gilgal
Hazor
Rabbath-Ammon
Lod
Rimmon
Bethhoron
Bethel
Michmash
Jericho
Beth-Nimrah
Gezer
Ekron
Ajalon
Gilgal
Shittim
Elealeh
Heshbon
Mizpah
Beth-Hoglah
JERUSALEM
Mt. Nebo
Timnah
Bethshemesh
Bethlehem
Medeba
Shoco
V. of Elah
Beth-baal-meon
Tekoa
SALT SEA
Lachish
Mts. of Judah
Hebron
Kirjathaim
Ziph
Juttah
Bezer
Dibon
Dumah
Debir
Carmel
SEA OF THE PLAIN
R. Arnon
Aroer
Rimmon
Pisgah Mts.
Abarim or
Ain
Wilderness of Judah
Arad
Rabbath Moab
Beer-sheba
Aroer
Moladah
MOAB
SIMEON
NEGEB
EDOM
ASHER
NAPHTALI
ZEBULUN
ISSACHAR
MANASSEH
EPHRAIM
DAN
BENJAMIN
JUDAH
PHILISTIA
REUBEN
GAD
ARABIA
BASHAN

Map IV

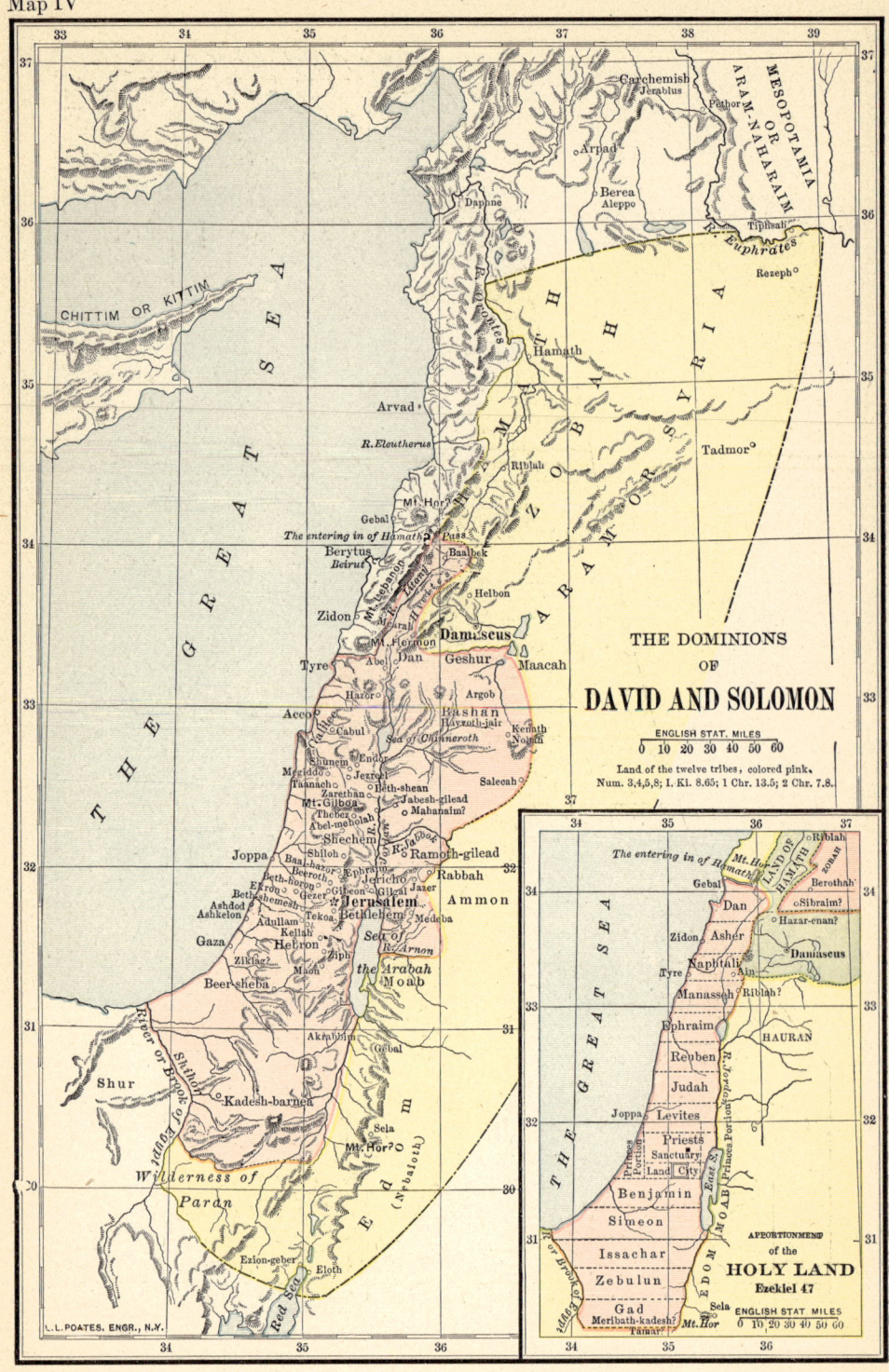

# THE DOMINIONS OF DAVID AND SOLOMON

ENGLISH STAT. MILES
0 10 20 30 40 50 60

Land of the twelve tribes, colored pink.
Num. 3,4,5,8; 1 Ki. 8.65; 1 Chr. 13.5; 2 Chr. 7.8.

APPORTIONMENT of the HOLY LAND
Ezekiel 47

ENGLISH STAT. MILES
0 10 20 30 40 50 60

L. L. POATES, ENGR., N.Y.

# The Kingdoms of Judah and Israel

Map V

Map VI

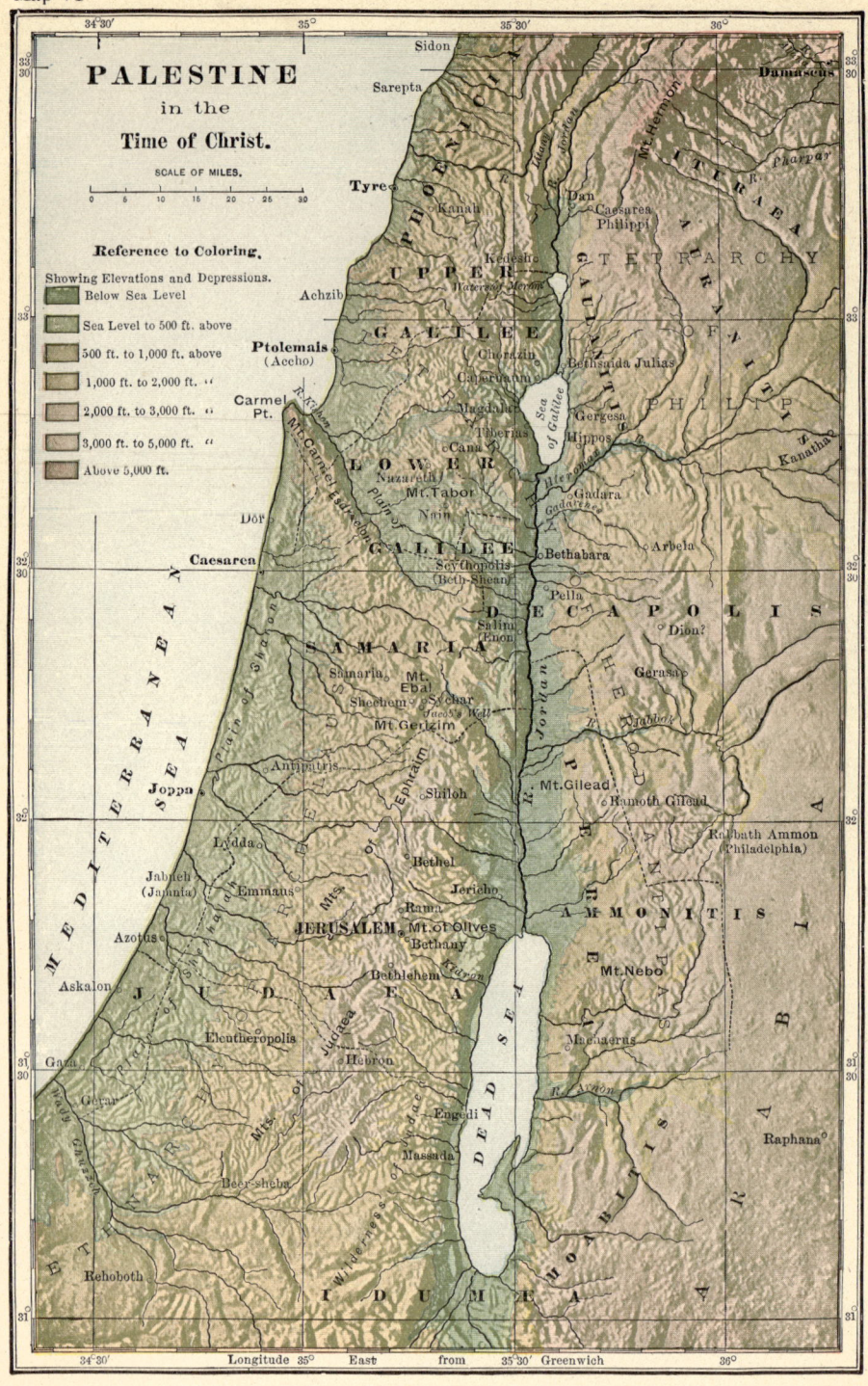

# Map VII

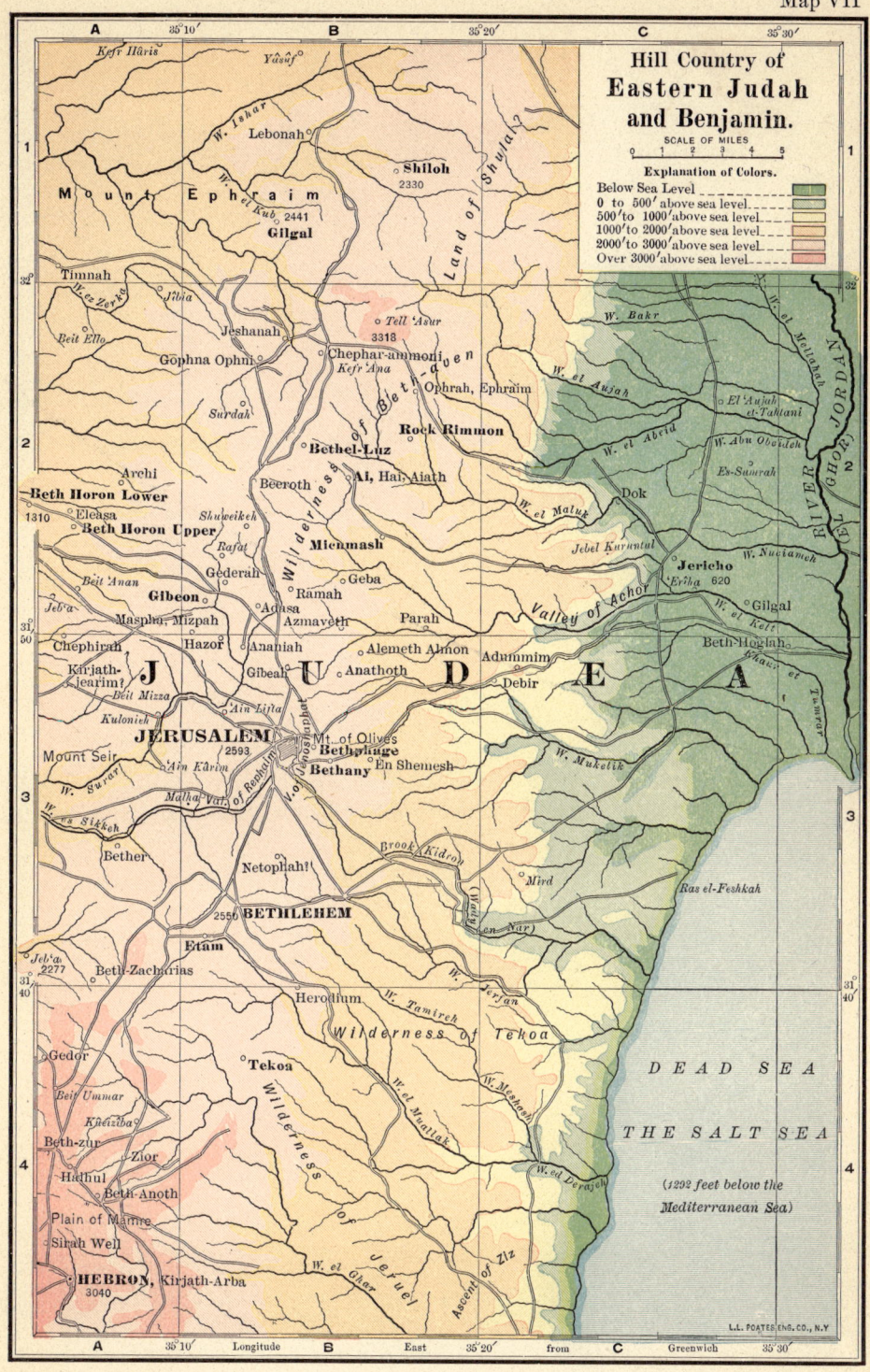

## Hill Country of Eastern Judah and Benjamin.

SCALE OF MILES

**Explanation of Colors.**
Below Sea Level
0 to 500' above sea level
500' to 1000' above sea level
1000' to 2000' above sea level
2000' to 3000' above sea level
Over 3000' above sea level

Kefr Hâris
Yâsuf
W. Ishar
Lebonah
Shiloh 2330
Land of Shulal?

**Mount Ephraim**
Kub. 2441
Gilgal

Timnah
W. ez Zerka
Jibia
Jeshanah
Tell 'Asûr 3318
W. Bakr
Beit Ello
Gophna Ophni
Chephar-ammoni
Kefr Ana
W. el Aujah
El Aujah et-Tahtani
Surdah
Ophrah, Ephraim
W. el Abied
Es-Sumrah
Rock Rimmon
Bethel-Luz
Beeroth
Ai, Hai, Aiath
W. el Maluk
Dok
W. Abu Obeideh
Archi
Shuweikeh
Wilderness
Michmash
Jebel Kuruntul
W. Nueiameh
**Beth Horon Lower** 1310
Eleasa
Rafat
Geba
**Beth Horon Upper**
Gederah
Ramah
Jericho Erîha 620
Beit 'Anan
Gibeon
Adasa
Azmaveth
Parah
Valley of Achor
Gilgal
Jeb'a
Maspha, Mizpah
of Bethaven
Beth-Hoglah
Chephirah
Hazor
Ananiah
Alemeth Almon
Adummim

**J U D Æ A**

Kirjath-jearim?
Gibeah
Anathoth
Debir
Ghawr et Tawarah
Beit Mizza
**JERUSALEM** 2593
Kulonieh
'Ain Lifta
Mount Seir
'Ain Kârim
Mt. of Olives
Bethphage
W. Surar
Bethany
En Shemesh
W. Mukelik
Malha Val. of Rephaim
W. es Sikkeh
Bether
Brook Kidron
Mird
Ras el-Feshkah
Netopah?
2550 **BETHLEHEM**
'Ain Nar

Etam
Jeb'a 2277
Beth-Zacharias
Herodium
W. Tamireh
Wilderness of Tekoa
**DEAD SEA**
Gedor
Tekoa
W. el Muallak
W. Mesheeh
**THE SALT SEA**
Beit Ummar
Kheizîba
Wilderness of Jeruel
(1292 feet below the Mediterranean Sea)
Beth-zur
Zior
Halhul
Beth-Anoth
W. el Derajeh
Plain of Mamre
Sirah Well
Ascent of Ziz
**HEBRON** 3040
Kirjath-Arba
W. el Ghar

Longitude East from Greenwich

RIVER JORDAN (EL GHOR)

L.L. POATES ENG. CO., N.Y.

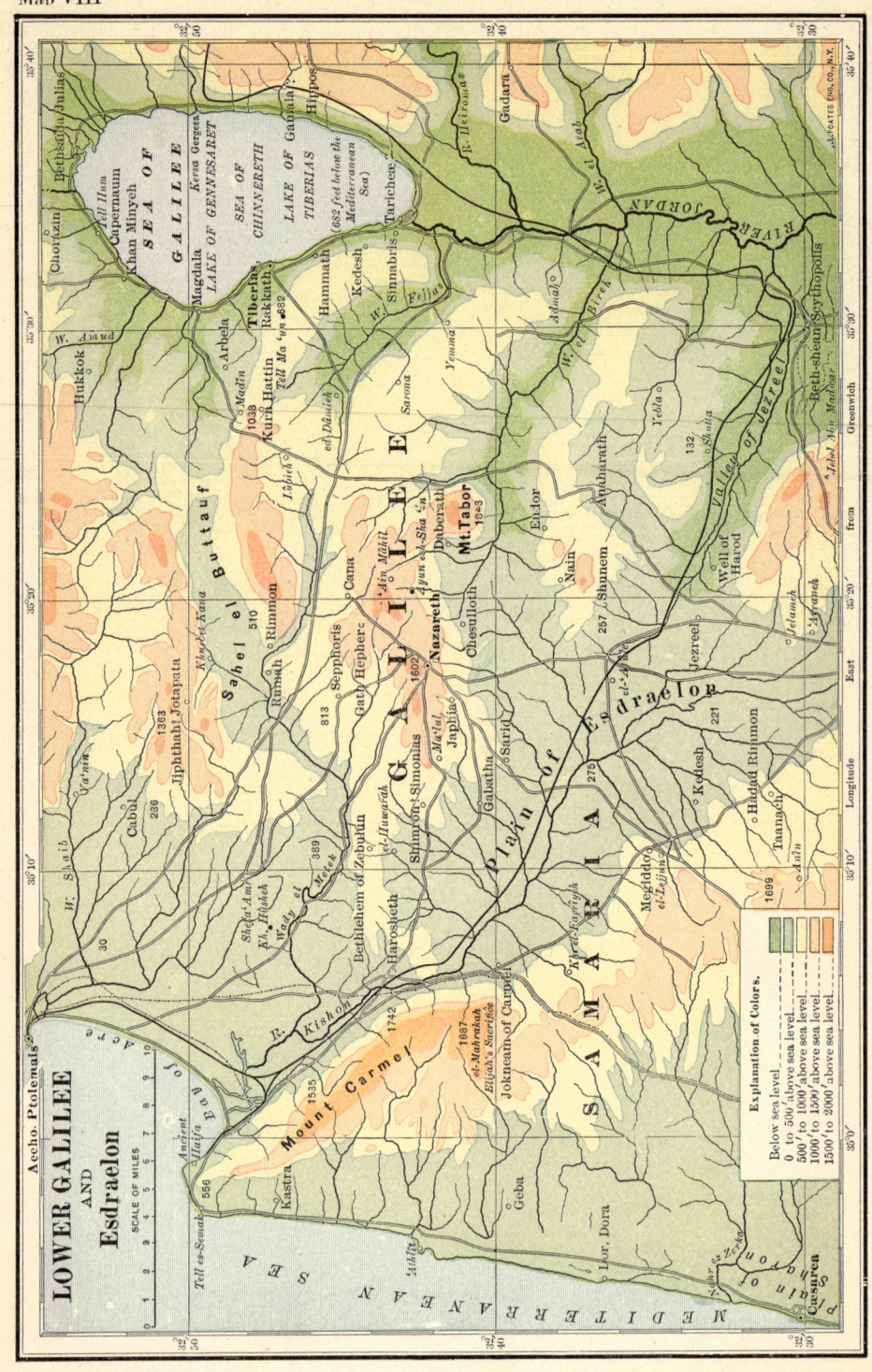

# Map VIII: Lower Galilee and Esdraelon

Map IX

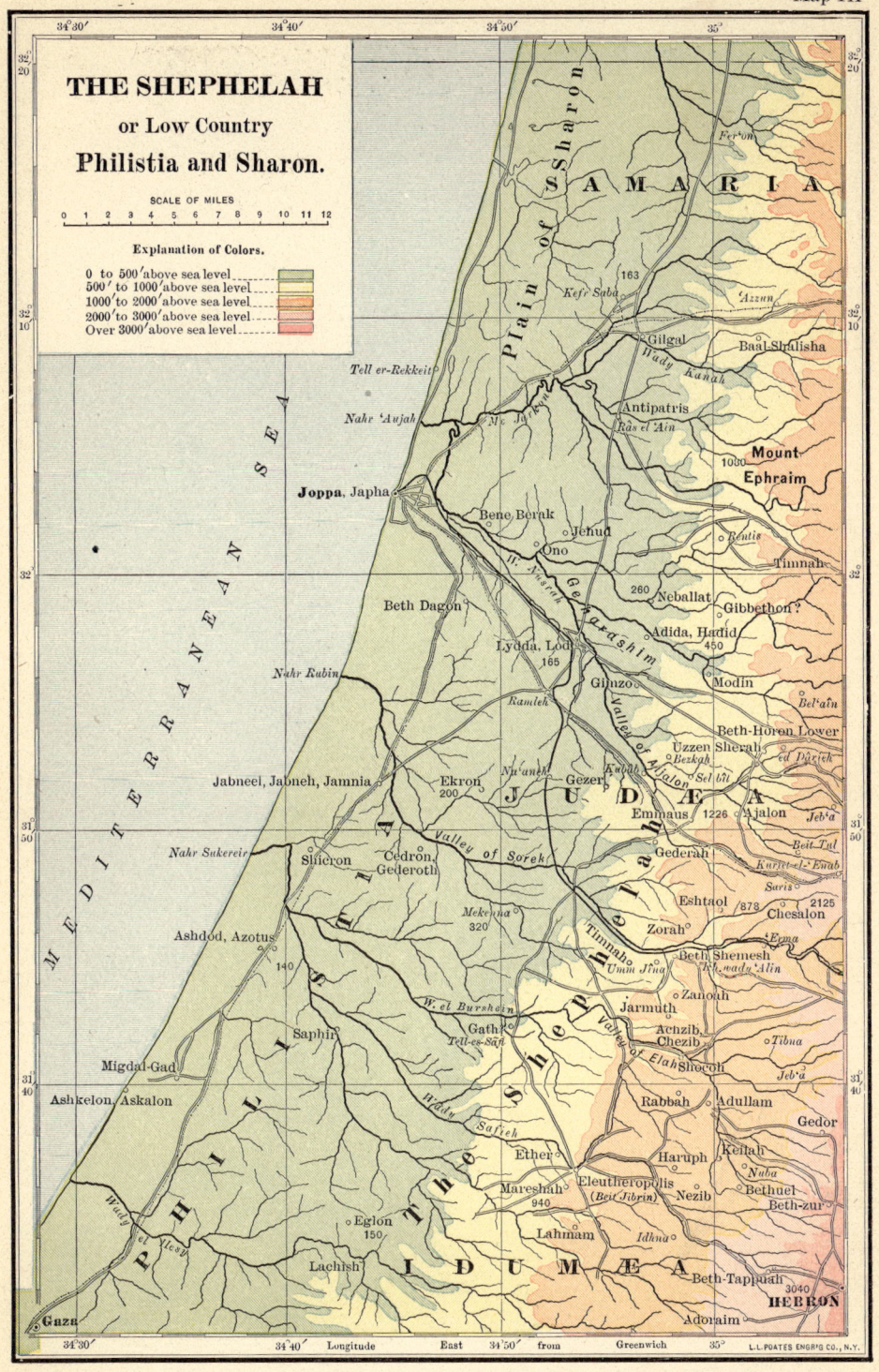

## THE SHEPHELAH
### or Low Country
### Philistia and Sharon.

SCALE OF MILES
0 1 2 3 4 5 6 7 8 9 10 11 12

Explanation of Colors.
0 to 500' above sea level
500' to 1000' above sea level
1000' to 2000' above sea level
2000' to 3000' above sea level
Over 3000' above sea level

Plain of Sharon
SAMARIA
Fer'on
Kefr Saba
163
Gilgal
Baal Shalisha
Wady Kanah
Tell er-Rekkeit
Antipatris
Ras el 'Ain
'Azzun
Nahr 'Aujah
Mt. Jarha
Mount Ephraim
1080
MEDITERRANEAN SEA
Joppa, Japha
Bene Berak
Jehud
Bentis
Ono
Timnah
Beth Dagon
Neballat
260
Gibbethon?
Adida, Hadid
450
Lydda, Lod
165
Modin
Nahr Rubin
Ginzo
Bel'ain
Ramleh
Beth-Horon Lower
Uzzen Sherah
Bezkah
ed Darieh
Sel bit
Jabneel, Jabneh, Jamnia
Ekron
Nu'aneh
Gezer
200
Aught
JUDAEA
Emmaus 1226
Ajalon
Jeb'a
Valley of Sorek
Beit Tul
Nahr Sukereir
Gederah
Shicron
Cedron, Gederoth
Saris
Kuriet-el-'Enab
Eshtaol
Chesalon
Mekenna
878
2125
320
Zorah
Eqna
Ashdod, Azotus
Timnah
Beth Shemesh
140
Umm Jina
R. wada 'Alin
Zanoah
Jarmuth
W. el Bursheir
Saphir
Achzib, Chezib
Tibna
Gath
Valley of Elah
Tell-es-Safi
Shocoh
Migdal-Gad
Wady Safieh
Jeb'a
Ashkelon, Askalon
Rabbah
Adullam
Gedor
PHILISTIA
Ether
Haruph
Keilah
Eleutheropolis
Nuba
(Beit Jibrin)
Nezib
Bethuel
Mareshah
Beth-zur
940
Lahmam
Idhna
Eglon
150
The Shephelah
Beth-Tappuah
Wady el Hesi
Lachish
IDUMAEA
3040
Gaza
Adoraim
HEBRON

Longitude East from Greenwich

L. L. Poates Eng'r'g Co., N.Y.

Map X

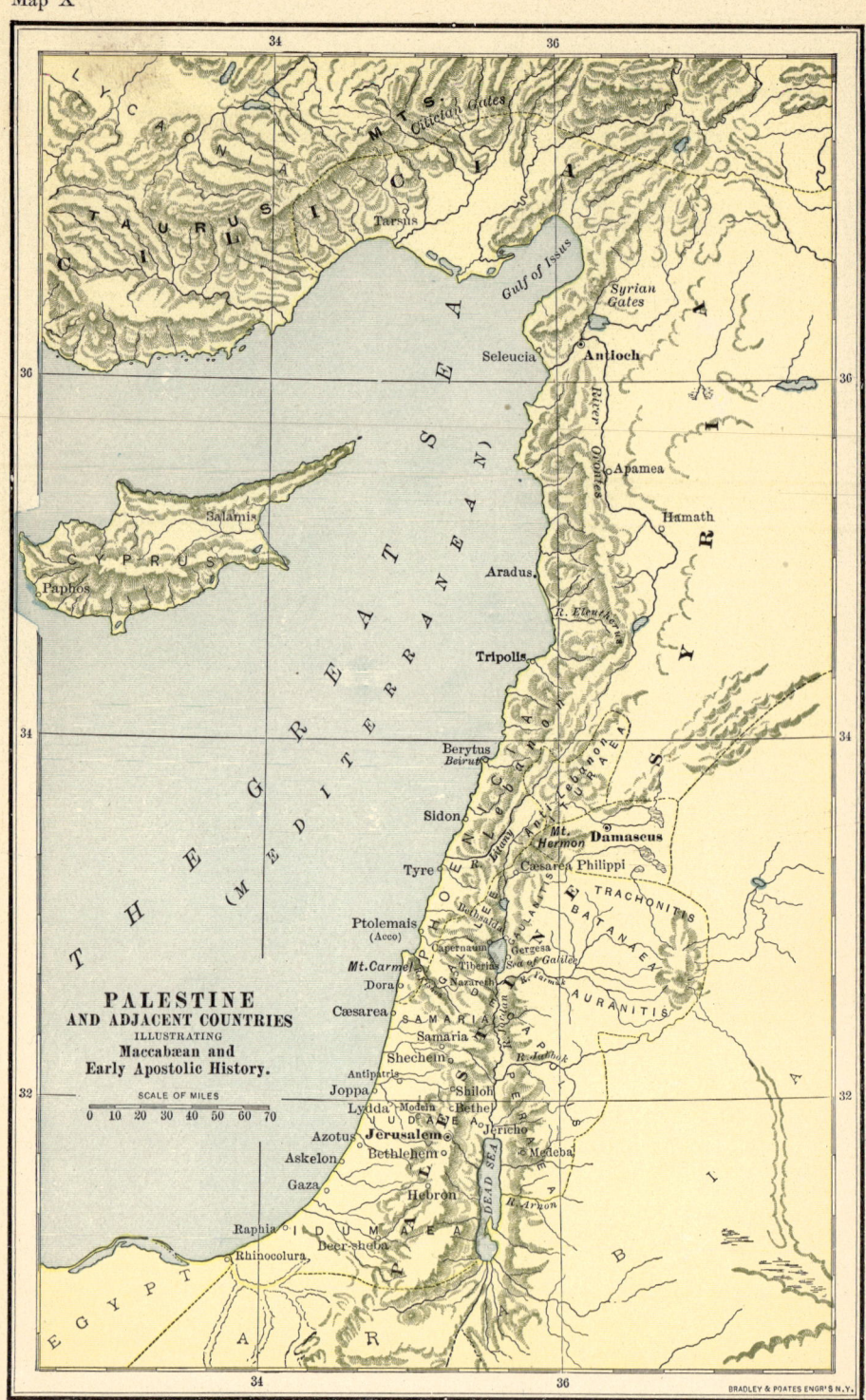

PALESTINE
AND ADJACENT COUNTRIES
ILLUSTRATING
Maccabæan and
Early Apostolic History.

Map XI

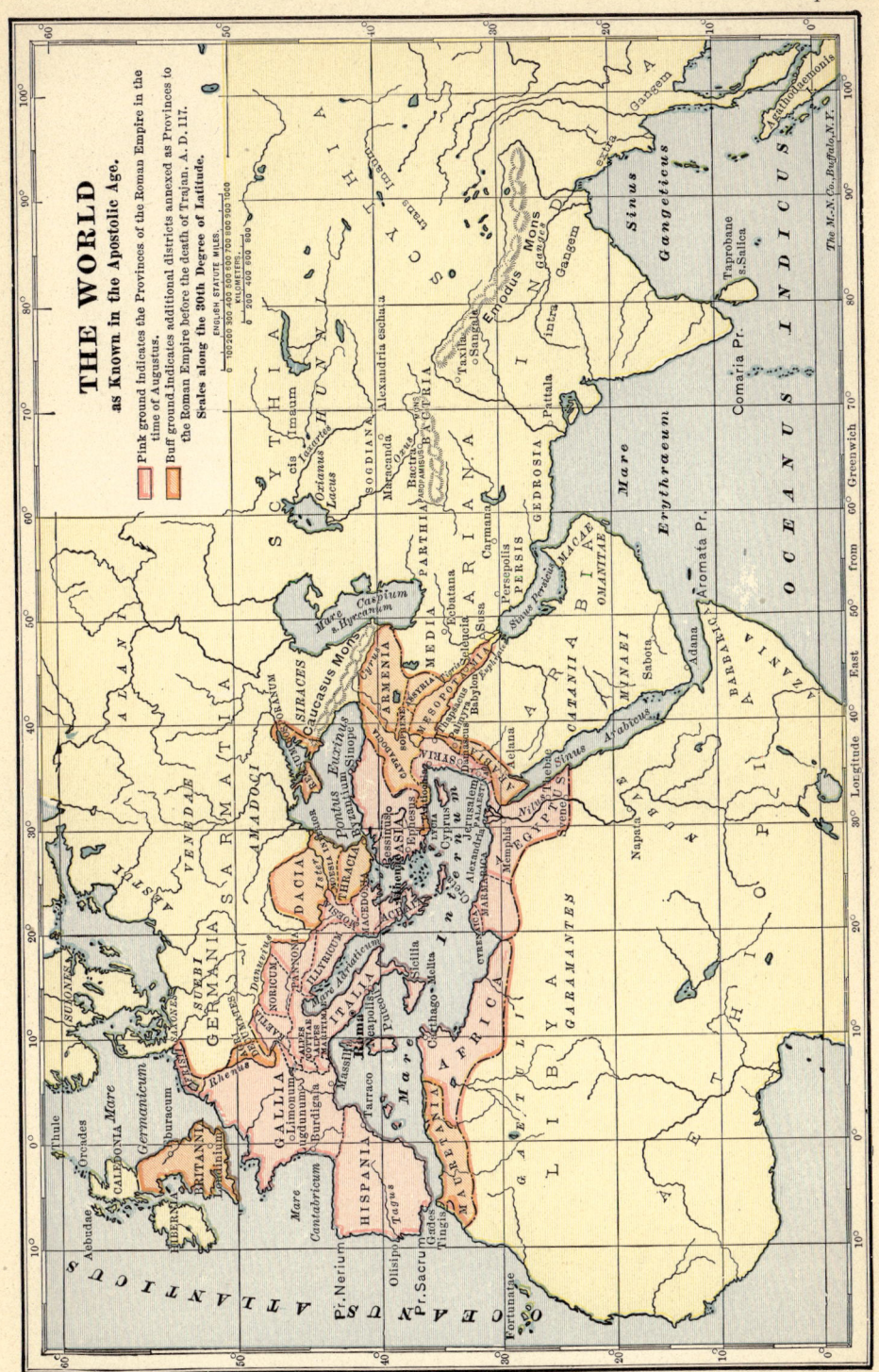

Map XII

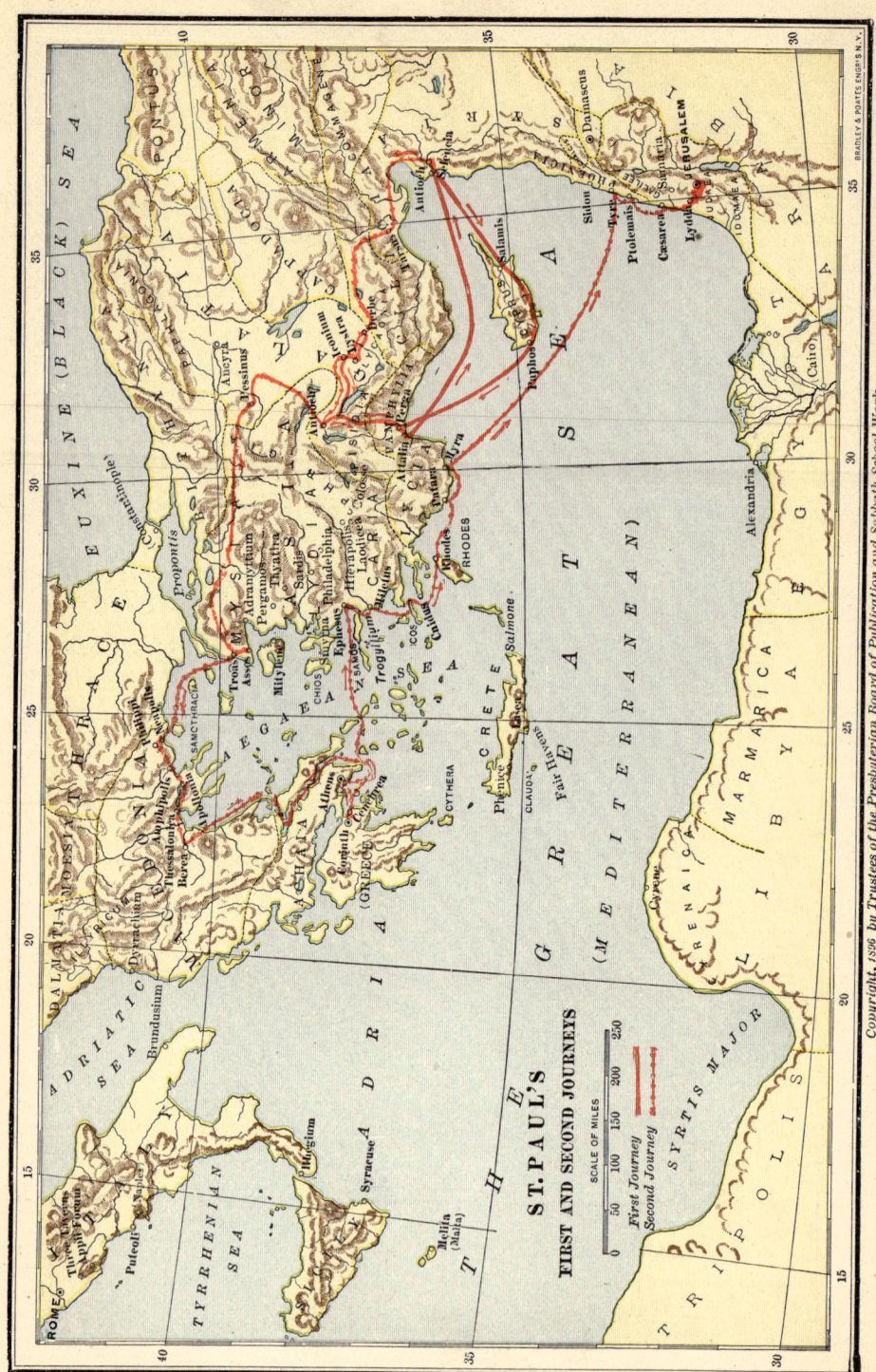

ST. PAUL'S
THIRD JOURNEY AND JOURNEY TO ROME.
SCALE OF MILES
0 50 100 150 200 250
Third Journey
Journey to Rome
EUXINE (BLACK) SEA
ADRIATIC SEA
TYRRHENIAN SEA
AEGAEAN SEA
THE GREAT SEA
(MEDITERRANEAN)
ADRIA
SYRTIS MAJOR
ROME
Three Taverns
Appii Forum
Puteoli
Naples
Brundusium
Rhegium
Syracuse
Melita
(Malta)
SICILY
ITALY
DALMATIA
MOESIA
THRACE
ILLYRICUM
Dyrrachium
MACEDONIA
Philippi
Neapolis
Amphipolis
Thessalonica
Berea
Apollonia
SAMOTHRACIA
ACHAIA
Athens
Corinth
Cenchrea
(GREECE)
CYTHERA
CRETE
Phenice
Lasea
CLAUDA
Fair Havens
Salmone
(Constantinople)
Propontis
BITHYNIA
PAPHLAGONIA
R. Halys
PONTUS
Tavium
Ancyra
Pessinus
GALATIA
CAPPADOCIA
ARMENIA MINOR
COMMAGENE
MYSIA
Troas
Assos
Adramyttium
Pergamos
Thyatira
Mitylene
Sardis
ASIA
LYDIA
CHIOS
Smyrna
Ephesus
Philadelphia
R. Meander
Hierapolis
Laodicea
Colosse
SAMOS
Trogyllium
PATMOS
COS
Miletus
CARIA
Cnidus
Rhodes
RHODES
LYCIA
Patara
Myra
Attalia
Perga
PAMPHYLIA
PISIDIA
Antioch
Iconium
Lystra
Derbe
LYCAONIA
CILICIA
Tarsus
Antioch
Seleucia
SYRIA
CYPRUS
Salamis
Paphos
Sidon
Tyre
Ptolemais
Cæsarea
Lydda
JERUSALEM
Samaria
GALILEE
PHENICIA
Damascus
JUDAEA
IDUMAEA
ARABIA
Alexandria
Cairo
EGYPT
LIBYA
MARMARICA
CYRENAICA
Cyrene
TRIPOLIS
15 20 25 30 35 40
BRADLEY & POATES ENGR'S N.Y.

Map XIV

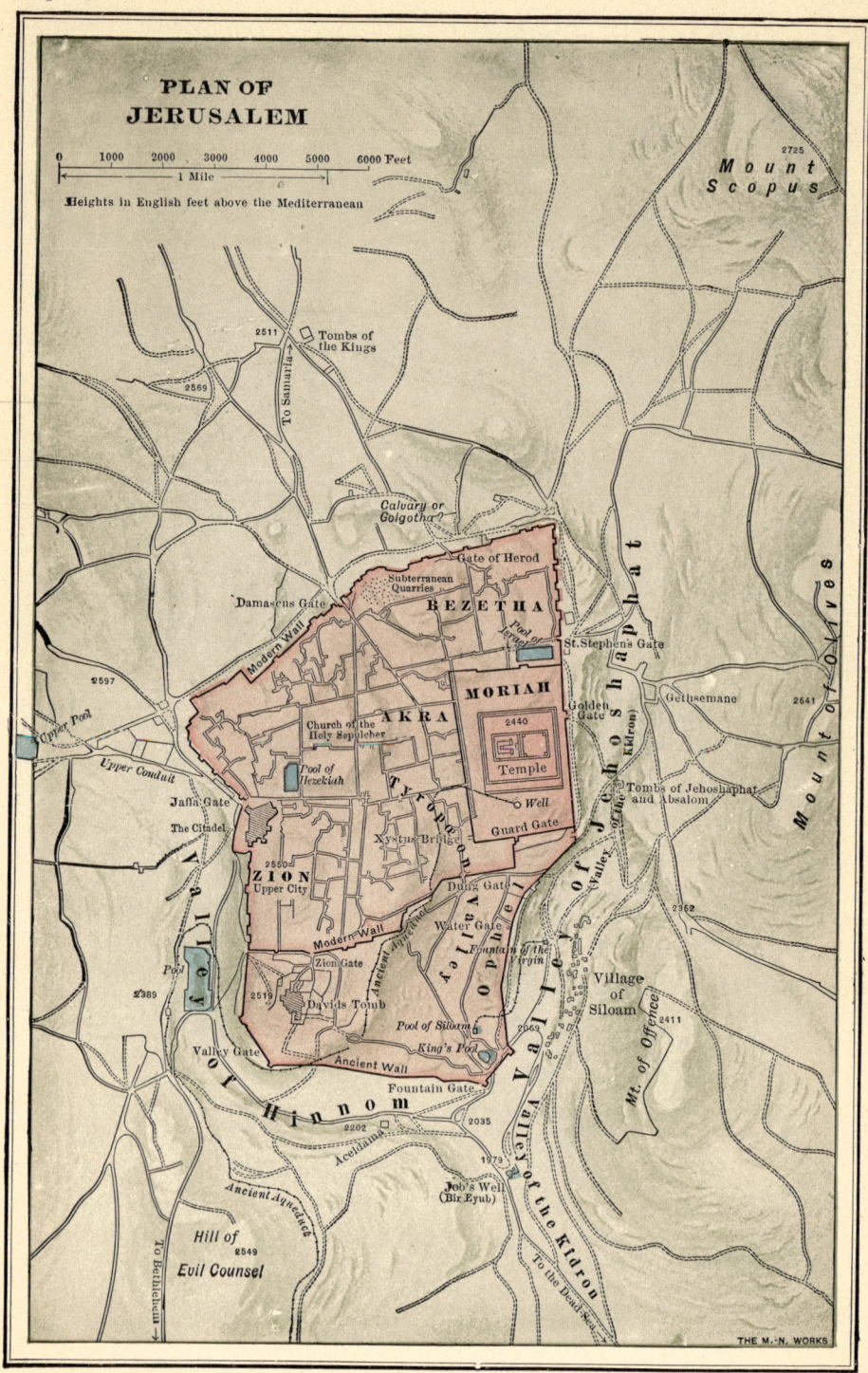

# PLAN OF JERUSALEM

FUNDERBURG LIBRARY
MANCHESTER COLLEGE

220.91
C129h

WITHDRAWN
from
Funderburg Library